A Texas Freethought Reader

A TEXAS FREETHOUGHT READER

A Selection of the "Lost" Writings of

J. M. Gilbert
Chas. H. Jones
T. V. Munson
& J. D. Shaw

A Companion to:
**GUIDED BY REASON:
THE GOLDEN AGE OF FREETHOUGHT IN TEXAS**

Edited & Introduced By
STEVEN R. BUTLER

The Freethought Press of Texas

RICHARDSON, TEXAS

The Freethought Press of Texas

"Shining the light of reason on the Lone Star State"

Cover design and Introduction
Copyright © 2017 by Steven R. Butler.
All rights reserved.

ISBN 978-0-9982065-1-6

For information about Freethought Press of Texas titles, please visit:

www.freethoughtpressoftexas.com

Additional copies of this book are available from:
Amazon.com and other online stores

All material in this book, with the exception of the Introduction, was originally written and/or published prior to January 1, 1923, and therefore, in accordance with U.S. copyright law, is in the public domain.

Cover photo: Two Texas cowboys reading a newspaper, circa 1907; courtesy Library of Congress, Washington, D.C.

"As yet Texas is the only southern state in which the Liberals have made a vigorous fight against priest-craft. But the Liberals of other states are falling into line, and the time is not far distant when they will be holding Liberal meetings all over the south."

—John E. Remsburg, 1886

Contents

Introduction	xi
JASPER M. GILBERT (Randolph, Texas)	1
News from Texas (1897)	3
Distracted Meetings (1897)	6
The Preachers (1897)	9
Conversation with a Parson (1897)	12
Materialistic Philosophy (1899)	15
Gift of Faith and Belief (1899)	17
Regarding the Death of Robert G. Ingersoll (1899)	26
Christianity as It Is (1899)	27
The Money is Safe! (1900)	32
Plain Truths for Preachers, Part I (1900)	33
Plain Truths for Preachers, Part II (1900)	40
Plain Truths for Preachers, Part III (1900)	52
How I Became an Atheist (1902)	58
Reply to Prof. C. J. Finger (1903)	70
Orthodox Baptist Preachers (1903	75
Teed the Humbug (1903)	79
Elijah (1903)	85
Those "Holy Men of God" (1903)	92
Prayer (1903)	100
Free Press & Free Speech (1905)	108
An Ex-Methodist Freethinker (1905)	110
Judas Iscariot, Part I (1905)	112
Judas Iscariot, Part II (1905	117
Why Cater to Ignorance? (1906)	122
Does a Believer Exist? (1908)	125

CHARLES H. JONES (Denison, Texas)   131
   One World at a Time is Enough (1916)   133
   As to Belief or Disbelief in the Inspiration of the
      Bible (1916)   134
   The Rev. J. E. Aubrey's Sermon Answered by Chas.
      H. Jones, first installment (1916)   136
   The Rev. J. E. Aubrey's Sermon Answered by Chas.
      H. Jones, second installment (1916)   139
   The Rev. J. E. Aubrey's Sermon Answered by Chas.
      H. Jones, third installment (1916)   142
   The Rev. J. E. Aubrey's Sermon Answered by Chas.
      H. Jones, fourth installment (1916)   144
   The Rev. J. E. Aubrey's Sermon Answered by Chas.
      H. Jones, fifth installment (1916)   147
   What Christians Say About Skeptics (1916)   150
   Is It a Fact That Christianity is the Hope of the
      Nation? (1916)   151
   Is the Bible Inspired Concerning Women? (1916)   155
   Is Christianity Opposed to Free Speech? (1916)   158
   That Talking Snake in the Garden of Eden (1917)   160
   If the Bible is True, the Persons Described Following Are
      Eternally Lost (1917)   163
   A personal letter from Mr. P. C. Preston (1917)   166
   A personal letter to Mr. P. C. Preston (1917)   167
   Is the Skeptic Honest Regarding the Bible? (1917)   170
   Rev. W. D. Darnell Ridicules Evolution… (1917)   172
   The Church News Editor and Committee Refuse
      Space for an Answer from Chas. H. Jones (1917)   175
   Darwin the Evolutionist Did Not Turn to the Bible
      and Christ (1917)   178
   How the Infidel May Convert Himself (1917)   181
   Jonah and the Whale Story, or Jonah and His
      Submarine Hotel (1917)   183
   Edison the Great Inventor Says, the Christian Gods
      are Myth (1917)   185

Being on the Safe Side, as to Belief, is a Childish Reason Born of Fear (1917)	187
Are Prayers Answered? Nobody Can Prove They Are (1917)	190
Are Prayers for Good Crops a Waste of Breath (1918)	193
Will One-Minute Daily Prayers Enable Us to Whip the Kaiser? (1918)	196
THOMAS VOLNEY MUNSON (Denison, Texas)	199
Evolution, Chapter I (1883)	201
Evolution, Chapter II (1883)	206
Evolution, Chapter III (1883)	213
What is God?—A Name, Nothing More (1884)	221
Spiritualistic Religion (1884)	224
An Interesting Correspondence (1886)	227
A Broader Philosophy Necessary, I (1886)	232
A Higher Philosophy Necessary, II (1886)	237
A Higher Philosophy Demanded, III (1886)	241
A Higher Philosophy Demanded, IV (1886)	247
A Higher Philosophy Needed, V (1886)	251
Are Liberals Progressive (1889)	259
Are Liberals Progressive, No. 2 (1889)	263
The Fiskean God (1891)	269
Why Theophilus Became an Infidel (1906 & 1910)	278
Dualism and Monism: Or Religion and Science in a Nutshell (1906 & 1910)	301
JAMES DICKSON SHAW (Waco, Texas)	307
The Bible Against Itself (1889)	309
Mr. Munson on Liberals and Progress (1889)	336
An Infidel's Confession of Faith (1896)	345

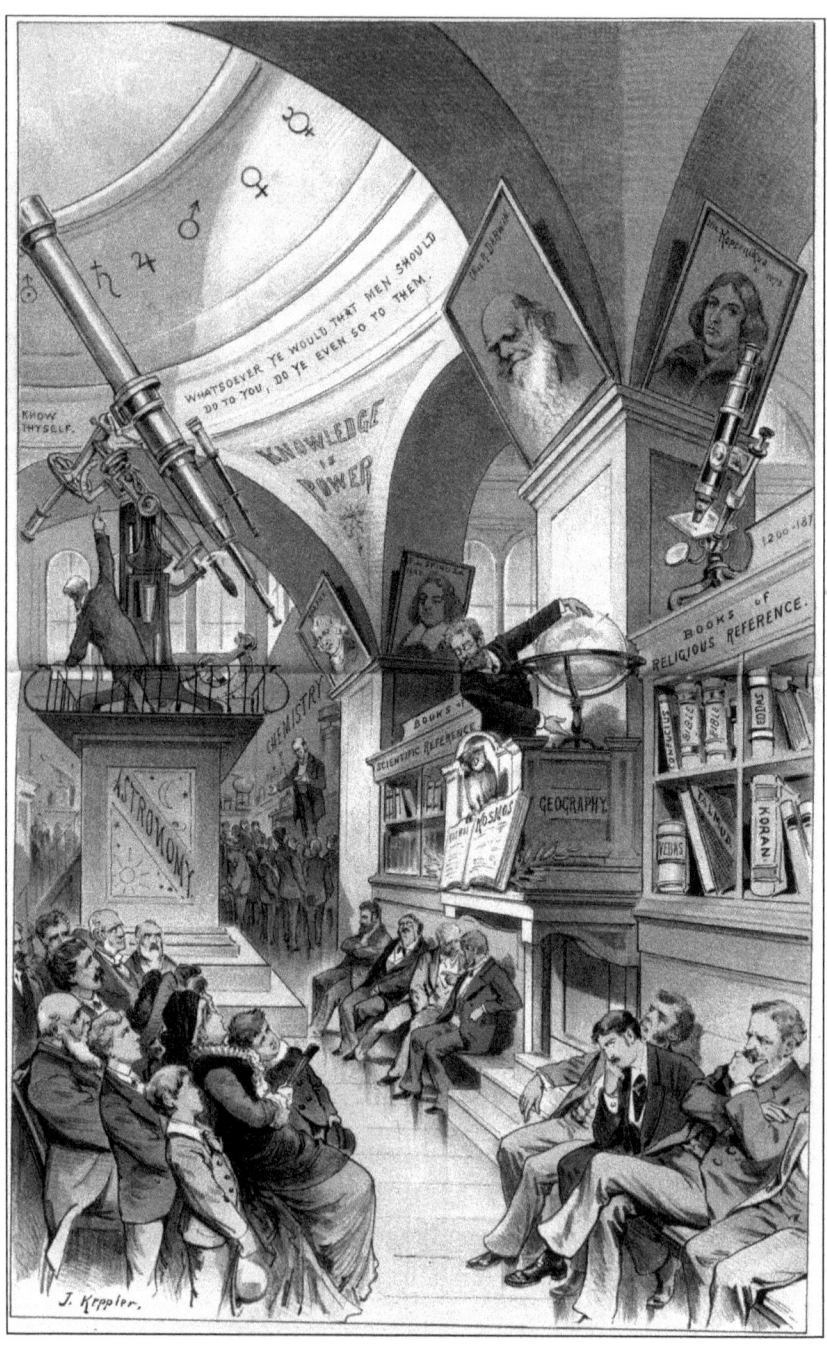

The Universal Church of the Future; from *Puck*, vol. 12, no. 305, January 10, 1883, centerfold.
Courtesy the Library of Congress, Washington, D.C.

Introduction

BY STEVEN R. BUTLER

If you have never heard of any the four freethought writers whose names are printed on the cover and title page of this book, it is hardly surprising. They are certainly not household names, even among the freethinkers of today. Only one somehow managed to make a living (albeit a spare one) using the pen, and even he has largely been forgotten in the slightly more than ninety years since he died. The other three—a doctor-turned-farmer, a merchant, and an eminent horticulturist—were occasional writers only, whose published work, even during their own lifetimes, had an unfortunately limited readership.

You may likewise be unfamiliar with the term "freethinker." *Chambers Twentieth Century Dictionary of the English Language*, defines it as "a person who professes to be free from conventional authority in religion." In 1924, in a presentation entitled "Lincoln the Freethinker," Joseph L. Lewis, lifelong president of the Freethinkers of America, explained the meaning of the term a little more thoroughly:

> In order to be a Christian, it is necessary to believe the Bible to be a divinely inspired book. To be a Freethinker it is essential that you reject the Bible as a revelation from God. To determine, then, whether a person is a Christian or a Freethinker should indeed be very simple. A person may believe in God and yet reject the Bible as a divine book. Such a person cannot be a Christian believer, but may be a Freethinker.
>
> A Freethinker may be any one of the following: A Deist, a Rationalist, a Pantheist, a Materialist, an Agnostic, or an Atheist.[1]

I think if Lewis were alive today, he would almost certainly broaden

---

[1] Joseph L. Lewis, *Lincoln the Freethinker* (New York: Freethought Publishing Company, 1924), 11.

his definition to include not only Christians but also members of all other religious faiths, and to include not only the Bible but also the Torah, the Quran, and the Vedas (and any other "holy" text) in his definition of what it is that freethinkers reject as the word of God (or gods).

I think it would be safe to say too, that if we were to place the four men whose work appears between the covers of this book in one of the six categories of freethought listed by Lewis, that they can all be classed as atheists, although the term "pantheist," i.e., a believer in Nature as "God," might be appropriate in one instance. The terms "rationalist" and "materialist" would likewise suit them all, I think. There is no question, however, in light of their own writing, that none of the four had much use for Christianity, nor the Bible, except to point out its copious flaws and contradictions to anyone willing to accept that even "holy writ" is not immune from critical examination.

The reason I term their writing "lost" is because it first appeared in print during America's approximately half-century-long "Golden Age of Freethought"—an era that lasted from the end of the Civil War until the beginning of U.S. involvement in World War One—and it has not been republished in any way, shape or form (to the best of my knowledge) in all the many years since—*until now of course*.

Throughout the so-called "Golden Age," freethought publications with titles such as *The Truth Seeker*, *The Index*, and *Free Thought Magazine* not only provided the nation's far-flung army of "freethinkers" with the latest in what was also termed "liberal" news and thought, but also a public forum where these self-styled "infidels" (a then-popular synonym for "freethinkers") could share their ideas and opinions in largely unsolicited articles, reviews, and letters that seldom, if ever, earned their authors any monetary recompense. Other popular titles included *The Blue Grass Blade*, *Lucifer, the Light Bearer*, and the *Humanitarian Review*. In Texas during this time, a monthly journal called *The Independent Pulpit*, founded in 1883 by one of the men whose work is included in this book—a former Methodist minister named J. D. Shaw,—enjoyed a remarkable readership that extended not only from one side of the state to the other, but also well beyond its borders.

Although Shaw and other infidel publishers enjoyed some slight degree of name recognition, at least among freethinkers, as did a small

Introduction

army of full-time freethought writers and lecturers, such as John E. Remsburg, Mattie P. Krekel, Samuel P. Putnam, and the celebrated "Great Agnostic," Robert G. Ingersoll, most contributors to these various "liberal" publications were obscure, irregular writers only. Largely unknown outside their own communities or professions, or their readership (if they had one), they are even less-known today than in their own era. The remaining three writers whose work is included in this *Reader* fall into this category. This should not be taken to mean, however, that their compositions are somehow inferior to that of the better-remembered full-time essayists, because nothing could be further from the truth!

There is another reason why the men whose work is included in this book were so little known by the masses in their own time, as well as today: As in our own time, most late nineteenth and early twentieth century Americans were Christians, or at the very least nominal Christians, who went to church, participated in religious rituals, and professed, perhaps even when they had doubts, to believe the dogma, creeds, and "revelations" that society expected them to accept as "the infallible word of God." Then, as now, Freethinkers were not likely to attend church services, but many, for the sake of their families and just as importantly, for the sake of their livelihoods, kept their critical opinions about religion to themselves. Few people were willing, or financially able, to accept the negative consequences that might almost certainly follow an open admission of religious "infidelity." (Americans like to think they are religiously tolerant, and that our ancestors were also, but unfortunately, both history and current events reveal that tolerance is more often a myth than reality.) Consequently, most nineteenth and early twentieth century Americans were almost certainly oblivious to the fact that there were any freethinkers living among them, or that any sort of freethought movement was taking place practically right under their noses! Although it would be difficult to ascertain their precise numbers, it is almost certainly a fact that self-identified "infidels" made up only a tiny fraction of the U.S. population, even during the "Golden Age." If the average American chanced to hear the terms "freethinker" or "freethought" at all, they most likely came from the lips of their priests or ministers, who, not unnaturally, were hostile to the movement and therefore warned their parishioners against it. It is equally unlikely then that the average American had any idea that freethought publications, all of which were available by subscription only, even existed.

This *Reader* has been published for two reasons. One is to serve as a companion volume to *Guided by Reason: The Golden Age of Freethought in Texas*. The other is to rescue four of these "lost "writers from the undeserved literary oblivion where they, and their work, have languished far too long. Today, extant examples of the infidel press of the late nineteenth and early twentieth centuries can be found only in state and local archives, special collection libraries, and private collections—and also perhaps in old trunks and boxes in dusty attics, where they were put away long ago and forgotten. In short, much of this sort of work is not easily accessible. Thankfully, *some* early-day freethought publications, all of which are now in the public domain, have been digitized and made available on the Internet, but not all, and even then, that does not mean that their existence is widely known. By making some of this heretofore "lost" writing available in print for the first time in more than a century (even longer in some cases), I am trying not only to resurrect (pun intended) the literary careers of some of Texas' best freethought writers and thinkers but also to awaken the current generation of freethinkers—as well as a generation of *potential* freethinkers—to insights, thoughts, and opinions, which in spite of the passage of so much time, are no less relevant today than when they were first published. The fact that such is undoubtedly the case, makes a book like this one all the more welcome and needed, I think, at this particular moment in history.

Although they followed different occupations and did not necessarily share the same political or social views, the four men whose work is included in this *Reader* did have three things in common. First of all, each one lived in North Central Texas—within a 100-mle radius of Dallas—during the "Golden Age of Freethought." Secondly, each of the four, judging by both the content and the composition of his work, was an adroit, intelligent critical thinker who possessed, in spades, the ability to express himself both clearly and articulately. Third: Each one was firmly and positively committed to the advancement of reason and rational thought in opposition to what they termed the "superstition" and

Introduction

"tyranny" of organized religion, particularly Christianity. We know too that at least two of them (Munson and Shaw), were also personally acquainted with one another. (It is possible, but not known, that Munson and Jones might also have known each other.)

I have arranged their work alphabetically by name of writer, rather than chronologically by age, or by the year each one began writing, because doing so enabled me to place the two most colorful and assertive of the four—Gilbert and Jones—at the beginning of the book. The work of Professor Munson, who comes third in the sequence, is more scholarly in tone and in substance, more complex and scientific, which is unsurprising in view of his academic background. For that reason, I thought it best to leave him for later. Munson was also more gentlemanly—not so much of a firebrand—in his approach to the opposition. It seems to me that Shaw, who brings up the rear, falls somewhere in-between these two poles.

I think readers will agree that Gilbert, the "village atheist" of a small town where nearly everyone was a Bible-toting churchgoer, was by far the most feisty of the four. To openly challenge the status quo by confronting believers, including local "sky pilots," daring them to debate, required both confidence and boldness. It is puzzling though, as to why he stayed in Randolph—a small, remote farming community in southwestern Fannin County—for almost all his life. Although it appears that he did not travel often, he *did* live briefly in both Los Angeles, California and St. Louis, Missouri—cities where he was far more likely to be intellectually comfortable than in rural, small-town Texas. How and where he acquired the critical thinking skills that are evident in his writing is another mystery. Indeed, it is astonishing, in light of the time and place in which he lived, that he became such an outspoken iconoclast, despite being raised in a conservative rural environment where conformity and unquestioning obedience to Biblical authority were far more valued and respected than investigative thinking.

Freethinkers, as well as anyone else who is willing to keep an open mind, will almost certainly find Gilbert's work interesting and engaging. Most of it is short and to the point, providing not only compelling arguments regarding the spuriousness of religious teachings, but also taking readers back in time to a rural, small-town Texas that apart from a lack of modern amenities, most of us would probably have no trouble recognizing. Conversely, if Gilbert could somehow be transported from his time to ours, apart from the automobiles, TV, and air conditioning and other technology that would no doubt catch his attention, he would probably likewise feel "at home" in the small-town Texas of today, although I feel certain that in terms of Texans' religiosity, he would be dismayed by how little that has changed over the course of a century.

More than a hundred years after the "Randolph Radical" and his cohorts were making an effort to open the minds of their contemporaries to more critical ways of thinking, it is quite evident that much of Texas, and particularly the small towns and rural districts, remains much the same as it was in the late nineteenth and early twentieth centuries. Churches still dot the landscape and there is plenty of other evidence that makes it abundantly clear that rural and small town Texans still take "that old time religion" quite seriously. One such place that comes to mind is the Panhandle community of Clarendon, where the main street is lined at intervals with gleaming white crosses made from oil well pipe, as well as by billboards proclaiming "God Loves You" and "Jesus—the Only Way to Heaven." There are similar signs and religious displays in other small towns, and even in Texas cities.

If Charles H. Jones, a Denison furniture store owner and real estate agent, could somehow see the Texas of today, he would also no doubt be disheartened, particularly in light of his three-year-long (1916-1918) newspaper campaign to bring his fellow Denisonians to the light of reason.

Like Gilbert, Jones' was not only unafraid to criticize the tenets of religion but also to challenge local ministers to defend their pronouncements. From time-to-time, the atheistic furniture store owner went to church, just to hear them preach, so that he could afterward refute what they had said in the pulpit on Sunday morning. One preacher who received particular attention was the Reverend J. E. Aubrey of Denison's First Presbyterian Church, whose sermons provided Jones with material for no fewer than five consecutive articles that were published in two Denison newspapers, as paid advertisements, which he later pasted into a scrapbook that I came across entirely by chance. I think Jones would be pleased that his work has been rescued from the

Introduction

oblivion in which it would have continued to languish if I had not seen and recognized it for what it was. I think he would be pleased too that a new generation will now be able to read, to learn from, and hopefully, be inspired by both his work and his example.

Thomas Volney Munson, another Denisonian, is better remembered today as a pioneering Texas viticulturist and savior of the French wine industry. A little older than either Gilbert or Jones, it is very clear, judging by both the style and substance of his writing, that the theological opinions of the respected plant nursey-owner were shaped largely by his study of science, which he frankly admits in one of the essays contained in this book. Many of his philosophical musings, most of them published in J. D. Shaw's *The Independent Pulpit*, are not only lengthier but also more cerebral than the works of Gilbert or Jones.

In addition to eleven examples of Munson's work that first appeared in J. D. Shaw's *Independent Pulpit*, and a three-part article on evolution first published in the Denison *Sunday Gazetteer*, this *Reader* includes two essays that form the bulk of a thin pamphlet, *The New Revelation*, which was privately printed for Munson in 1906 by a close friend and fellow "infidel," Bredette C. Murray, publisher of the *Sunday Gazetteer*—the closest thing to a freethought newspaper in Far North Texas during this period.

Written under the pseudonym "Theophilus Philosophius," *The New Revelation* also included poetry, as well as a eulogy that Munson wished to be read aloud at his funeral. When he died of natural causes in 1913, it was. Three years earlier he observed: "Man creates for himself his own proper monuments in his works and children." Clearly, he intended *The New Revelation*, in which he reveals how and why he gave up the religion in which he was raised, to be such a monument. In 1910, after making some corrections, revisions, and additions to this very personal work, he called for 10,000 copies to be printed and mailed "to as many preachers that they may learn to teach truth rather than fable." He also asked that copies be sent " to each of the leading magazines and journals," adding: "The religious theories must be reformed in order for man to make better progress." Owing to the fact that copies of *The New Revelation* are now quite scarce, it appears his wish was unfulfilled.

By publishing *The Independent Pulpit*, as well as writing for it,

Munson's contemporary, a former-Methodist minister named James Dickson Shaw, can be likened to those ex-smokers, recovering alcoholics, and former drug users who are often some of the most passionate, as well as effective, advocates for personal reform. Why? Because knowing from personal experience not only what it is like to be on the wrong road, but also how difficult it can be to make major changes in one's life, has the effect of bestowing on such people an extra measure of credibility, which means their words and actions carry far more weight than someone who has not had the same experience. There is no question then, that as a Christian minister-turned-atheist, James Dickson Shaw of Waco, Texas was certainly possessed of such integrity when it came to matters of theology. Unfortunately, this *Reader* includes only three examples of his work. It is not due, however, to any shortage of material but rather, in order to keep this book to a manageable size!

Although it includes both introductory and summary paragraphs, the first Shaw piece is not so much an essay as a list of contradictory Bible verses, which the former cleric compiled expressly for his readers so that they could refer to it whenever they had a chance to challenge the claim by believers, amazingly still being made today, that the Bible is the "infallible word of God." It is no less useful today and I feel completely certain that he would approve its inclusion herein.

In the second piece, which is a critique of an article written by T. V. Munson and published in the same issue of *The Independent Pulpit*, Shaw not only offers his opinion of a contributor's essay but also defends as "legitimate" the much-needed work of challenging organized religion and calling its dogma into question. He also identifies a situation that was problematic in his own time, and from all appearance, remains so to this very day, i.e., the difficulty of organizing disbelievers.

> The trouble with Liberals [i.e., "Freethinkers"] is that they lack unity of thought, aim and purpose. In the transformation from some branch of superstition, each one has developed his individuality to such an extent that any organic movement looks to him oppressive. It is but natural that this should be so, and it will require many long years of effort, crowded with failures innumerable, for us to overcome this evil. The transition from one habit of thought to another is a slow one and cannot be otherwise. We need to have patience and a mind to work with little hope of reaping the reward of our labors in person.

Introduction

The third piece, "An Infidel's Confession of Faith," which appeared in *Public Opinion* magazine in 1896, largely explains how Shaw lost his religious faith. It likewise addressed the problem of organizing freethinkers and spurring them to take action, something that is difficult to do even today.

Although this *Reader* was compiled and published primarily to serve as a companion volume to *Guided By Reason: The Golden Age of Freethought in Texas*—wherein the lives and careers of the men whose work is presented here are laid out in more detail—I think it stands very well on its own—as an example of some of the best freethought literature produced in the Lone Star state during the late nineteenth and early twentieth centuries. It also provides evidence that contrary to popular belief, early-day Texas was not populated entirely by men, women, and children who obediently marched in lock-step to church each Sunday morning, but also by thoughtful, articulate independent thinkers who dared not only to challenge the status quo but also to advance the seemingly radical notion that logic and reason, combined with belief based on scientific evidence rather than "faith" or religious dogma, provides a better, more certain path to progress and peace in the world. As we now living in the early twenty-first century well know, that vision was not realized during their own era—nor has it yet. This does not mean however, that they were wrong, just simply ahead of their time. With the publication of this *Reader*, they have been given a second chance—and consequently, so have we. The question is, *will we embrace it*?

Jasper M. Gilbert

"Those who try to explain existence by the meaningless word 'God' and those who try to explain mind and mental phenomena by 'spirits' are simply taking refuge behind ignorance. The words 'God' and 'spirit' are used to cover up things not yet understood by those who use them. They are no explanations at all, but simply make matters more complicated."

JASPER MONROE GILBERT was born January 1870 in Fannin County, Texas, the son of Jasper Gilbert, Sr., who died the very same month, and Rebecca Lindsey Gilbert. His paternal grandfather was Capt. Mabel Gilbert, an early day pioneer in both Dallas and Fannin counties. He was raised as a Presbyterian in Randolph, Fannin County, Texas, by his mother and stepfather Woodruff P. Hall.

Around 1880-1890, Gilbert traveled to California. While residing in Los Angeles he began attending Unitarian church services and also took some interest in spiritualism.

A few years after returning to Randolph, Gilbert began to have doubts about the authenticity of the Bible and religion in general. After reading Volney's *Ruins*, John William Draper's *History of the Conflict Between Religion and Science*, and works by Ingersoll, Darwin, Huxley and Haeckel, he not only became an atheist but also an outspoken opponent of organized religion. In politics he embraced Populism before converting to Socialism, and then finally Anarchism.

In 1897 he wrote the first of several letters and articles that were published in D. M. Bennett's *The Truth Seeker*. During the early 1900s his work also appeared in *Free Thought Magazine* and other "infidel" publications.

In 1898 Gilbert enrolled at the American Medical College in St. Louis, Missouri. In 1902 he was graduated with a degree in "eclectic" medicine. After living briefly in Homer, Indian Territory (present-day Oklahoma), he returned to Randolph, where it appears he remained for the rest of his life. Unable to make a living as a doctor, he turned to farming.

During the second decade of the twentieth century many of the "infidel" publications Gilbert wrote for began to close down. With no outlets for his work, his writing seems to have ceased.

Between 1919 and 1921 Gilbert was treated for a cancerous growth on his face, doubtless the result of exposure to intense sunlight while working in the fields. For a while he thought he was cured but after the cancer returned, he grew despondent. On May 19, 1943, he committed suicide in Dallas. He is buried at Randolph, Texas.

NEWS FROM TEXAS.

From *The Truth Seeker*, July 3, 1897

To the Editor of The Truth Seeker.

I thought I would write you the way things have been around this place. There were only three of us outspoken Infidels in this community, but one of them moved away last fall and left only two of us that were not afraid to let people know where we stood. We have some sympathizers, but they are afraid of public opinion. We have a kind of mushroom-revival here every summer, whose only effect is to make a great many hypocrites and a number of fools. A traveling evangelist by the name of C. O. Jones came here with his tent and held a revival last summer. He was a hellfire howler; he ranted about Infidel deathbeds, and said that when they were dying they raved, foamed at the mouth, experienced all the horrors of hell; indeed, their souls were on the embers burning while they were passing away. He called all honest doubters "dried-up skeptics." He foamed at the mouth when talking about the saloons; he said that all women who went to dances were indecent, and implied in very plain language that they went there for illegal purposes. It is astonishing how much people will bear. While they were holding this meeting the depot agent, J. K. McCarty, another friend, and myself wrote a note to the men who were holding prayers out in the woods, that if they would pray for us, and we felt any change, we would renounce ourInfidelity. We told them this would be a good test as to the efficacy of prayer, and we quoted the New Testament to them, telling them what they could do if they were believers. This aroused the venom of the hypocrites and fools, and the next morning Mr. McCarty found a notice stuck on the door of the depot signed by "The 8 Undertakers," stating that he must quit talking his Infidelity or get out in so many days, threatening to silence him, "God being their helper." It is needless to say that he did not get out or quit talking Infidelity either. Since then they have cooled off and will not have arguments with us. I think that they have taken counsel among themselves and come to the conclusion that the more their holy fraud is stirred the louder the stench, and all the way they can do anything with unbelievers is to let them alone.

Randolph is thoroughly Christian. They all became converted last summer at the distracted meetings, even all the little children, if crying is conversion to religion, and they have become the most cowardly set to be found anywhere. They are afraid to meet their God. We had a few storms this spring, and a great many of the people have been in abject terror. The majority of them could not rest until they had storm-houses, into which they scramble at the appearance of every little whirlwind, and those who have no storm-houses will get up at all hours of the night and rush to their nearest neighbor's. The Christian parents are making a race of cowards out of their children.

We commenced to have a debate here, but could not run it for lack of attendance. The Christians must attend religious services four or five nights out of every week, besides Sunday, in the worship of a phantom God whom they can neither see, hear, feel, taste, nor smell; go through hollow ceremonies and utter vain prayers to a nonentity. They must waste all of this time in repeating nonsense and trying to learn something about that of which nothing can be known, which is worse than time thrown away. It keeps their minds imprisoned and dwarfed by a degrading superstition; it keeps them from attending a debate or anything else that has the possibility of doing them any good intellectually. Thus it is plain to be seen by all not blinded by this religious folly that Putnam [S. F. Putnam, a well-known Freethought lecturer] was right when he said, "Religion is a curse, religion is a disease, religion is a lie."

I received the first copies of The Truth Seeker and the "Pictorial Text-Book" all right. I am well pleased with the paper and the book. The pictures very forcibly illustrate what churchism, the perpetuator of ignorance and superstition and opponent of freedom, has been in the past, what it is now, and what we may expect of it in the future. The reading matter contained in the book forms almost a library in itself.

Yours fraternally,

J. M. GILBERT

Randolph, Tex.

"DISTRACTED" MEETINGS.

From *The Truth Seeker*, September 4, 1897

To the Editor of The Truth Seeker:

At the present writing they have just finished having two *distracted* meetings at Randolph, Texas, but I do not think that they succeeded in working their hoodoo very successfully on many. They had one of their meetings at the C. P. church and the other at the Baptist. Some deluded people look upon these churches as speaking well of the community, but I look upon these with their spires pointing heavenward as monuments to ignorance and superstition. It is humiliating to those not blinded by superstition or addicted to mental cowardice, to look behind the scenes and observe the deep-rooted superstition, whose mother is ignorance, that has such a firm hold upon the minds of the people; and it fills one with indignation to see those hypocrites, the preachers, who by deceit and falsehood, are keeping their minds infused with these soul-destroying dogmas in order that they may continue to reap in the future, as they have always done in the past, the earnings of their ignorant dupes. This is the secret why religion has always opposed scientific knowledge, and why it still continues to be the enemy of science; why it has slandered, persecuted, imprisoned, tortured, and burned at the stake some of the greatest and noblest humanitarians that the world ever saw—martyrs in the cause of humanity, which is infinitely greater than a mere religious martyr. The religious martyr dies with the belief that that he is only giving up his short stay here, which is but a few fleeting years at best, and that he will be rewarded with eternal life; while the Freethinker goes down to his grave in reconciled submission to the course of nature, believing that death ends all, without the thought of a reward after death. Christians, in their conceit and egotism, pity us poor Infidels, but that is only a make-believe;

the inward thought of most of them is directly the opposite. They pant to unite church and state, draft God in the Constitution, and if they only had the power they would close the mouth of every heretic and of every Infidel; all real progress and real enlightenment would be brought to a stand-still, retrogression would set in, and the conditions of the dark or middle ages would again make their appearance. Christianity has been always on the side of tyranny and oppression, as is well attested by the pages of history. It claims to be the *summun bonum* of all good, but it has been a curse instead; not one good that it contains can be pointed out; it has not one redeeming feature. It has given us no inventions, except the rack, the thumbscrew, the wheel, the iron boot, and the stake; no art except the fiendish art of torture in which the victim was made to writhe and suffer the agonies of a thousand deaths.

They always hold their revivals (orgies) here in the summer time; that is the period when their monomania seems to make its periodical return. I do not know why it is always in the summer, unless the returning heat recalls to their memory their imagined hell, while the winter season, when so many backslide, gets them to thinking that hell would not be such a bad place after all. The holiness people have been holding meetings all over this country, and great many are growing demented over it, claiming to get sanctified. One girl at Bonham got sanctified and then killed herself. These revivals always turn out hypocrites whenever they make conversions or succeed in deluding people. They work upon the sympathies just like a political speaking, pervert their minds in making them believe that this is the operation of some supernatural agency. These people, if they ever realize that they have been deluded, will never acknowledge it, and, in most cases, will go through life a hypocrite, countenancing a fraud all their lives because they are ashamed to acknowledge that they have been fooled, for they fear public opinion, or have not the courage to boldly meet the stinging slanders of the lying, scorpion tongues of the rest of the hypocrites.

I look upon Christianity as a species of insanity which, like an epileptic fit, makes its periodic return here every summer. Now is the time that the dog is returning to his vomit, the fool to his folly, the fakirs (preachers) with renewed energy to their hoodooism and the monomaniacs to their "particular superstition." I want to emphasize what Putnam [S. F. Putnam, a prominent nineteenth century Freethought writer and lecturer] has said: "Religion is a disease. Religion is a big burning boil, preachers are pimples, churches are cancers, and piety is pus." Never will the people be completely free and happy, never will they get the reforms they so badly need until every vestige of superstition is wiped away, or the people learn to stop referring to all their evils to other than natural causes, and learn that for every effect there must be a natural cause, and that by constant application they will be able to find the cause and apply the remedy. Then it will be possible for them to become a free, prosperous, and happy people.

Yours for Freethought.

J. M. GILBERT

THE PREACHERS.

From *The Truth Seeker*, November 6, 1897

To the Editor of The Truth Seeker.

The article in The Truth Seeker by John Peck is indeed a sledge-hammer blow to that pious fraud Christianity. Such thoughts as are therein expressed have been uppermost in my mind ever since I became convinced of the truths of Liberalism. I look upon orthodox preachers as one of the most worthless classes under the sun. Instead of being useful for any thing they are a hindrance and a curse to civilization, a clog to stop the wheels of true progress. They drain the country of untold millions in salaries, the foreign mission fraud, and in a worse than useless outlay to build expensive churches for themselves to preach in, thus continually creating places for themselves where they make strenuous efforts to keep the minds of the people imbued with the superstition of the Dark Ages. They keep their ignorant dupes gazing at the cross, keep their attention riveted to a spectacle of death and suffering claimed to have taken place eighteen centuries ago, while they filch their pockets of their hard earned cash. They prostitute both time and energy by preaching over and over again the same old stale nonsense of myths that have no foundation in fact. They preach submission in tyranny in order that such men as Rockefeller may contribute to their support; thus they keep on the side of the plutocrats. They preach economy and thrift that they may live a life of luxury and ease; they preach virtue and morality and it is violated by more of their class than any other. The morality that they preach, however, has a false foundation, in that they teach that all immoral acts will be forgiven believers, thus leaving an open road to vice and crime. "The Gleaner," Cuero, Texas, credits the Rev. Thos. Dixon, Jr., with saying: "The decline of the ministry is a great factor in the decay of the ecclesiastical machinery. If there is a runt in the family, who is of no earthly use for anything else," note the words of the last clause which implies that anything will do for the ministry, "the parents make a preacher of him, there are one thousand preachers in this city out of a job." Why is there a decline? Is it not because one great preacher after another who does his own thinking on the existing problems of to-day and who has the moral stamina to tell the people his honest thoughts, is denounced by the rest of the orthodox clergy as a heretic and is voted out of the pulpit by his congregation? Such occurrences are frequent. Those preachers that hide facts and preach fiction or who are willing to preach the ignorant dogmas believed in by men that lived in a more ignorant age of the world are still retained in the orthodox fold. Ignorance, credulity, and superstition are inseparable and Christianity is their consummation.

We have here in Randolph (Tex.) a man who taught school several years ago. He held a second grade certificate. He did not keep up with the advancement of the times and he quit teaching and became a politician and succeeded in getting elected to the legislature of this state. His constituents never heard his doing anything except voting. When his time expired and he came home they did not run him any more, but left him at home. He remained a year or two, without any visible occupation. He finally got ordained by the Baptist church to preach, as that was all the avenue he saw open by which he could get his living without work. He is now a worthless parasite upon the body politic. While he taught school he was of some use to the community, but now is no earthly use. Many incompetent or otherwise lazy school teachers become deadbeat preachers.

The difference between a paid preacher and a tramp is, a tramp is very often a person forced out of employment by the introduction of improved machinery, while the majority of men preach in order to get out of hard labor; a tramp does his own begging, while preachers generally have women and children do theirs for them. How much better is a preacher than a robber who takes your property by stealth—the result is the same, they both get something for nothing? What is the use of a country complaining of *hard times*, as long as these useless parasites are allowed to fatten upon the unrequited toil of the millions? "Take theology from the world," says Ingersoll, "and millions of men will be compelled to earn an honest living. Impudence will not tax credulity. The vampire of hypocrisy will not suck the blood of honest toil."

J. M. Gilbert

CONVERSATION WITH A PARSON.

From *The Truth Seeker*, November 27, 1897

Editor's note: It is both ironic and unfortunate that in this short piece, Gilbert reveals in his statement regarding evolution that although he was a well-read, intelligent, and seemingly open-minded man who deplored slavery (see p. 16), his apparent belief that white people were more intelligent than black people was in line with the majority white opinion of his era, at least in 1897, when this letter was written.

To the Editor of The Truth Seeker.

I was a forced listener the other day to a conversation between an ordained Baptist exhorter and a citizen who had lately been converted to Christianity. All that they said was mere lot of rubbish that one can hear every day in the South. They talked for some length, seemingly for my benefit, when one of them said, "I do not believe that an honest man can doubt the existence of a creator." This seemed to be making it personal enough for me to put in, which I did by saying, "Men, I think you are mistaken on that." One of them asked, "What makes men believe in a God?" I told him that was more a matter of education and the result of living among people of that belief, and that children were natural unbelievers until they were taught religious ideas. The parson then spoke up and said, in substance, that all peoples of every degree of civilization and of every caste and of every country and nation on the globe have innate ideas of a God and a future life. I told him that he was making a purely gratuitous assertion, asserting more than he could prove. He says, "Of course I cannot prove it to one who denies all history"—another gratuitous assertion. I told him that Darwin, Humboldt, and other great travelers found numerous instances where the natives did not believe in a God or a future life. He then asked me who Darwin was. When I told him, he asked, "Do you know what Darwin taught? He taught that man came into existence from an inferior animal." I said, "Yes, and I believe that to be true." He then dished out a lot of irrelevant words about cross-breeding the canine species and getting a better blooded animal, but could not produce human beings, which showed that he had never read Darwin and that he was utterly ignorant of what he really taught, and it also became apparent that he had no clear idea of evolution. I told him, "You take the whites, negroes, cannibals, aborigines of Australia, the gorilla, the chimpanzee, and there is a descending scale of intelligence." He wanted to do all the talking, the way he always does when in an argument, thinking that those listening will take an idle clatter of words for an argument, and great many do.

To cut the argument as short as possible I said, "One thing I do know, and of which I do not have a particle of doubt, and that is, your Bible is false." He asked, "Can you prove it?" I answered that I could prove the falsity of a great many things in it. He did not ask me for any proof, for he is a school teacher and knew that what he had taught in school on astronomy and geography that contradicted the Bible. He then left, but turned around to say, "We see the grass growing but cannot understand it, which proves the existence of a higher ruler." He did not stay for me to reply, but I called to him and said in substance, "It is our ignorance, because we cannot understand what is going on around us, but ignorance is no proof of a God."

Once this very man came up to where a friend and myself were talking about the Bible and he said to us, "If it were not for the Bible, we would not know that we were men, we would be no more than brutes." I told him that if the Bible said he was a jackass he would believe it. What a silly argument the above is for a man who has taught school, been to the legislature, and is ordained to preach. Is he so ignorant of the origin of languages? Does he childishly believe the fairy tale about God taking Adam by hand then giving him a ready-made language? As to being so much above the brutes as to deserve another life, I ask him to take the inspired testimony of Job vii, 9: "As the cloud is consumed and vanisheth away, so he that goeth down to the grave shall come up no more." That ought to be plain enough, but let him listen to Solomon, the wisest man, and if any one is inspired it cannot be denied to him: "The dead know not anything; neither have they any more reward; for the memory of them is forgotten; also their love, and their hatred, and their envy is now perished. There is no work, nor device, nor knowledge, nor wisdom in the grave whither thou goest. For that which befalleth the sons of men befalleth beasts; even one thing befalleth them: as the one dieth, so dieth the other—yea, they have all one breath; so that a man hath no pre-eminence above a beast. All go unto one place; all are the dust, and all turn to dust again." (Eccl. ix, 5, 6, 10; iii, 19, 20).

The above person referred to received a sample copy of The Truth Seeker, and he made about the following remarks to a friend of mine: "It is pictured off nicely and looks very plausible and it would hardly do for a person weak or undecided to read it. I can read it; it cannot turn me because I am fixed." This is just about as sensible as sending a boy to school and telling him that he must not believe that the world is round; that it moves and that the sun stands still in its relation to the earth, because the Bible says the earth is flat and that sun moves and that he must remain *fixed* and believe the Bible or he would go to hell. It was because the churches and their congregations were fixed and had the power, that Bruno, Vanini, and men who taught advanced truths were burnt at the stake or, like Galileo, languished and died in loathsome dungeons. If everybody were like my friend above, there would be no need of schools, colleges, and teachers, for they would be of no benefit to people who were already "fixed."

J. M. Gilbert

MATERIALISTIC PHILOSOPHY.

From *The Truth Seeker*, March 4, 1899

I greatly admire Otto Wettstein's philosophy. I think it is a solid foundation—one that cannot be shaken by all the theologians in the world, nor Spiritualists either.

The explanation of many things which the world once thought inexplicable is now simple, and so will it be with all the phenomena now shrouded in obscurity. The best explanation in most things is the simplest, the longest in being found out, and which the world is last in accepting, so prone are the people to believe in the mysterious, because of misdirected past education and unreasoning prejudices in consequence.

It has been found by long and careful research that natural laws act the same throughout the whole universe. These are called forces, which Buchner shows cannot be separated from matter. We cannot conceive of matter without force, or *vice versa*. Abundant experience shows that one atom of matter cannot be annihilated. If matter cannot be destroyed it cannot be created, and it necessarily follows that matter and the forces inseparable from it must have existed eternally. It is a self-evident truth that something cannot come from nothing. A so-called God, or any other imaginary being, is impotent to create and impotent to destroy. We cannot have a God and all it implies and at the same time have a universe, because of the self-evident fact that two things cannot occupy the same place at the same time. We must give up one or the other. We have the universe, we know that it exists and it is conceded by all to be infinite. By having a universe there is no room for an infinite God to exist.

Those who try to explain existence by the meaningless word "God" and those who try to explain mind and mental phenomena by "spirits" are simply taking refuge behind ignorance. The words "God" and "spirit" are used to cover up things not yet understood by those who use them. They are no explanations at all, but simply make matters more complicated.

When the world learns to "let the ghosts go," it will be a grand victory for humanity. It will place us far on the road to happiness, prosperity, and perfection. The blatant, hypocritical priests, parsons, chaplains, and imposters will have to work or starve. The world will support no more churches, but will establish in their places institutions where useful knowledge will be taught instead of guesses and degrading superstition.

The religious bigots, who are trying to get God in the Constitution, and thereby reestablish religious tyranny, are preparing to reap the inevitable storm unless they discontinue. It took Infidelity to free us from kingcraft, it took Infidelity to free us from black slavery, and it will yet take Infidelity to free us from the first, last, and greatest curse of all—religion.

This republic was founded by such Infidels as Paine, Jefferson, Adams, and Washington. All were to be free to worship or not to worship, but Christians, not content to enjoy their own rights, must violate the highest law of the land in trying to force all to bend to their ignorant creed. Infidels have a perfect right to resist such lawlessness.

I think it is time for all lovers of liberty to speak out plainly and show these narrow-minded bigots wither they are drifting. Yours for Freethought.

J. M. Gilbert

GIFT OF FAITH AND BELIEF.

WHAT FOLLOWS IF THE PROMISES ARE TRUE.

From *The Truth Seeker*, March 11, 1899

Works Not Necessary to Salvation, But Are Rather a Hindrance—Sin Not Possible to Those Born of the Spirit, Which Is to Say of God, as All True Believers Are—Communism of the Apostles—How One May Know of a Surety That He Is a Christian.

BY J. M. GILBERT

A Christian's belief and his faith are the same thing. The terms "belief" and "faith" are used synonymously, and one term can be substituted for the other, "for there is no difference." (Rom. iii, 22). Faith and belief are said to come alike by hearing: "How can they believe in him of whom they have not heard? So then faith cometh by hearing and hearing by the word of God." (Rom. x, 14, 17). The Christian's faith is said to be the gift of God. "God hath dealt to every man the measure of faith. Jesus, the author and finisher of our faith. It is the gift of God." (Rom. xii, 3; Heb. xii, 2; Eph. ii, 8).

Sufficient Unto Salvation

There is one unpardonable sin—the sin of unbelief. "He that believeth not shall be damned. For if you believe not that I am he, ye shall die in your sins." (Mark xvi, 16; John viii, 24). "He that believeth on the Son hath everlasting life, and he that believeth not the Son shall not see life. And by him all that believe are justified from all things, from which you could not be justified by the law. Therefore we conclude that a man is justified by faith without the deeds of the law. But to him that worketh not, but believeth on him that justifieth the ungodly, his faith is counted for righteousness. For Christ is the end of the law for righteousness to everyone that believeth. That if thou shalt confess with thy mouth the Lord Jesus, and shalt believe in thine heart that God hath raised him from the dead, thou shall be saved." (John iii, 36; Acts xiii, 29: Rom. iii, 28' iv, 5; x, 4, 9).

These passages plainly teach that *belief is sufficient unto salvation*, and that *works are not necessary*. Works without belief are counted for nothing, but belief without works is counted sufficient to justify "from all things."

> Try every art of legal thieving;
> No matter—stick to sound believing.
>   —Burns

How to Know Believers

We cannot tell them by their occupation or their morality, for they have a special license to the effect that they will be "justified from all things" immoral if they only believe with all their heart. Human beings, however, do not believe with their hearts any more than they see with their ears or hear with their eyes. Believers must have some gift or power that unbelievers do not possess, otherwise how much better off are they than the Infidel? By searching the scriptures we have hit upon an infallible rule by which to know these supernaturalized beings called believers.

"Whomsoever believeth that Jesus is Christ is born of God" (a spirit). "Whosoever is born of God doth not commit sin…and he cannot sin, because he is born of God." (I John v, 1; iii, 9). There is no sin for a believer, for "Christ is the end of the law." Being "born of God" is what Christians call being "born again," or being "born of the spirit." God is said to be a spirit, and being born of him could not be anything else but the spiritual birth. Christians, if you are "born of the spirit" you are the "sons of God" and you "cannot sin." If you are "born of the spirit," you are not men, for "who can say, I have made my heart clean; I am pure from sin? There is not a just man upon the earth, that doeth good, and sinneth not. He that committeth sin is of the devil. For there is no man that sinneth not." (Prov. xx, 9; Eccl. vii, 20; John iii, 8; I Kings viii, 46). If you are "born of the spirit" (God) you are a spirit, for "that which is born of the spirit is spirit." You can come and go like the wind and no one can see you (except believers who have the power of "discerning of spirits"); they can hear the sound of your coming and going, but you will be invisible; "so is every one that is born of the spirit," "for a spirit hath not flesh and bones" to make it visible. If you sin you are "not of God," but "of the devil;" if you cannot come and go without being seen, you are not "born of the spirit." In other words, you do not believe.

"And the multitude of them that believed were of one heart and one soul; neither said any of them that aught of the things which he possessed was his own; but they had all things in common." (Acts, iv, 32). Now, Christians, are you all of one mind? Are there no dissensions among you? Do you have all things in common, none claiming private property? It is true, you can agree only too well when it comes to suppressing and denying facts against your religion and interfering with the individual rights of those who will not conform to your absurd superstition, but you do not agree on your own doctrines. The reason is plain enough, your old paper fetich [sic] is full of contradictions.

Thieves may disagree and fight when it comes to dividing the spoils, but when they are about to be convicted they can all turn liars and agree that the mouth of the witness must be closed or he must be put out of the way. All thoughtful and industrious people take thought for the morrow, but you are commanded not to do so. When smitten on the cheek do you turn the other? If you are "born of the spirit" it cannot hurt you any more than you can hurt the wind by striking it. When your horse is stolen do you give the thief your cow also, or do you have him put in prison? If you do not come up to these requirements can you be Christian?

What Believers Can Do

But let us take another step. "Verily, verily, I say unto you, he that believeth on me, the works that I do shall he do also; and greater works than these shall he do. If you ask anything in my name I will do it." (John xiv, 12, 14). "And these signs shall follow them that believe: In my name shall they cast out devils; they shall speak with new tongues; they shall take up serpents; and if they drink any deadly thing it shall not hurt them; they shall lay hands on the sick and they shall recover. All things are possible to him that believeth." (Mark xvi, 17, 18; iv, 23). Compare Matthew xxi, 21, 22; xvii, 20. Luke xvii, 6; Mark xi, 23.

Now, Christians, if you are believers, you ought to be able to demonstrate it according to the rules laid down by Christ. Step forward and let us see you perform "greater works" than Christ is said to have performed. Let us see you bring a decomposed corpse back to life. Let us see you cast out a devil. At this day and time this would be an extraordinary feat, indeed, seeing there are no devils to cast out. No one but the insane now believe in devils inhabiting the bodies of men and causing them to be afflicted with diseases. Medical science has settled that question. All physicians, and those who send for them, are practical Infidels on that bead.

If you are a believer, you have the gift of the Holy Ghost. Give us an exhibition of the linguistic performance that is said to have taken place on the day of Pentecost—let us hear you "speak with new tongues." If you are what you claim to be, why don't you heal your own sick instead of sending for a doctor? Why don't you trust in prayer and laying on of hands, and let medicine alone? (James v, 14, 15). Why should you mourn the loss of your dead relations and friends? Why don't you raise them up? Why don't you give us proof of a resurrection and of a future life? Raise up some dead friend and let him give us the desired information. A believer is in demand in this poverty-stricken country. He could command a fortune by moving mountains out of the way of railroads. Life insurance companies would want to monopolize him; the coffin trust would want to bribe him. Uncle Sam greatly needs such a man to feed his army and to remove obstructions that the enemy has thrown in the way without endangering life. A believer could feed the many millions of tramping, starving, and unemployed from a few biscuits. Why in the name of suffering humanity is it not done? It is because a believer does not exist and never did, except in the imagination of the stupidly credulous.

A False Claim

Christians, knowing full well that they cannot come up to the requirements of a believer, as described in the passages just cited, try to evade the plain statements by making the unwarranted assertion that the things enumerated above only applied to that day and time, and not to this age. They cannot explain away the gospels as applying to another age and still truthfully say they also apply to this. Christ was a false prophet. He taught that the end of the world was near at hand. He taught that that generation (the one he was talking to) would not pass away until he would be seen coming in his glory, and that some of those standing there should not taste of death until it should come to pass (See Matthew xxiv, 29—34; x, 23; xvi, 28; Mark xiii, 28—30; ix, 1; Luke xxi, 25—30; ix, 27). If Christ existed he was an imposter for saying things not true, or he was a poor, deluded, crazy mortal. He left his dupes in the suds. As he was to come and set up his kingdom during the lifetime of some of those then living, we may justly say that all of his teachings about being saved by belief could not hold good any longer than the time he was to come, which was to be the end of the world. But as this prophecy, by which all his other promises were to be fulfilled, proved false, can any sane man put any trust in them? If any of the gospels apply to this age, those parts describing the powers of believers, and the "signs" which were to follow, also apply to this age. Christ said: "Go ye into all the world, and preach the gospel to every creature. And these signs shall follow them that believe." The terms "he that believeth," "him that believeth," and "them that believe" will then apply to "every creature" of "all the world" to whom the gospel is preached, and the "signs" which were to follow were to assure such as believed that they were really believers. If "all the world" does not include people living now, then we live in an entirely different world, are out of the boundary of the gospel, and have no business to bother out heads with it. If "all the world" only meant countries then known, then the declaration that "God sent not his Son into the world to condemn the world, but that the world through him might be saved," does not apply to this age.

The Scriptures Not True

We have seen that according to the scriptures belief or faith comes by hearing; that it is sufficient unto salvation, and a believer would possess supernatural powers. But belief does not come by hearing, except to the stupidly credulous. Some are silly enough to believe, or pretend to believe, every falsehood, every lie manufactured in the interest of religion. Mosheim says that the early fathers of the church esteemed it an "act of virtue to deceive and lie when by that means the interest of the church might be promoted." Christians have kept this practice in the holy family so long that it has become almost second nature for them to practice deception and falsehood in the interest of the church. They still keep up the practice.

These stupidly credulous people, however, are extremely incredulous when it comes to believing scientific facts which will destroy their absurd superstition. Rational people do not believe everything they hear unless evidence or sufficient reasons are given. Belief is not subject to the will. No two persons can believe alike, because their cerebral organizations are not alike. There are several faculties of the brain which must cooperate in weighing evidence for and against, and then the scales turn in spite of ourselves. There is no chance for a person to be dishonest in the formation of a belief, but many are dishonest in expressing it. Belief is not knowledge, when we know a thing, it ceases to be a belief. Where knowledge ends belief begins. Our desires, hopes, and beliefs will not make anything true. They are impotent to change one natural fact. An almost universal belief did not make the earth flat, did not make it the stationary center of the universe, nor the sky a solid, although it was so taught by the scriptures. The beliefs in a God, in immortality, in a place of eternal reward and of eternal punishment, are not as plausible as the belief in a flat earth. It is puerile to think a thing is so just because it is believed by many, or because it was written, especially if you go back into ignorant antiquity for authority. It is a false and pernicious doctrine that teaches that belief merits eternal reward and unbelief eternal punishment. It is idiotic to think that belief or unbelief can change our destiny after we are dead.

Fruits of Christian Belief.

Because they believed in a vengeful tyrant God, in witchcraft, that unbelief was an unpardonable crime, and that their God would punish such with endless torment, their belief has been, and still is, a great curse to the world. They became intolerable, treacherous, and deceitful like their imaginary God; they devastated and drenched the earth with the blood of good and noble men and women, and of helpless and innocent women and children; they carried on wars of extermination against all heretics, philosophers, and men of science who dared to advocate facts contrary to a book written by ignorant barbarians. As God would burn unbelievers in hell, they thought they were doing his will by beginning it here, and that they would be rewarded for it.

This is the black record of Christianity. It is in its very nature to be intolerant, to persecute, and to make everything bend to their ignorant dogmas and all to worship their tyrant God. Its God was so intolerant that he commanded all who worshipped other gods to be stoned to death. Its Christ was so intolerant that he commanded: "Those mine enemies, which would not that I should reign over them, bring hither and slay before me," and all those who had brains enough to think for themselves and could not believe on him he said he would damn. Christianity now lacks power to do all it would wish, but the same old spirit of intolerance and hatred still rankles in its bosom.

Christianity is founded upon the false geocentric system of astronomy. Astronomy has shown us that the earth is not the immovable centre of the universe, and that the rest of the planets, suns, and stars were not created purposely for it. We know that the sky is not a solid crystal with windows in it. The heaven of the ancients, which they thought was only a few miles above the earth, has played out, and its twin idea of hell must go with it. The ignorant ancients, deceived by appearances, thought they could build a tower to the sky—to heaven—and God ignorantly thought so too, for he had to come down from his crystal throne and confuse their language, for fear they might succeed. They could then pour through the windows in great numbers, and he would thereby lose the pleasure of committing suicide to redeem only a small portion of them, according to his predestined plan, and damning the rest.

Christianity is founded upon the false heathen fable of creation. Geology shows that the earth must have been many millions of years in forming, that life and death existed millions of years before man, and that man existed many thousands of years before the time of creation according to Genesis.

Something cannot come from nothing. One of the scientific truths is matter cannot be annihilated, and that which cannot be destroyed cannot be created, and must have existed eternally. Rev. J. W. Chadwick says: "Science teaches us how from primal germs the world has been evolved into its present shape…Think of all the precious time wasted to endeavor to make the Bible echo the great truths of science." The fall of man has been shown to be false, and that which is founded upon a falsehood must also be false. Rev. M. J. Savage says: "It is well known that the Jews did not attempt to tell any story of Adam or the fall until after they had borrowed it in the days of their captivity. These things are only pagan traditions, and there is no more reasonable basis for them than there is one of the tales of the Arabian Nights…The first man is now found close on the borders of the animal world, and in the light of this discovery the utterly baseless tradition of the fall becomes absurd. No *fall*, but the ascent of man is what now appears…In the light of to-day the plan of salvation has no rational excuse for continued existence one day more."

LETTER REGARDING THE DEATH OF ROBERT G. INGERSOLL

From *The Truth Seeker*, August 26, 1899

To the Editor of The Truth Seeker.

The report of the sudden death of Col. R. G. Ingersoll came like a shock to all lovers of Freethought and liberty. It pains us all to know that his mighty voice has been hushed, that we will never more hear the eloquent words from the lips of this great champion and hero of Freethought and foe to superstition and tyranny. He met the most able defenders of Christianity and they were beaten. Liberalism has sustained a great loss by his death. Although the Ingersoll of flesh and blood has passed into an eternal sleep his influence will be perpetuated in the memory of his friends, be extended, and continue to be felt all over this broad land. His sublime words and thoughts will still be read by many thousands yet to come, and wherever read they cannot help but bear good fruit. My prayer is that the works of this noble man may be read more than ever, and they will be widely circulated by friends who have the means. I greatly regret my inability to do much in this grand work. Had I a million dollars I would rather give it all and see every vestige of religion wiped out than to retain one cent. We will never get perfect liberty and justice until this is accomplished. Those reformers who are turning their attention to politics and are known by the many "isms" are simply wasting time. The most of these are too cowardly to print anything against religion, the greatest enemy of reform, and which will have to be fought and subdued before they can accomplish the ends they have in view. Yours for success.

J. M. Gilbert

CHRISTIANITY AS IT IS.

The Followers of that Faith Persecute Because They are Zealous and Sincere

From *The Truth Seeker*, October 14, 1899

[I wrote a letter which was published in the Farmers' Review, a Socialist paper, at Bonham, Tex. The letter was criticized by one of the editors, who admitted, or did not deny, most all that I had to say except what is explained by the inclosed article. He admitted that Christna and Gautama "taught about the same theory of ethics as did Jesus," thus conceding that Christianity is a borrowed and plagiarized system from the older religions and needed no revelation, which strongly implies that Christ was a myth. He could not deny that the Bible is full of contradictions, that the Jesus of Matthew, Mark and Luke could not have been the Jesus of John. He thus gives up the infallibility of the Bible. On account of the innumerable contradictions that it contains it both sanctions and condemns many vices and crimes, and is absolutely unfit for instruction in philosophy, morals, or economics. Washington and the whole army of patriots resisted "the powers that be," and if Christianity is true, "shall receive to themselves damnation." He does not deny that religion has opposed every scientific fact and every radical change for the betterment of the human race, because they were contrary to the teachings of an ignorant book. Religion is not the force that causes progress, but always follows in the rear, and advances just as it is driven to do so by a progressive civilization. He says that "no religion has ever risen above the civilization that professed it." Then religion has been and is a curse. It is a lock and a barrier to the upward striving of mankind from ignorance, superstition, and slavery. I then sent a rejoinder which he refused to publish. He gave as his reasons that it would not do, and that it would ruin any Socialist paper that ever was. This illustrates the fact that the people are yet too ignorant, prejudiced, and intolerant to hear the truth in regard to their religion. It shows the amount of education that is yet needed before it is possible to have a just and equitable government. It shows the extreme need of supporting Liberal publications which show up the curse of religion in its true light, and how very weak and mild must be the articles that obtain admission into the common newspaper. Socialist papers claim to favor and advocate the right of the free speech and a free press, but fear to publish anything criticizing or showing the lie of religion.—J.M.G.]

The editor of the Farmers' Review says: "I see he [meaning the writer of this article] charges up to Christianity the unfortunate mistakes of a false Christianity. The underlying truth of Christianity is in no wise responsible for the enormities of Constantine or the persecutions waged in the dark ages…nor for the Spanish Inquisition, nor the murder of the Huguenots in France, any more than the principles of democracy are responsible for mob violence and the stuffing of ballot-boxes by a lot of traitors to political freedom."

Now, there is no such analogy between Christianity and democracy. Democracy never has said that all who would not be ruled by it should be killed. It never has said that all who would not believe in it shall be damned to an eternal hell. Here is a very wide difference which forbids the one to be compared with the other. The intolerance, persecutions, and murders of Christianity are not due to corruption of it or to a "false Christianity," but are due to its intolerant qualities and true principles, which will not out as long as all of the teachings of Christ are implicitly believed in.

Some of his reputed sayings are: "Suppose ye that I am come to give peace on earth? I tell you nay, but rather division. If any man come to me, and hate not his father and mother, and wife and children, and brethren and sisters, yet and his own life also, he cannot be my disciple. Think not that I am come to send peace on earth. I come not to send peace, but a sword. I am come to send fire on the earth; and what will I, if it be already kindled? Those mine enemies which would not say that I should reign over them, bring hither, and slay them before me. He that hath no sword, let him sell his garment and buy one. He that believeth not shall be damned."

There would just as much truth in saying that the command, "Thou shalt not suffer a witch to live," was not responsible for the horrible tortures and deaths for the "crime" of witchcraft as to say that the teachings of Christianity did not cause believers in it to persecute, butcher, and burn heretics and unbelievers. As God would burn all unbelievers forever, his adherents thought they were doing him a service by initiating his work here, and they were certainly carrying out the express commands of Christ by unsheathing the sword and lighting the fagot.

The "sword" that Christ came to send was wet with human blood for more than a thousand years, and has hardly yet had time to dry since a more humane principle called a halt. It was this sword that was used to murder the Huguenots. The "fire on earth" was kindled during the Dark Ages and during the Spanish Inquisition.

A pagan priest was too just to offer absolution to the murderer Constantine, and he turned to Christianity, which said that all sins will be forgiven believers, thus offering a license for crime. But in this Christian system there was no pardon for honest unbelief, either in this world or in the world to come. The main difference between Protestantism and Catholicism is, one believes in an infallible church and the other in an infallible book. One granted indulgences for nominal fee, while the other said that sinners would be forgiven with price, except belief. As to the empty rites and ceremonies, it matters not what form they take, they are worse than heathenish in this age, when a fair degree of enlightenment is with the reach of all.

Christ, if he lived, was ignorant of the workings of the human mind. He did not know that it required evidence to convince rational beings; that our beliefs are not subject to our wills, that the scales turn in spite of us; or that there was no possible chance for anyone to be dishonest in the formation of his beliefs. He did not grasp the great truth that no one can justly be held responsible for honest unbelief, even if it is founded upon error. He was unconscious of the fact that we are not all constituted alike, and can no more think alike and act alike than a savage and Humboldt. He did not say, He that hath brains to think, let him think, but "He that hath ears to hear, let him hear." If the New Testament is true, Christ was unjust and intolerant. He taught in parables, that the multitudes hearing might not understand, and seeing might not perceive. Would any just teacher who wanted to do the most good for mankind speak in language so enigmatical that the people could not understand and become converted? He taught the use of brute force to make the people become his subjects, just as tyrants do.

"Intolerance is a crime accursed." Some of Christ's teachings are curses, and Christianity is the greatest curse that ever existed. If intolerance is a "crime," Christianity is criminal. It is not the "unfortunate mistakes of a false Christianity," but the unavoidable acts of a true Christianity—as true as any part of it—that are responsible for the ages of intolerance, persecution, and bloodshed. Why is it thousands conceal their honest opinions and beliefs? For fear of ruining their business and of being slandered and calumniated. Why is it that a great incentive of the times is to lie and act like a hypocrite? Because this lying and intolerant system of Christianity has made it so.

Just in proportion to the sincerity of the Christian is his zeal, just in proportion to his zeal is his intolerance, and it is unavoidable. Gibbon, in his history, gives as one of the causes of the spread of Christianity "the inflexible and, if we may use the expression, the intolerant zeal of the Christians, derived, it is true, from the Jewish religion." Bishop Watson said, "with respect to the inflexibility and intolerance of Christian zeal," that he "would refer it to a more adequate and a more obvious source, a full persuasion of the truth of Christianity." If Christians are convinced that unbelief is a crime, and the great cause of sending souls to hell, they want to crush it out. The Puritans were intolerant, they persecuted, and they established Blue laws because they believed in the Bible. They established these wicked laws because Christ said, "Think not I am come to destroy the law or the prophets; I am not come to destroy, but to fulfil."

It is the very nature of Christianity to be intolerant, to persecute, and to exterminate its enemies. The most successful arguments it ever used were the rack, the wheel, the dungeon, the sword, and the stake. Brute force was the power more than any other used to convert. We see the same spirit manifested today in the National Reform Association, the Young Men's Christian Association, the Women's Christian Temperance Union, and Christian Endeavor societies. They would make the world conform to their ideas, believe in their creeds, and worship at the same shrine. They are endeavoring by every means, fair or foul, to bring the strong arm of the law to their aid, thus reuniting church and state, which in this republic were meant to be forever separate. Not content with exercising their own rights, they must infringe upon the rights of others. Yet they have the same rights as the adherents of any other religion, or as those who do not believe in any religion, and no more. Mohammedans or Buddhists have the same right as the Christians to use the law to establish their religion, but neither has any such right. In passing their odious Sunday laws, in teaching religion in our public schools, in exempting church property from taxation, and in hiring chaplains in the army, navy, Congress, and the legislatures, these bigoted zealots are traitors to the spirt of '76; they are lawbreakers and violators of the Constitution—the highest law of the land. They want to get God and the Bible in the Constitution and, like the Puritans, govern by this relic of barbarism. They are a standing menace and a source of danger to a republic and to liberty. If they could accomplish their designs liberty and freedom of conscience would be a thing of the past and intolerance would reign supreme.

St. Louis, Mo.   J. M. GILBERT

THE MONEY IS SAFE!

From *The Truth Seeker*, April 21, 1900

To the Editor of The Truth Seeker

The thousand dollars' reward offered for a Christian is entirely without danger of being claimed. There are no Christians and never were any when tested by the book they profess to believe. I would like to see this morsel thrust down the throats of all the sanctimonious pretenders and make them go through the test, to their utter chagrin, humiliation, and mortification, and to the unavoidable acknowledgment of the humbug, falsity, and lie of Christianity. If this was done those who honestly think they believe could have the veil of deception lifted from their eyes and be shown the true nature of the abominable thing they have been promoting by their clamor for religious class legislation and hard-earned cash, which is worse than wasted when given to such enterprise. Long live The Truth Seeker. Yours truly,

J. M GILBERT

St. Louis.

Jasper M. Gilbert

PLAIN TRUTHS FOR PREACHERS

A LETTER TO A CLERGYMAN ON BIBLICAL FALSITIES.

From *The Truth Seeker*, December 1, 1900

A Review of the More Conspicuous Absurdities Found in the Bible and the Christian Religion—Passages that Are Totally Irreconcilable With One Another or with Fact—Christ, the Central Figure of Christianity, a Myth Who Did Not Exist Even as a Man.
BY J. M. GILBERT.

I think I will employ a little of the present time in writing you another letter to again call your attention to the character of the book which you make a business of expounding. I wrote you a letter once before and kindly requested you to answer it, but not to take an unfair advantage in the pulpit. But that is what you did. If you could not give me a direct and fair answer to show me where I was in error, honesty would have prompted an honest confession or else silence, and not an unfair spouting about it in the pulpit. You know as well as I do that the account of the creation of the world about six thousand years ago is nothing more than a fable borrowed from the older legends of the heathen nations of antiquity. It was an attempt of ignorant men to account for the existence of the universe. All the natural sciences, such as astronomy, geology, and even physical geography, as taught In our schools, agree that our planet is millions of years old. Chemistry teaches us that matter cannot be created or annihilated, but is eternal and self-existing. You know this as well as I do. When you continue to teach this old fable as truth you are teaching something that is false. Why cannot you teach the truth in this matter? If your present calling will not let you, why don't you find one that will?

If you know anything about the Bible at all, you know that it is filled with numerous contradictions which cannot be harmonized. The first and second chapters of Genesis contain two different and contradictory accounts of creation. Their language and style are different, and it is plain to be seen they were collected from different sources. In one the earth was created wet, in the other dry; in one the birds were made out of the waters, in the other out of the ground; in one the lower animals were created first, in the other the order is reversed. The same two accounts can be traced through the description of the fabulous deluge. Witness the forty days' rain in one instance, and the one hundred and fifty days' rain in the other; the command to take the animals in by twos, and the command to take them in by sevens. The same with the history of Joseph. In one place it is said his brethren sold him to the Ishmaelites who sold him into Egypt, and in another place his brethren hid him in a cave from which he was stolen by the Midianites who sold him into Egypt. What man of sense can believe such contradictory accounts to be the inspired word of a truthful God?

What sensible person would believe in such a God as that depicted in the Old Testament? A fickle, changeable God, who said to the first man and woman, "Every tree in which is the fruit of a tree yielding seed, to you It shall be meat," but soon changed his mind and said, "But of the tree of the knowledge of good and evil, thou shalt not eat of it, for in the day that thou eatest thereof thou shalt surely die." Who would believe in a God who is a liar ? Here In this last verse is the primal lie of time. God is the first liar on record. Adam and Eve did not die the day they ate of the forbidden fruit, for God said unto Adam, "Cursed is the ground for thy sake; in sorrow shalt thou eat of it all the days of thy life." "All the days of thy life" here clearly means that Adam was to live more days than one, and God told a falsehood. If the record is true, they did live hundreds of years longer and reared a lot of children. The serpent, however, told the truth. He told them, "Ye shall not surely die" (meaning the day God said they would), "for God doth know that in the day ye eat thereof, then your eyes shall be opened, and ye shall be as gods, knowing good and evil." "And the Lord said, Behold, the man is become as one us, knowing good and evil." Doesn't this prove that the serpent told the truth and that God did not? According to the whole book, the devil is the best character of the two. You cannot show where he ever told a lie. He never was guilty of ordering the wholesale slaughter of innocent men, women and children, killing everything that breathed, except the virgins, telling them to save these for themselves. He never made the mistake of creating a world so that it would end in wickedness, and then got angry because things went just as he knew they would, repented, and sent a flood to drown the world. But this was a failure, for the world was soon just as bad as it was before. Then to appease the wrath of himself he committed suicide by sending his son to die, who was a part of himself and as old as himself. This last act was a failure, for nine-tenths of the world refuse to believe it. What a sorry God this is, anyway! a God getting angry and repenting because the world went just as he knew it would before he created it, and then taking vengeance on his creatures for what he alone can be held responsible. Worse than a peevish child at play. There is good excuse for the child, but none for a God. The devil is said to be the author of evil, but it is not true. "I make peace and create evil. I, the Lord, do all these things. Shall there be evil in the city and the Lord hath not done it ?" (Isaiah xiv, 7; Amos iii, 6.)

Byron, in his poem, makes Lucifer thus discourse to Cain:

> I tempt none.
> Save with the truth; was not the tree, the tree
> Of knowledge? and was not the tree of life
> Still fruitful? Did I bid her pluck them not?
> Did I plant things prohibited?
> Within the reach of beings innocent, and curious

By their innocence ? I would have made ye
Gods; and even he who thrust ye forth, so thrust you
Because "ye should not eat the fruits of life,
And become God as we." Were not those his words?

Again, he speaks as follows:

He as conqueror will call the conquered
Evil; but what will be the good he gives?
Were I the victor, his works would be deem'd
The only evil ones.

The New Testament is founded upon the Old. Upon the fable of creation depend its fundamental doctrines of the fall of man and the need of a redeemer. As the account of the creation is not true, so the fundamental doctrines of Christianity are false, and Christianity is a false system. No well-informed person now believes in the table of creation. Any person of ordinary sense can see the connection that, the table of creation given up, there is no longer any excuse for the existence of a priestcraft to preach a plan of salvation founded thereon. "In the light of to-day," says the Rev. M. J. Savage, "the plan of salvation has no rational excuse for continued existence one day more." Priestcraft is a burden to the tolling millions and an obstacle to progress and learning. It has always opposed every scientific discovery.

Just take the two imaginary localities, heaven and hell. The writers of the Old Testament took the apparent for the real, were deceived by appearances. They thought the blue sky was a solid, a firmament. They thought the earth was a flat circular plain, that it was stationary, and the centre of the universe. Heaven, according to them, was only a few miles above the earth, and they tried to build a tower to it. God's throne and heaven rested upon this imaginary firmament. From the phenomena of volcanoes, earthquakes, and boiling springs was conceived the idea of hell and its locality. Heaven was just above and hell beneath. The writers of the New Testament adopted this crude notion, as can be shown by many passages. Those were the times of ignorance and credulity. They had no telescopes or instruments of investigation by which they could have learned the facts. When the telescope was invented, with one sweep heaven vanished Into nothingness; it was found to be a myth and purely imaginary. As heaven and hell are twin ideas, they stand or fall together. Knowledge has destroyed the Christian's selfish bribe of heaven for stupidity and their malignant threat of hell for genius and sense. You know as well as I do that the Old Testament heaven does not exist. As that of the New is identically the same, it is nonexistent. When you continue to preach the existence of these two places you are preaching what you know in reason to be false.

The central figure of the Christian religion is clearly a myth. The gospel stories told of him are so contradictory that they cannot be accepted as history or taken as evidence. Such evidence would not stand in any court to-day. Matthew says there were twenty-eight generations from David to Christ and that Joseph was the son of Jacob; Luke says there were forty-three generations from David to Jesus and Joseph was the son of Hell. All the way through these genealogies the names are all different except David, Joseph, and Jesus. If Jesus was the son of a ghost, what was the use of these genealogies?

The doctrine of divine paternity was old to the world at the beginning of the Christian era. The oldest religions depend upon exactly such an origin. The gods of Greece and Rome frequently descended to become fathers and mothers of fabulous demi-gods and heroes. This was claimed for Augustus Caesar and many others. The claim that Christ was the son of God was nothing new or remarkable, or no more true than the rest of these tales.

"Although there were so many examples of supernatural birth to serve as a pattern for the fable of Jesus, still various circumstances in the story of his life seem to suggest particular instances as the chief sources of the imaginary details.

"These instances are Krishna, Mithra, and Buddha.

"The Magi belong to the story of Mithra, a deity of the ancient Persians, originally a personification of the sun.

"He was said to have been born of a virgin in a cave, on the twenty-fifth of December, an allegorical representation of the emergence of the sun from the darkness of the winter solstice. At the period of the composition of the gospels the cult of Mithra was familiar to the Western nations, and had long been established in Rome.

"The Roman catacombs contain a picture of the virgin seated holding the infant on her lap, and before them three men in Persian dress are kneeling and offering gifts.

"The massacre of the Innocents is taken from the story of Krishna, the favorite deity of India, the eighth incarnation of Vishnu, and also the personification of the sun.

"Krishna was miraculously conceived by divine agency, and his uncle, the Rajah of Madura, fearing to be supplanted in his kingdom, determined to slay the infant at birth, but this plan being frustrated by the vigilance of Krishna's protectors, the rajah ordered the massacre of all the male children of the same age among his subjects. Such a deed might be performed under the despotic Indian ruler in ancient times, but not in a Roman province in the time of the Caesars.

"If such a wholesale murder had been accomplished there would have been some mention of the event in profane history, and the silence of three of the four evangelists respecting the visit of the Magi and the succeeding massacre by Herod is sufficient proof of the mythical character of the story."

This is taken from "The Christ Myth," by Elizabeth E. Evans. It should be read by all who are in search of truth. But those who are interested in keeping up a false system will pay no attention to it.

Matthew says that Joseph took Jesus and his mother into Egypt, but Luke says that after making a journey to Jerusalem they returned to their own city, Nazareth. Matthew leaves the idea that they had never been in that place before, but that this was done " that it might be fulfilled which was spoken by the prophets. He shall be called a Nazarene." There is no such prophecy. There are no prophecies of Christ, and those quoted by the New Testament as prophecies are all impositions and frauds.

Take Matthew i, 22, 23, claiming Christ being born of a virgin as a fulfillment of prophecy. This Is found in Isaiah vii, 14. Read Isaiah vii, 1-16. It becomes perfectly plain that two kings, Pekah and Rezin, were making war upon Ahaz, and that this was a sign to Ahaz that these two kings should not prevail against him. A sign must precede the thing signified. The sign was the birth of a child and the thing signified was that Ahaz would be rid of these two kings before the child knew to refuse the evil and choose the good. It is no such thing as a prophecy of Christ. Anyone can see the fraud practiced by this writer. No doubt it was in that day as it is in this—the people did not read and investigate for themselves, and this writer felt secure in committing the fraud. The book at that time was only in manuscript and limited in copies, and these were in the hands of the priests, who felt doubly secure against detection. The people took the words of the priests, as they do that of the preachers to-day, and were deceived. But read Isaiah viii, 2, 3, 4, 18. It shows that the child meant was Isaiah's own child and the virgin his own wife. But this prophecy proved false anyway. These two kings did prevail against Ahaz and he was taken captive, and they slew" a hundred and twenty thousand" (2 Chron. xxviii, 5, 6).

PLAIN TRUTHS FOR PREACHERS

A LETTER TO A CLERGYMAN ON BIBLICAL FALSITIES.

A Review of the More Conspicuous Absurdities Found in the Bible and the Christian Religion—Passages that Are Totally Irreconcilable with One Another or with Fact—Christ, the Central Figure of Christianity, a Myth Who Did Not Exist Even as a Man.

BY J. M. GILBERT.

II.

From *The Truth Seeker*, December 8, 1900

Take Matthew ii, 15: It says that Christ was taken out of Egypt "that it might be fulfilled which was spoken of the Lord by the prophet, saying, Out of Egypt have I called my son." This is found in Hosea xi, 1. This has reference to the children of Israel when captive in Egypt, and speaks of their deliverance. The passage is in the past tense.

Take Matthew ii, 18: This is made into a prophecy of the murdering of the children by Herod. This is found in Jer. xxxi, 15. By reading verses 15, 16, and 17 it becomes plain that this has no reference to the slaughter told by Matthew, but has reference to the time when the children of Israel were taken captive to Babylon, and refers to their return. It would be perfectly absurd to say that murdered children could again return to their border. The translator knew better than to make this into a prophecy of the time of Christ, for he headed the chapter " The Restoration of Israel." But the writer of Matthew imposed it upon the world as a prophecy.

Take Matt, xxvii, 35, where it says they parted Christ's garments, casting lots, that the prophecy might be fulfilled,

"They parted my garments among them, and upon my vesture did they cast lots." This is found in Ps. xxii, 18. David, or the person here speaking, is lamenting about his own misfortunes. This passage is in the present tense, and does not refer to the future. It is not a prophecy.

Take John v, 46, 47: "For had ye believed Moses ye would have believed me; for he wrote of me." Moses nowhere mentions Christ. The passage referred to in Deuteronomy is speaking of Joshua, as can be seen by reading Num. xxvii, 12-23. Moses was speaking of his immediate successor. We have shown you at the beginning of this letter that Genesis was not all written by the same person, as it contains different accounts of the same things. Gen. xxxvi, 31, speaks of kings reigning over Israel. This passage could not have been written until kings began to rule, and that was long after Moses. A history mentioning the presidents of the United States could not have been written until after this country became a republic. The last chapter of Deuteronomy gives an account of the death and burial of Moses, and he could not have written that account. To teach that Moses wrote the Pentateuch is teaching falsehood.

Take John xix, 36: "For these things were done that the scripture should be fulfilled, A bone of him shall not be broken." This is found in Ex. xii, 46. By reading the whole chapter we can see it is speaking of a lamb or a goat. It is instructions how to keep the Passover. Who ever saw a greater fraud perpetrated than the making of this into a prophecy? What a set of impostors these New Testament writers were! All of these so called prophecies are impositions and frauds.

Mosheim says: "Not long after Christ's ascension into heaven, several histories of his life and doctrines, full of pious frauds and fabulous wonders, were composed by persons whose intentions, perhaps, were not bad, but whose writings discovered the greatest superstitions and ignorance." Again he says one of their maxims was, " that it was an act of virtue to deceive and lie when by that means the interest of the church might be promoted" (Mosheim's Ecclesiastical History).

M. Daille says, "They made no scruple to forge whole books." The internal evidence of the New Testament shows that the four gospels were likewise forgeries full of pious frauds. The passages which we have been examining prove this to be strictly true. Besides, the maxim to lie and deceive to promote the interests of the church is still in vogue.

"Of the three fathers who contributed most to its (the canon's) early growth Irenæus was credulous and blundering, Tertullian passionate and one-sided; Clement of Alexandria, imbued with the treasures of Greek wisdom, was mainly occupied with ecclesiastical ethics." "Their decisions were more the result of pious feelings, biased by theological speculations of the times, than the conclusions of sound judgment. The very arguments they used to establish certain conclusions show weakness of perception. What are the manifestations of spiritual feeling compared with the result of logical reasoning ?" "The three fathers of whom we are speaking had neither the ability nor inclination to examine the genesis of documents surrounded with an apostolic halo. No analysis of their authenticity and genuineness was seriously attempted" (Davidson on the Canon).

These were the kind of men who voted the four gospels into the canon as the word of God. They were "credulous and blundering," "passionate and one sided." They had "weakness of perception" and were " biased." They had "neither the ability nor inclination to examine," and their decisions were "the result of pious feeling" and not "the conclusions of sound judgment."

I derived my information in regard to these so called prophecies from Thomas Paine's "Examination of the Prophecies." What he said about them was to the point, and all the theologians in the world cannot answer him. I will quote from his concluding words: "I have now, reader, gone through and examined the passages which the four books of Matthew,

Mark, Luke, and John quote from the Old Testament and call prophecies of Jesus Christ. When I first sat down to this examination I expected to find some cause for censure, but little did I expect to find them so utterly destitute of truth, and of all pretensions to it as I have shown them to be.

"The practice which the writers of those books employ is not more false than it is absurd. They state some trifling case of the person they call Jesus Christ and then cut out a sentence from some passage of the Old Testament and call it a prophecy of that case. But when the words cut out are restored to the place they are taken from and read with the words before and after them, they give the lie to the New Testament. A short instance or two of this will suffice for the whole.

"They make Joseph to dream of an angel, who informs him that Herod is dead, and tells him to come with the child out of Egypt. They then cut out a sentence from the book of Hosea, 'Out of Egypt have I called my son,' and apply it as a prophecy in that case.

"The words 'And called my son out of Egypt' are in the Bible, but what of that? They are only part of a passage and not the whole passage, and stand immediately connected with other words, which show they refer to the children of Israel coming out of Egypt in the time of Pharaoh, and to the idolatry they committed afterwards.

"Again, they tell us that when the soldiers came to break the legs of the crucified persons they found Jesus already dead, and therefore did not break his. They then, with some alteration of the original, cut out a sentence from Exodus, 'A bone of him shall not be broken,' and apply it as a prophecy of that case.

"The words 'Neither shall ye break a bone thereof' (for they have altered the text) are in the Bible, but what of that? They are, as in the former case, only part of the passage and not the whole passage, and when read with the words they are immediately joined to, show it is the bones of a he-lamb or a he-goat of which the passage speaks.

"These repeated forgeries and falsifications create well-founded suspicion that all the cases spoken of concerning the person called Jesus Christ are made cases, on purpose to lug in, and that very clumsily, some broken sentences from the Old Testament and apply them as prophecies of those cases, and that, far from his being the son of God, he did not exist even as a man, that he is merely an imaginary or allegorical character, as Apollo, as Hercules, Jupiter, and all the deities of antiquity were. There is no history at the time Jesus Christ is said to have lived that speaks of the existence of such a person, even as a man.

"Did we find in any other book pretending to give a system of religion the falsehoods, falsifications, contradictions, and absurdities which are to be met with in almost every page of the Old and New Testaments, all the priests of the present day who supposed themselves capable would triumphantly show their skill in criticism and cry it down as a most glaring imposition. But since the books in question belong to their own trade or profession they, or at least many of them, seek to stifle every honesty and the courage to do it.

"Were the New Testament now to appear for the first time, every priest of the present day would examine it line by line and compare the detached sentences it calls prophecies with the whole passages in the Old Testament from whence they are taken. Why, then, do they not make the same examination at this time as they would make had the New Testament never appeared before? If it is proper and right to make it in one case it is equally proper and right to do it in the other case. Length of time can make no difference in the right to do it at any time. But instead of doing this they go on as their predecessors went on before them, to tell the people there are prophecies of Jesus Christ, when the truth is there are none.

"They tell us Jesus rose from the dead and ascended into heaven. It is very easy to say so. A great lie is as easily told as a little one. But if he had done so, those would have been the only circumstances respecting him that would have differed from the common lot of man, and consequently the only case that would apply exclusively to him as prophecy would be some passage in the Old Testament that foretold such things of him. But there is not a passage in the Old Testament that speaks of a person who, after being crucified, dead, and buried should rise from the dead and ascend into heaven. Our prophecy mongers supply the silence the Old Testament guards upon such things by telling us of passages they call prophecies, and that falsely so; about Joseph's dream, old clothes, broken bones, and such trifling stuff.

"Let us grant for argument's sake that Jesus was a man. Those who have the least insight into the growth of myth and fable can easily see how traditions, myths, and fables could have been collected around such a personage and have been believed. Even to-day, in this enlightened age of the world, impostors or deluded persons rise up and claim to perform miracles, and even claim to be Christ or God. It makes no difference how absurd or extravagant their claims may be, they can always obtain followers. If such can obtain credence now, how much easier it would have been in that age of unbridled credulity at the incipiency of Christianity? Such traditions, myths, and fables were grouped around many persons before the beginning of Christianity, and there is nothing remarkable about such things being said of a person called Christ. He might have been a real person or only imaginary, it makes no difference which, we are not justified in believing such tales.

"But," says some theologian, "if you grant that Christ lived as a man, you will have to admit that he was the greatest teacher that ever lived; and, considering the age in which he lived, he must have been more than human." Nothing of the kind. History attests the fact that as great and greater teachers lived before his time, and much better ones since. Christ taught the observance of a part of the Decalogue and ignored the rest. He taught the Golden Rule. Many others before his time taught the Golden Rule, and all the rest of his teachings that are of any value. Confucius taught as good moral maxims without as much admixture of superstition which characterized his, and in that respect Confucius was superior. They needed no inspiration, because these things grew out of the experience of mankind through their many social relations. It is an admitted fact that there is not a rite, dogma, or precept in Christianity which cannot be found in some of the older pagan and heathen religions. Whoever created the character of Christ and invented his fictitious history had only to pattern after and borrow from these others.

The "Sermon on the Mount" is extolled as the greatest thing ever uttered. Was this a sermon on the mount (Matt. v. 1), or was it a sermon on the plain (Luke vi, 17)? I cannot do better than to quote from "The Master's Masterpiece," by Daniel K. Tenney.

"'Blessed are the poor in spirit for theirs is the kingdom of heaven.'

"What does this mean? Where is the kingdom if heaven? What is it? Modern scholarship says there is no such place. But if there be, why should those poor in spirit possess it, to the exclusion of those rich in spirit? Can no one possess a seat in the kingdom of heaven but the depressed and downcast, the gloomy, those who in this world are given to melancholy? Can cheerful souls gain no admittance? What sense or merit is there in this opening sentence?

"'Blessed are they that mourn for they shall be comforted.'

"Why should they that mourn be blessed instead of those who do not? Is mourning for things which cannot be helped so surpassing a virtue that it should be specially rewarded? Mourning is a natural emotion. So is the cessation of mourning. One always follows the other. Did not the hearers of Jesus on that occasion know this without telling it to them? It seems impossible to discern a new or valuable thought in this tame expression.

"'Blessed are the meek, for they shall inherit the earth.'

"Is this true, or has it ever been? Who ever heard of anyone, by reason of meekness, inheriting the earth, or any portion of it? Are the meek noted holders of real estate? Is there any reason why they should be? To be meek is to be humble. It takes something besides humility to buy land. Was this expression of the Master the product of wisdom or a feeble mind?

"'Ye are the salt of the earth...Ye are the light of the world...Let your light so shine among men that they, seeing your good works, may glorify your father which is in heaven.'

"Here we are again. Where is heaven, and who and what the father located there? Why glorify something which has no existence; or, if existing, what good will it do to universal power to be glorified? Among the audience addressed, there was probably not one in a thousand who could read and write. All semi-barbarians at best, and almost inconceivably ignorant. Why flatter them that they are the salt of the earth and the light of the world? Did not the Master comprehend their stupidity, or was he in that respect but little, if any, above their level?

"'Lay not up for yourselves treasures on earth, where moth and rust doth corrupt and where thieves break through and steal. Take, therefore, no thought for the morrow, for the morrow shall take thought for the things of itself.'

"If these commands of the Master had been observed, in what condition would be the human race at this day? Groveling in caves, naked or clothed in skins, searching daily for their daily food, hungry and savage. No dwellings for permanent occupancy. No homes. No government. Nothing but wild tribes roaming over the earth. No science. No inventions. No education. No ambition. No advance in human achievement. No money, no credit, no enterprise, no property, no anything but some visionary treasures in heaven, laid up there in imagination only. Every church, every cathedral, every temple, every building devoted to education and charity, every block, every home, all these and every other thing indicating the progress of the race, have been constructed in violation of this wonderful rule of the Master, to take no thought for the morrow and to lay up no treasures except in heaven. Yet the Christian stomach has been swallowing these things for centuries as sacred and solemn, and though paying no attention to their observance, would consign to eternal torture any man who doubts their divine authority. Do not lay up a cent. Don't order anything for breakfast. Do not think what you will wear to-morrow. God does not want you to. He will take care of that. Believe in Jesus and his Sermon on the Mount or be damned?

"'Ask and it shall be given you. Seek and ye shall find. Knock and it shall be opened unto you. For every one that asketh receiveth, and he that seeketh findeth, and to him that knocketh it shall be opened.'

"Is there any one who does not comprehend the falsity of these statements? They refer to divine favors. Have men and women always received what they devoutly asked or sought for, or has one of them? Could delusion and falsehood be more complete than those embodied in these strange statements of this sermon?

"'Therefore, all things whatsoever ye would that men should do to you do ye even so to them. For this is the law and the prophets.'

"This is the Golden Rule, so-called. It is all right, except that the Master got it wrong end foremost. As it reads, it is as much as to say, 'If you would that a man should lend you a dollar lend him one instead, whether you have it or not.' Confucius stated it much better centuries before the Master was ever heard of: 'Do not unto others what you would not that they should do unto you.' This is sublime and to the point. Briefly stated, 'Do no harm to any one.' It does not require a Master to invent so plain a moral axiom. But this is not the 'law and the prophets,' as stated. One of the divine laws, as given by Moses, was 'Ye shall not eat of anything that dieth of itself.' 'Thou shalt give it unto the stranger that is in thy gates, that he may eat it, or thou mayest sell it unto an alien, for thou art an holy people unto the Lord thy God.' How does this comply with the Golden Rule of the Master? Give our bad meat to strangers or sell it to foreigners. As to the prophets, they were the most infamous old wretches possible to imagine. Under the guidance of the Lord in war they killed every one that breathed, but in exceptional cases saved the lives of the virgins and turned them over to be ravished by the soldiers, thus disposing in one instance of thirty and two thousand virgins. That is the way the prophets construed the Golden Rule. A hundred similar instances might be cited from holy writ. So the Master was mistaken about the 'law and the prophets' favoring that rule.

"Christ was certainly a poor teacher in many things. He said, 'Resist not evil. Unto him that sinneth thee on one cheek offer also the other. If any man sue thee at law, and take away thy coat, let him have thy cloak also. Of him that taketh away thy goods ask them not again. Agree with thine adversary quickly.'

"Christians themselves completely ignore all these teachings. We were set free from kingcraft by manly resistance of evil, and that is the only way we will ever be rid of priestcraft, the ally of injustice, slavery, and despotism. The fathers of this republic did not gain their independence by submitting to evil; they did not gain it because they were poor in spirit, because they were meek, or because they did nothing but mourn. When England taxed them unjustly they did not say, 'Take more, take all we have.' When armies were sent to force them into obedience they did not throw down their arms and turn the other cheek like a lot of cowardly curs. They counted England as an adversary, but they did not agree with her. What causes all the furor in politics to-day if the people are not resisting evil?

"'Blessed be ye poor.'

"In what are the poor blessed? Are they blessed in being in a starving condition; in having poor food, poor clothing, poor shelters, crowded In dingy tenement houses, all of which breed misery, crime, disease, pestilence, and death? Would any wise man say that the poor are in a blessed state of existence?

"Christ is called the 'Prince of peace.' He said to honor father and mother and to love one another; to be meek, poor in pocket, poor in spirit; to submit to oppression and robbery, and to be submissive menials and slaves. This was a good doctrine for tyrants to teach their subjects. For all this they were bribed with a promise of visionary happiness and glory in a mythical heaven.

"Considering the last teachings mentioned, how can we account for the hatred and intolerance manifested by Christians, their persecuting and putting to death of heretics, their hanging of witches, their punishing people for the non-observance of the Sabbath, their killing of the heathens because they will not accept Christianity and choose to worship a different God? This is because the New Testament abounds in contradictions, and a different set of doctrines were put into the mouth of the mythical Christ. Here are some of them:

"'Suppose ye that I am come to give peace on earth? I tell you nay; but rather division. If any man come to me, and hate not his father and mother, and his wife and children, and his brethren and sisters, yea, and his own life also, he cannot be my disciple. Think not that I am come to send peace on earth. I come not to send peace, but a sword. I am come to send fire on earth, and what will I, if it be already kindled? Those mine enemies which would not that I should reign over them, bring hither and slay before me. He that hath no sword, let him sell his garment and buy one. He that believeth not shall be damned.'

"These teachings have been responsible for the hatred, intolerance, persecutions, and murder committed by Christians.

No other religion has been as bloody. These were responsible for the Inquisition and the blackest of crimes. The Puritans were intolerant; they persecuted, they murdered, and they established the Blue Laws because they believed the Bible. They had Christ's sanction to all this in the words, 'Think not that I am come to destroy the law or the prophets; I come not to destroy, but to fulfill.' What is the law? To kill witches, to enslave human beings, to put disobedient children to death, to rob other nations and not leave a soul to breathe; if any one sought to find a better god than the fiendish Jehovah, he was to be stoned to death.

From *The Truth Seeker*, December 22, 1900

A Correction.

To the Editor of The Truth Seeker.

    I write this letter to call your attention to a slight mistake made in the second part of my letter in the current issue of The Truth Seeker [Dec. 8, 1900]. At the end of the first paragraph in the second column on page 771 the quotation from Mr. Tenney ends at the words " favoring that rule." The language from there on is mine. I do not wish to appear as making Mr. Tenney say something he did not say, and that is the reason I call your attention to it. I thank you for publishing the letter. Yours truly,

J. M. GILBERT.

PLAIN TRUTHS FOR PREACHERS

A LETTER TO A CLERGYMAN ON BIBLICAL FALSITIES.

A Review of the More Conspicuous Absurdities Found in the Bible and the Christian Religion—Passages that Are Totally Irreconcilable with One Another or with Fact—Christ, the Central Figure of Christianity, a Myth Who Did Not Exist Even as a Man.

BY J. M. GILBERT

III.

From *The Truth Seeker*, December 15, 1900

Was it an evidence of greatness or wisdom to curse a fruit tree for not bearing fruit at the wrong season of the year? A man who would do such a thing to-day would be counted a fool, and that justly too. The case is so much worse for Christ, who was said to be God who knew all things.

Would a wise teacher, who claimed to preach a doctrine upon which the salvation of the world depended, teach in parables purposely so that the multitude hearing might not understand, and seeing might not perceive, and, therefore, for that reason could not believe and would be damned?

"He that believeth not shall be damned."

If Christ uttered those words he was ignorant as well as intolerant. He was ignorant of the workings of the human brain. He did not know that it required evidence to convince rational beings. He did not know that our beliefs are not subject to our wills, and that the scales turn in spite of ourselves. He did not know that there is no possible chance to be dishonest in the formation of belief. He did not grasp the great truth that no one can be justly held responsible for honest unbelief. He was unconscious of the fact that we are not constituted alike and cannot possibly believe alike. He showed the spirit of intolerant despot in wanting to slay all who would not become his subjects. Any intelligent person knows that belief cannot change the laws and facts of nature; therefore, no belief can change our destiny after we are dead; nature will take care of that regardless of our beliefs, hopes, or actions.

The doctrine that salvation depends upon belief is the fundamental lie of Christianity. Upon that lie depends the preacher's trade. "All that believe are justified from all things." As Burns says:

"Try every art of legal thieving;
No matter—stick to sound believing."

In other words, a believer has a special license to commit all manner of crimes. Search the universe and you cannot find a doctrine more odious, more destructive of the world's happiness, or a doctrine more false. Just let a believer commit any manner of crime and he is excused with the words, "To err is human." But let an Infidel do the same thing, and there is no excuse for him; it is peddled around by the mouths of all the hypocrites, and held up to the gaze as most horrible. The crime is diminished and covered up as much as possible in the one case, magnified and narrated as much as possible in the other. Don't this tend to show that Christians expect better morals of an Infidel than they do of one another?

I say without fear of successful contradiction that a believer does not exist. I do not mean an ordinary believer who must have evidence, but I mean, in this case, one who must take his credentials from the New Testament. Do you believe? then give the signs. Cast out a devil, speak the foreign languages, take up a serpent whose sting is death, drink a cup of deadly poison, raise up the dead. "All things are possible to him that believeth"

(Mark ix, 23). If these words are true, a believer has as much power as God. Chemistry teaches us that matter cannot be created nor annihilated. Let us see you refute this Infidel science by creating something new, create a world and people it with a race of beings. You say God did these things, you say all things are possible with God. If you are a believer you have as much power as God, or was Christ a liar when he said, " All things are possible to him that believeth?" If you cannot give the signs you are not a believer; then read your doom, "He that believeth not shall be damned."

But I hear you already saying, "These things do not apply to this age." You have absolutely no authority for saying that a part of the description of believers applies only to that age and another part of the same description applies to this. The language of the New Testament bears no such interpretation as Christians put on it in order to evade this plain statement. Christ said : "Go ye into all the world, and preach the gospel to every creature. And these signs shall follow them that believe" (Mark xvi, 16, 17, 18). I want to call your attention to the words, "them that believe." It is a prevarication of the worst sort to say a believer is one thing in one sentence and quite a different thing in a sentence just below it. If the command to go "into all the world and preach the gospel to every creature" applies to this age, then the description which immediately follows also applies to this age, and there is no way to get out of it. The terms "he that believeth," "him that believeth," and "them that believe" will apply to "every creature" of "all the world " to whom the gospel is preached. All believers were to have the "signs," so that they must really know they believed, and if they could not give the signs it would be known that they were pretenders, hypocrites, and impostors.

But I agree with you when you say that these things do not apply to this age. Not one of Christ's teachings applies to this age, and not one of his promises was made to the people now living. They have no part in them. I will endeavor to show this to be strictly true.

Christians tell us that Christ prophesied of things now taking place. They put forth as proof of this the wars and rumors of wars we are now having; the famine, pestilences, and earthquakes; desolation, tribulation, and the spread of iniquity; people betraying and hating one another; the arising of false prophets and false Christs, showing signs and wonders.

These things are not prophecies at all. Any man of ordinary sense could have told of those things; it did not take a seer, a prophet, or a God. There never has been an age of the world in which these things have not been wholly or partially true, and it is no evidence of greatness or wisdom to be able to tell of them. If Christ had ordinary intelligence he knew there had always been wars and rumors of wars; he knew people had always betrayed and hated one another; he knew there had always been desolation, tribulation, famine, pestilence, and iniquity in some portion of the inhabited world; he knew also there had been many instances of persons claiming to be prophets, Chrlsts, and Gods, showing great signs and wonders and performing miracles. If false prophets and false Chrlsts can show signs and wonders and perform miracles, how can such evidence prove Jesus to be a true prophet and a true Christ? If people could be so easily deceived by these others, could they not be just as easily deceived in regard to Jesus?

But it is only necessary to read the twenty-fourth chapter of Matthew in order to see that Jesus was only speaking of things which were to take place at the end of the world, and these were to be no longer than a generation in being fulfilled. Christ no doubt had witnessed eclipses and the falling of meteors. Ignorant people always thought the falling of meteors was the falling of the stars. The people at that time no doubt shortly expected another eclipse or another shower of meteors, and this was what Christ meant when he said the "sun shall be darkened, and the moon shall not give her light, and the stars shall fall from heaven, and the powers of heaven shall be shaken." Impostors have always made use of such phenomena of nature to frighten their credulous hearers to make them believe these things are evil omens or portentous of some great disaster or event. But earthquakes, comets, showers of meteors, and eclipses are in the order of nature, and are not signs of anything or subjects of prophecy.

The people of that day thought the world was coming to an end in their time, and that some of them would live to see it, and Christ thought the same thing. To prove that Christ thought these things were soon to take place it is only necessary to quote his words, "Verily I say unto you, this generation shall not pass till these things be fulfilled." Christ was a false prophet. He taught his hearers that some of them would live to see the end of the world. He told them, " There be some standing here which shall not taste of death till they see the son of man coming in his kingdom."

That generation did pass away, tasted of death, and a hundred generations since, and the prophecy was a complete failure. The fulfilment of this prophecy was to be the time when all his other promises were to be fulfilled. It was the time when believers were to reap their "reward," when their " redemption " was to take place. It was the promise upon which all the rest depended was a complete failure, there is no sense or reason to longer trust or depend upon any of them. The time for the reward and redemption of believers is past. The time for the damning of unbelievers is past. The Christian's hope is in vain; his hopes are founded upon the false. We have nothing to fear; our fears were founded upon the false.

No one has lost anything. The world will be the gainer by giving up a religion founded upon falsehood. We still possess all the good things we ever did have and the capacity to make them better. Let us be thankful! At last the light is breaking through the dense clouds of superstition; the mists of myths are clearing away; the ghosts are vanishing, and fear is being banished from the human brain. "Let the ghosts go. Let them cover their eyeless sockets with their fleshless hands and fade forever from the imaginations of men." Our imaginations are now free to fly, swifter than lightning's speed, to every recess of the universe without the least danger of once running counter to ghosts, devils, or gods. We must thank scientific investigation for this great blessing, and no blind faith which shuts its eyes to realities and sees anything its morbid imagination can invent.

HOW I BECAME AN ATHEIST.

BY J. M. GILBERT

From *Free Thought Magazine*, August 1902

I was born in a strictly Christian community. I do not recollect my father, and I do not know what his religious opinions were. My mother belongs to the Presbyterian Church. There was not to my knowledge and infidel in the whole country. All either belonged to the church or were nominal Christians. Those who were not converted fully resolved to become so at some future time. The idea was universal that it made no difference how moral a man was he would be damned unless he became converted. This they called getting religion. A person reared among such people nearly always holds to Christianity. It is a surprise to me that I did not become prejudiced in favor of religion like the rest.

The change in religious belief is nearly always by slow degrees, but it is sure when once started on the road with a determined effort to know the truth. Christians recognize the fact and they show it in their actions. Their custom is not to let any book or periodical come into their houses which criticizes or throws doubt upon the Bible or their long-cherished superstitions. They make strenuous efforts to keep such things out of the hands of their children. When they receive such literature they will not venture to read it from fear that they may be made to doubt. They declaim against reason and will not accept its conclusions on religious dogmas. They say that such literature and such trusting to reason, is the work of the devil. God cannot defend himself at the bar of reason.

I suppose that most all who have freed themselves from religion (superstition) have traveled pretty much on the same road. All such cases are interesting, instructive and convincing.

I do not know whether my case will prove interesting to others or not, but it is of great interest to me.

When a very small boy I remember of hearing about Ingersoll. From the way they talked I would think that he was the only Infidel in the whole world. They would say that no one but a Christian had any right to exist in this country. They would say, "Let the Infidel go to Africa and there, among the cannibals and fierce savages, who are without religion and without God, ventilate his views." They claimed that Infidels owed the very preservation of their lives to Christians. The way they said it suggested the idea that if Christians should exterminate the Infidels they would be justified in the act. The way they caricatured Ingersoll would make me think of the pictures of their mythical devil which I had seen. They said that he could not be honest, that he was out for the money. They gave it as their candid opinion that he would masquerade a few years as an Infidel and finally turn Christian. Then he would call in the money, as every one would go out to hear the converted Infidel.

At an early age I was a regular attendant at Sunday school. I received many cards of merit for reciting Bible verses and for having good lessons. I did not know what they all meant, neither did I seem to care. This sort of thing soon became monotonous. Going to Sunday school and having to stay to hear long, dry sermons at last became unbearable. I dreaded to see Sunday come. I resolved to go in as little as possible. In the summer time I would slip off to the woods with their giant trees, flowers, birds and brooks. I thank my parents for leaving me to enjoy these things instead of forcing me off to the horrid Sunday school, for which I had an aversion almost akin to hate. My parents would admonish me about the sin of breaking the Sabbath, but I could not see why I should not be allowed to enjoy myself on that day.

Every summer we would have a long series of protracted meetings, and at such times the people would become distracted.

They would build brush arbors, spread straw underneath, and placed planks across logs for seats. The first two or three meetings were held for the purpose of receiving lukewarm and backsliding Christians so as to get in working order. Some good sister would break out shouting and keep it up until she became exhausted. She would faint and some brother or the minister would have to lend support. The parson would exhort, plead, threaten, and tell some pious tale about the fearful agony of those who died unconverted. While some pious hymn was being sung he would call for mourners. Many Christians would go out through the audience and almost drag their friends to the mourner's bench. For this they would leave a vacant seat in front. The penitents would get down upon their knees with their hands resting up on their hands. Christians would go and talk to them, and in their frenzy would sometimes beat the mourners on their backs with their hands. Their actions would make me think of the Bible tale which I had read about a man possessed with devils. Some of the most excitable mourners would be so overcome with emotion and frenzy that they would get up shouting. Then all would shout and praise God, and the show would be at its fever heat. Before this I would often be asleep upon the soft straw, but when the excitement grew most intense I would get up to observe their antics. I have never seen a lunatic asylum, but I imagined the scenes there enacted would be something similar to these protracted meetings. But I never questioned religion; I thought probably it might all be true. I never had any serious thoughts about it, and was only a silent observer. I never felt any inclination to go to the "mourner's bench," and I am glad to say that it is one piece of foolishness I was never guilty of.

They would tell us that if we wanted to become converted to pray at home, to pray in the field, to pray anywhere, and that God would hear our prayers. But I never could see how I was to become converted, it looked impossible to me. I thought that there might be a devil and a hell, but I could not feel any fear. Once I thought that I would see if there was any truth in prayer for conversion. I would try to gratify a curiosity. I went out one night to pray. By some means I fell asleep. When I woke my folks were out with a lantern searching and calling for me. The future destiny of my soul weighed so heavily upon my mind that I went to sleep. I did not tell them why I was there. I was ashamed of being so foolish as to pray. After that I thought I would give it another trial. I thought I would pray while in bed. But the thing looked so ridiculous that I could not utter a word. God was represented as being invisible and omnipresent. Such a person was beyond my comprehension, and I could not pray to a thing I could not understand. Besides, my conscience was clear, I felt no remorse or guilt, and I could not see anything to pray for. I said to myself, "if I am damned, I will just have to be damned—that's all." I never again was guilty of such foolishness as trying to pray.

Several years now passed, during which I never troubled myself about religion. I sometimes went to religious services, but not often. My parents had been to California before the war. I heard my mother talk so much about the beauties of the country that I resolved to go, and I went the first opportunity that offered. I lived a year in Lordsburg. During that time I seldom went to church. The place was in a beautiful valley. I spent my Sundays roaming and hunting over the foot-hills, through the valleys, and up the large canyons. The State had a free Sunday and a person could do anything which was lawful on any other day. This I greatly appreciated. I lived several months in Los Angeles. There I spent Sunday in going to the theaters, or on excursions to the beach. A comrade of mine was a Spiritualist, and I sometime went with him to their meetings, sometimes to the Unitarian Church. The mediums claimed that spirits could materialize, and that they could permeate any solid substance. I went to one séance where the medium promised us that he would have the departed spirits of our dead friends to materialize. He had us to form a circle and to join hands. The effort was a signal failure. The medium said that the conditions were not right. In all of these meetings I saw nothing to convince me that there were such things as spirits or a spirit-world. The conviction was forced upon my mind that these mediums were the most deluded of persons, or else very great frauds.

I came back to Texas and spent several years in indifference as to whether Christianity was true or false. The first one to interest me was a "Restitutionist." I went several times to hear that doctrine preached. The minister denied the doctrine of "eternal torment." He claimed that heaven was not to be set up on earth. He would say, "My friends, my soul weighs 149 pounds. If the breath is the soul, then a cow has a larger soul than a human." I guess he forgot that many animals also have much larger bodies than men. I thank this man for starting me on the right road to investigation.

I next read a lot of Unitarian and Universalist literature sent to me from Boston. I began to see things in the Bible which could not be harmonized. Their doctrines, it is true, are far superior to the orthodox creeds, and they at least want a God who is a gentleman and not an infinite fiend. But try as they may, they could not explain away the doctrine of eternal torment and still retain the complete Bible. They tried to make the Bible agree with science, and said the days spoken of in the account of the creation meant geological periods, but upon that theory the command to keep the seventh day holy was perfectly absurd and directly contradictory. This was the first fact which called my attention to the hopeless contradictions between religion and science. Before this I had paid no attention to the teachings of the Bible. I found that the Bible taught the creation of all things out of nothing; that the earth was flat and stationary; that the sun revolved around the earth; that the sky was a solid and only a few miles above the earth. This brought vividly to my mind what

I had learned in the school room. There I learned that matter was indestructive and, therefore, self-existing. I learned that the earth had once been a molten mass which took millions of years to cool before it could be inhabited; that the earth was round and revolved before the sun; that the sun was the center of our solar system; that the sky was no firmament, that men gazed through it in observing the motions of the planets and stars.

I now began to perceive why theology had changed its front, and why theologians taught that the Bible meant just the reverse to what the authors meant. It was because science had gained a victory, and they were forced to accept her teachings or lose their occupations. That is why they teach the days to mean geological periods, but they are still grossly inconsistent in insisting upon the observance of the Sabbath. I knew the writers of Genesis clearly meant a day of twenty-four hours duration. I knew that the Bible taught that heaven rested upon the sky and that hell was underneath. But this proved to be false, and they were forced to relegate heaven and hell to some unknown mysterious place. I could now understand why apologists claim that the Bible was not revealed to teach science but to teach religion and morality. But there was not the shadow of an excuse for such an apology. I could not see why ignorant men, so mistaken in things they could see, could instruct us any better in morals, or be any wiser about things invisible. I learned that the Bible taught no better morals than it did scientific truths. If these apologists are wise enough to know that the Bible was not meant to teach science, why do they still continue to try to make it agree with science? Why do they still talk of a creation?

I was surprised that I had not seen all this before. But it was because I had not paid any attention to the Bible, and had not compared its teachings to what I had learned in school. And this is the principal reason why a majority of people still cling to the Bible as inspired truth, and why they do not recognize it for what it really is—the product of an ignorant age.

I began to seek for an explanation of the origin of these beliefs. I could not think that they were revealed. I could not comprehend an invisible and omnipresent God. Such a thing, according to my notion, must be in the nature of a gas. I could not conceive how this could have intelligence, or how it could reveal anything. I dismissed revelation as being worthless. I used to firmly believe in Santa Claus. I thought he knew all of our actions and whether we deserved any presents. I thought he could be everywhere on the same night, and that his power was unlimited. But curiosity one night prompted me to watch. I saw my parents placing the presents and my belief in Santa Claus was at an end. In thinking upon the question about the existence of God, I remembered this old belief. I began to compare the belief in God to the belief in Santa Claus. I saw that the two beliefs were taught to children in exactly the same way, and were held to be equally true. Eventually the child catches on to the deception in the one case. It occurred to me that the belief in God was a much greater deception held by adults, just like the belief in Santa Claus was held by the child. I now observed Christians when they prayed. At the end of each prayer they would say, "Not my will be done, but thine, O, Lord!" This made me think that those who uttered this prayer knew that nature paid no attention to prayers, and that everything would run the same course as if no prayer had been said. I saw more clearly the utter foolishness of prayer.

I knew the first people who began to think at all would seek for an explanation of the cause of the natural phenomena around them. I began to observe the things around me. The earth appeared to be flat and motionless; the sun appeared to travel around the earth; the sky appeared to be a solid. These things would present themselves in the same way to the first philosophers. These men, not having any means of knowing better, naturally believed the earth to be flat and stationary, that the sun moved, and that the sky was a solid. Not understanding the cause of rain they thought the windows in the sky opened to let the water pour through. This is the way the story was first written. Even to-day people who know better are in the habit of speaking of the rising and setting of the sun. The old Bible writers took the apparent for the real, they had no means of learning the facts. But those men who wrote this story could not understand how the sun and the moon could move without some agency. So they peopled the regions above with anthropomorphic beings for this purpose. But how could such beings themselves move through space? They observed the flight of birds, and they gave these beings wings also. As these beings were invisible they must have habitations upon and above the firmament, and this place they called heaven. The ancients imagined that the beings who had charge of these affairs to be good. They observed the actions of volcanoes, earthquakes, and boiling springs, and they imagined these things to be caused by bad beings or demons. As these were also invisible they must have their habitations in the bowels of the earth, and this they called hell. These people at first believed that they received all of their rewards and punishment on earth. They did not believe in immortality, or that they would go to heaven or hell. From their observations they very naturally thought that a dead man had no pre-eminence above a beast, they all died alike, all breathed the same air, and all went to the same place—back to the natural elements out of which they were composed. They said that "the dead know not anything, neither have they any more reward," and "he that goeth down to the grave shall come up no more." The doctrines of resurrection, eternal happiness, and eternal torment had their origin from the speculations of men, or were the inventions of men full of cupidity. They could thus fatten upon the hopes and fears of the people. In that age of unbridled credulity they could make the people believe almost anything. Those were some of the thoughts which had been passing through my brain.

About this time I was reading a Socialist paper published in Tennessee. It had an advertisement of "Volney's Ruins." I sent for the book. It was entirely different and a much better book than I expected to receive. I read this book through carefully. The honesty, earnestness, pure motives, sound logic, and scholarship of the author could not be doubted. This was the first book that I had ever read which denied the truth of Christianity. It convinced me that all religions had originated in the same way, and that all were equally false. I had heard of the "Age of Reason," but I did not know the character of the book. I borrowed this book from a depot agent and read it. Paine showed the books of the Bible to be written without any known authority. He refuted its claims to divine inspiration. He showed that all the so-called prophecies of Christ were impositions of the most glaring kind. When I had finished reading this book the impression was left upon my mind that no such a character as Christ ever existed, even as a man. I knew that all of the theologians in the world could not answer Paine. I now understood for the first time why Christians had willfully lied about this great man. No one, who will lay aside all religious prejudices, can read this book and not pronounce him noble and great. I learned that it was the common practice among Christians to lie about every great man who has given his reasons for rejecting their religion. But, on the other hand, when the beliefs of great men are not generally known, the church claims them as her own. I learned that the church lied in claiming Washington, Jefferson, Franklin, Lincoln and others to be Christian. If it had not been for the innumerable lies the church has told, which she resurrects every year and keeps perpetually green, she would have been dead to-day. It is true, as Ingersoll has said, that these lies are the most valuable assets of superstition.

I afterwards read Draper's "Conflict." I learned that the other claims of the church, that she was the most devoted friend to learning and science, that she was a friend to liberty of conscience, were also completely false. I learned how the church had been the bitter enemy to learning and philosophy. How she had persecuted, imprisoned and exterminated heretics and philosophers. How she had murdered the Hypatias, applied the fagot to the Brunos, and let the Galileos perish in her foul dungeons. I learned that the Inquisition was a natural result from Christian teachings. God said kill all who worshipped other gods, and Christ was made to say that he did not come to bring peace but fire and sword; that he came to fulfill the law and the prophets, and the law said kill. This is the way heretics and Infidels owe the protection of their lives to the church when she had unlimited power and religion was in flower. I read the history of the "Middle Ages," and learned of the dense ignorance, cruelty and piety of that period; how religion had opposed learning and philosophy because they had discovered truths which conflicted with a book of ignorant traditions. I learned that almost every great truth and reform had been first advocated by Infidels, and that the church had always opposed with stubborn hate. When at last any victory had been won for liberty and humanity, in spite of the church, she always stepped in and claimed the honor. The church always plays false in everything. I learned that the doctrines of Christianity had been borrowed from the older religions and were now masquerading under another name. The utter conceit and gall of Christians sending missionaries to heathen lands now stood out boldly.

 I read the lectures of Robert G. Ingersoll. These were grand. I saw that this man was one of the greatest thinkers and orators the world had ever produced. I knew at once that all of the calumnies that had been circulated against him were false. I did not have to be told—I knew the source from which these slanders had come—from the church, an institution whose stock in trade is nothing but lies. Its very foundation is false, and this begat the necessity of continuous lying through all the ages of its existence. I read Ingersoll's debates with Field and Gladstone, I read Huxley's debate with Gladstone. I read the Bennett-Mair debate. I found that the greatest defenders of the faith were completely vanquished and could not stand before the champions of reason and truth. The proof of the pudding is in the eating. These debates were circulated only by Freethinkers—this was proof of the victory. I read some of the works of Darwin, Huxley and Haeckel and became convinced of the truth of evolution. The only difficulty in the way to keep a person from accepting evolution is to remain ignorant. I attended a medical college and there became thoroughly confirmed in these views. Anatomy and physiology presented facts to prove evolution, and there I could see the anatomical facts with my own eyes, which could have no other intelligent explanation than that given by Darwin and Huxley. I have read many other excellent Free Thought books and pamphlets. Last of all, I have read Haeckel's "Riddle of the Universe." He conclusively shows that all the natural sciences converge towards the same goal, and that they link together in perfect harmony in teaching the unity of nature. The idea of an anthropomorphic God the church has about given up. Haeckel shows the preposterous absurdity of its substitute, the "Gaseous Vertebrate." For how could a gas have brains? How could a thing without brains be intelligent? A thing which permeates all space must be in the nature of a gas. It now appears to me that I must have been unconsciously an unbeliever in Christianity all my life.

Once convinced of the falsity of Christianity is to be always convinced. Once brought to see the ignorant and superstitious origin of one religion claiming to be supernatural, is to see the origin of them all. Some of the world's great religions are superior in many respects to Christianity, and some of them are more widely accepted. This is why philosophers in heathen lands, brought to see the fallacies of their own particular superstition, reject Christianity along with all the rest. They know that making proselytes to Christianity is nothing more than substituting one superstition for another. This is why Christian converts in heathen lands are confined to the most ignorant and vicious.

It is the most silly thing in the world for Christians to talk about converting Freethinkers, because most of them have reached their intellectual convictions and mental growth from investigation, study, and philosophy. A Christian who supposes such a thing is most densely ignorant of the process of mental growth and the status of mental liberty. As well try to change the planets in their course as to attempt to persuade a Freethinker back into the mental bondage from which he has escaped. Such a thing is impossible. The mind once set free can never go back.

Randolph, Texas.

REPLY TO PROF. C. J. FINGER.

BY J. M. GILBERT

From *Free Thought Magazine*, January 1903

The October number of The Free Thought Magazine contains a reply to an article of mine which appeared in the August number. He says: "The essay contains nothing, and left me wondering 'Why he became an Atheist.'" He only wishes to call attention to its "utter worthlessness." This is his opinion, but others may be different, whose opinions are worth just as much as his own. Does he jump upon me as an easy mark? Why did he not select some other from among your contributors more worthy of his steel? And where is his glory to come from? Is he a God and can create it out of "nothing?" I can as readily believe that as I can believe that a God created anything. All the emotional gush which he has dished out cannot make me "blush" for anything which I said that article. Why should anyone be ashamed of their honest convictions as to whether there are gods, many, one, or none?

He says that I fail to "trace any steps of mental evolution leading to the change." It was not my purpose to tell why, but how, I did this by stating some of my thoughts and mentioning some of the books which I had read, accepting the opinions of the authors in whole or in part. This should have prevented him from falling into the error of asking "Why?" It was not my purpose to portray the psychological processes, even had I been competent. This would have required one well versed in that branch of study. I left that for the reader to work out for himself. Those who had traveled the same road would understand something of it. Slaves to orthodoxy could not understand until they had laid aside their unreasonable prejudices and investigated for themselves. Prof. Finger's "wondering" is out of place.

He says that I treat religion as one grand organized scheme of willful deception. It has become so to-day, no matter what it was originally. A majority of intelligent ministers do not believe what they preach. Many of them only wish an easy time, regardless of the welfare of the people. Others claim that it would be dangerous to morality to tell the whole truth, as though the most religious of times, replete with belief in God, was not the most degraded and immoral. I know that there are many honest ministers who were reared in the lap of orthodoxy, who know nothing else, and whose prejudices will not permit of further investigation on their part.

By the term "religion" I mean a belief in a God who demands worship, belief in the supernatural, and all those empty rites, ceremonies and prayers insisted on by the creeds. I do not include in that term the "cherishing in the heart of man of love, sympathy, kindness, kinship, veneration and service to man." Atheism includes all of that. Atheism insists upon "the noble service of mankind," not to a myth, but the general good. Atheism necessarily destroys the false beliefs in gods and religious fallacies. But that is the inexorable consequence of all progress to play havoc with some popular error. If truth must hide itself because error becomes mortally wounded, all progress must cease. Atheism destroys nothing worth having. It places no limit upon the reasonable hopes and aspirations of man. It leaves man in possession of the entire universe, with all his capacities for growth and improvement, unimpaired. "Atheism," says Bacon, "leaves a man to sense, to philosophy, to laws, to reputation." It is clear that Prof. Finger has given us a misconception of Atheism when he says that it "represents the blank wall at which all progress must stop." It is not Atheism, but revealed religion, which says, "Here we stop!" In this direction the knowledge of man is complete." It knows just what the beginning was and just what the end will be. It would put an end to investigation, to discovery, and to the accumulation of knowledge. It has ever tried to do so in the past. It has branded the fearless searchers after truth as heretics and infidels. It has been intolerant, has persecuted nearly all and exterminated many with sword and fagot. It is intolerant still.

Prof. Finger says that I will not see, or do not "realize that all forms of theology are but guesses at the great question, and that the religion of man is but reverence for the assumed authors of nature." That is just what I do realize. God is nothing but a "guess," and his existence cannot be proved, but must be "assumed." Savages, in trying to explain the phenomena around them, assumed that they were caused by gods, beings in their own image, but much more powerful. As man began to trace phenomena to natural causes the gods began to disappear. What is not yet understood is said to be caused by God. The idea is the same—there is only a difference of degree and not in kind. The word "God" explains nothing; it represents the sum of ignorance of those who believe it; Christians worship their own ignorance.

Prof. Finger accepts evolution. That destroys the very basis upon which Christianity is founded. There was no creation, no fall of man, and no need of an atonement. "In the light of to-day," Says Rev. M. J. Savage, "the plan of salvation has no rational excuse for continued existence one day more." Prof. Finger rejects the idea of an anthropomorphic God. But that is the kind of a God that the Old Testament teaches. He is represented as having a local habitation, comes and goes to find out the truth of reports, and tried men to find out their hearts. He is often angry and sometimes repents. He talked to men face to face and they heard his voice. He took away his hand and allowed Moses to see his back parts. All of this is utterly irreconcilable to a God of omnipotence, omnipresence and omniscience.

Gladstone said: "Unless you accept the testimony of the Bible as conclusive, what evidence have you of God's existence and man's immorality? Rev. Mr. Moody said: "If you are going to throw out one of the Testaments, it will not be long before the whole will go. * * * The shortest way is to give up the whole thing." Henry Ward Beecher said: "The God of the Bible is a moral monstrosity." Rev. Theodore Parker said: "Vishnu, with a necklace of skulls, is [a] figure of love and mercy, compared to the God of the Old Testament." Rev. J. W. Chadwick says: "Every clergyman in the Protestant church knows that these books (of the Bible) have no validity." Science, logic, reason, analogy, observation and experience furnish no proof of God's existence.

Prof. Finger calls the opposing forces of nature "brothers in arms." Man tediously and painfully labors to produce and build for his welfare, and the destructive forces of nature quickly swallows them up, cyclones rend them to pieces, and volcanic eruptions convert them into cinders. Plagues, famines, and pestilence destroy millions as if they were nothing but flies—the good and the industrious as well as the wicked and indolent. It is the worst kind of nonsense to speak of all these as "brothers in arms." It is special pleading resorted to in order to justify the goodness of an assumed God who would be guilty of such conduct. We are forced to conclude that nature is devoid of intelligence, and there is no overruling Providence, which makes for righteousness. We are forced to conclude that nature cares no more for the welfare of man than she does for the lowest worm that crawls. The hiss of a venomous serpent is just as pleasing to her as the earnest prayer of a human being. Man is left to his own resources to contend against the blind forces of nature, and to use his reason to the best of his ability to overcome them if he can. He obtains no supernatural aid.

To say that there is an Unknowable, Infinite Power" that is intelligent, and that makes for righteousness, is mere sophistry. If it was unknowable you could not know what it was like or its attributes. If you know all these things about it, it cannot remain unknowable. An unknowable thing might as well have no existence, and we cannot be far wrong when we called such an assumed thing nothing. This is the last proposition that the God idea has been forced to assume, and it, too, must go, as there is not a particle of evidence in favor of it. The universe of nature, as a whole, is infinite, eternal, impersonal, and devoid of intelligence. Science has taught us to know that laws of nature are the same throughout the entire universe. The same to-day as in the past, and will remain so in the future. Matter, with its properties of force, form and motion could not have been created. The Atheist denies that there is a being that is omnipotent, omnipresent and omniscient, either inside or outside of nature. Gods are figments of the imagination. The burden of proof rests upon those who affirm the existence of such a being. The Atheist simply denies, and here he is invincible.

Homer, I. T. [Indian Territory; present-day Oklahoma]

ORTHODOX BAPTIST PREACHERS.

BY J. M. GILBERT

From *Free Thought Magazine*, March 1903

I once had an argument with a Baptist preacher upon the subject of Evolution. He was one of those aquatic fowls that wanted to make all of the noise so that nothing else could be heard, and getting through with this harangue, would hide himself away. To get a fair show at him I wrote him a letter, giving my reasons for believing in Evolution, also my reasons for disbelieving in a God. I requested a private reply, stating that if he had any convincing arguments to produce them. He made no attempt to do so, and I learned afterwards that he had admitted his inability to answer. Said that it would not do to circulate such as that among the people.

Not long after that my brother had a little child to die. He, like a majority of the people, though he must follow the old custom of getting a sky pilot to make a talk at the grave. He procured the preacher mentioned above. The preacher indulged in a lot of high-sounding but empty words about the budding and blooming the trees and flowers in spring as being proof of immorality. But any one gifted with a grain of common sense ought to see that a revivification of vegetation in spring cannot possibly be analogous to a resurrection of the dead. These things cannot be proofs of immortality. Dead once is to be dead forever. There is no analogy in Nature for a future life of any invidual, be it animal or vegetable.

The preacher, to get even with me for the letter which I had written him, quoted the passage in Psalms: "The fool has said in his heart there is no God." It is my opinion that he wished to retaliate for my letter, and no doubt he thought it would sink deeper upon this particular occasion. It is the way of priestcraft to slander and insult in such places and under such circumstances that should any one rise to remonstrate they would be indicted for disturbing holy worship. But the use of the above words was nothing more than I expected and was not surprised.

Another young Baptist preacher was helping to hold a revival at my town. In one sermon he said a person could not live without sin. If the Bible taught that a person could live without sinning, it contradicted itself. That if it contradicted itself he would quit preaching. I thought that, if he was sincere, it would be a good opportunity to do some good work for the cause. I wrote him a letter in which I pointed out many contradictions, and asked him to be good enough to keep his word. I told him that any time he felt competent to harmonize the contradictions which I gave him that I would come out to hear him, or he could answer by letter. He made no attempt to harmonize them or to answer a single argument, but about a month afterwards he wrote me an abusive letter, comparing me to the devil, and using a vulgar name, and said, "I am commanded not to cast pearls before swine."

Such phrases, "The fool has said," etc., and the one just quoted from the last preacher, are really the inventions of the priestcraft. They hurl them at their opponents instead of producing arguments, and the silly and unthinking greedily gulp them down as unanswerable arguments. And their Bible contains many phrases of like import, inventions of priestcraft, to be used as occasion demands.

This alone, it seems to me, is good evidence that the Bible is largely a work of priestcraft, compiled in such a way as to support them in their nefarious business of making people willing dupes and slaves to support them in idleness and luxury. "Behind a wall of obscene Bibles they skulk and sling their slanderous libels." And their blind followers parrot these stereotyped phrases at every opportunity and imagine that they are using sound arguments.

I wrote to this last preacher a letter in reply to his abusive one, but I have never received anything more from him. He asserted that he could harmonize all of the contradictions. I wrote him that nothing could exceed the egotism of an upstart like himself, who counted himself greater than Chadwick, Savage and Ingersoll, whom I had quoted. I wrote him that he might have given us any example of the facility by which he harmonized the contradictions. Those have asserted that Colonel Ingersoll was fighting a man of straw must be densely ignorant of the orthodox preachers in the South. I find that a majority of them are more intolerant, conceited, arrogant and bigoted than any other class of people. A great many of them are insincere. The South is my native country, but it is more religious because more ignorant. It is a truism that ignorance is the mother of devotion. A Methodist preacher in our town stated in the pulpit that he was never called to preach, but that he was preaching because that was easier than to get out and work. He stated the exact truth and that fully applies to all preachers who live by that means alone.

Another Baptist preacher took dinner at our house one day. I came in just in time to hear make the remark, that so many different churches and creeds were the cause of Infidelity. I took issue with him as to the real cause of Infidelity. The real cause of Infidelity, we all know, is a recognition by us of the falsity of the fundamental doctrines of Christianity. I told this preacher that the contradictions contained in the Bible were the cause of so many warring sects and so many conflicting creeds. For this cause no two people could understand the Bible alike. I said that Paine had proved the so-called prophecies of Christ to be glaring impositions and fraudulent. I pointed out the one about the virgin bearing a son, and he could not get around it. I also showed him that Christ, if a real person, was a false prophet, if the New Testament writers had correctly reported his words. I gave him Paine's "Examinations of the Prophecies" to read, and he said that he would read anything. He returned the book without comment. I noticed that in the last Baptist revival, referred to above, that he took no part, neither do I believe they invited him. It is my opinion that he had become too liberal for those narrow-minded bigots.

Homer, I. T. [Indian Territory; present-day Oklahoma]

TEED, THE HUMBUG.

His Interpretation of the Bible More Foolish than the Original.

BY J. M. GILBERT.

From *The Truth Seeker*, August 8, 1903

The following quotations, which we place in contrast for a purpose, are extracts from a letter before us, written perhaps at one sitting. A man who is not sure of the ground of his belief may unwittingly contradict himself in admissions here and assertions there, especially if he is undertaking to defend the conclusions of modern astronomy: "The defenders of the Copernican system do not claim to know it all. They thus show their modesty and their wisdom. They admit that the Copernican concept)s an hypothesis. It has been a good working hypothesis; It has been modified, and will be modified as greater knowledge is acquired. It is the beginner, or tyro, in science who claims to know it all." The admission that the Copernican conception is a hypothesis is an admission that the system has no certain foundation; that its premise is not demonstrated. An hypothesis is a supposition, something taken for granted, a guess, upon which a system of conclusions may be made to rest; it is a false foundation, a something "placed under," because of lack of a true foundation. The fact that the Copernican hypothesis has been modified, and will be modified as greater knowledge is acquired, shows the Copernican foundation to be uncertain. But before the writer saw fit to close his letter he grew more bold in his declarations, and, therefore, we find these words: "Any person of ordinary intelligence and observation, unless deluded by some attractive vagary, knows that we do not live in a hollow shell of an earth. He knows that we are on the outside instead of on the inside. He knows that the curvature of the earth's surface is convex instead of concave. He knows that the sun, moon, and planets are many thousand times farther away from us than Koreshanity says there is space." Now, does any person of ordinary intelligence, or even extraordinary intelligence, *know* that a thing is true if it be only an hypothesis subject to modification through further investigation? We judge that if the most eminent advocates of the Copernican system are both modest and wise in this admission that the system is founded on an hypothesis, be who asserts that any one knows that: the earth is a convex body must be a mere tyro in the study of even the popular system. Thousands of tyros are turned out of modern educational institutions every year!

The above appeared as an editorial in the Flaming Sword of April 10, and the quotations it contains were taken from a letter which I had written to a friend at Chicago in a private correspondence, and not for publication.

To call a thing an hypothesis does not argue that it is untrue. Teed's system does not rank high enough to be called an hypothesis, and he has not the good sense or honor to admit, as eminent astronomers have done, that he does not know it all.

When I said that the Copernican system had been modified from time to time, any one but a Koreshan might have understood that details were meant, and not the fundamental principles upon which it is based. I am not an astronomer or a scientist, but I can see enough to convince me that Koreshanity is a complete fallacy. I leave astronomy to be defended by those who make that their business. What concerned me most was the theological part of Koreshanity, and this the editor passed over in silence. Why did he not air that portion of the letter in his paper? This creates for me the conviction that I had punctured to the core of the Koreshan falsehood and found another false prophet. I now offer the letter which I wrote to my friend:

Koreshanity.

This, like all previous theologies, denounces the physical sciences as "figments and vagaries of pretended science It speaks of "the gigantic fallacy and farce of the benighted Copernicus." It claims to "alone scientifically defend the scriptures." It says that "the Bible is scientifically correct," and that Koresh (Dr. Cyrus R. Teed), "the divine and natural scientist, is its sole interpreter and expositor." Here we find the arrogance of the Roman Catholic church and of the pope. No one but Koresh is allowed to interpret the scriptures. " Koreshanity declares and defines the law of immortality...The first step is recognition of the Messiah and the application of his truth. As much as to say, "He that believeth not in Cyrus R. Teed (the Messiah) will be damned." Unless you do this, you cannot obtain immortality. This is the same old intolerance of Christianity; the same arrogance and bigotry characteristic of all impostors who have claimed to be messiahs or sons of God.

"All that is opposed to Koreshanity is Antichrist." It would seem that Teed claims to be a reincarnation of Jesus. All ideas opposed to his are heresies. He has all the truth. He was once reported to have said, "We have got it all [all the truth]. It is impossible to know a part of the truth till you are in possession of all the truth." This is enough to brand him as an impostor, whether he is conscious of it or not.

Absurdity could hardly go further than the talk of "dematerializing through a biological electro-magnetic vibration,...brought about through the direction of one mind." Teed claims to be that mind. Like Dowie, he claims to be Elijah, and they are both frauds. Strange it is that rational beings can believe in such gross impositions!

I read in the Flaming Sword an attempted explanation of the translation of Elijah. It was to be explained by the above law. Can any rational person now believe that such a thing ever happened? Why doesn't Teed prove it on some one now? It is safe to say, this he has never done and cannot do. Koreshanity becomes a preposterous absurdity when it seeks to prove that all the traditions, legends, fables, and myths of the Bible were actual facts.

The Koreshans say that the Copernican concept of astronomy is based upon unsupported assumptions. But can there be assumptions more completely unsupported than that the earth's crust is one hundred miles thick; that "there is nothing outside—no heat, cold, light, darkness, temperature, condition, entity, quality of substance—nothing;" that there is no space except inside the earth; that "mercurial discs" float between the metal layers of the earth's "shell?" And such nonsensical drivel as this claims to be the only true science!

"The Messiah [Cyrus R. Teed] is now in the world." He claims to demonstrate the scientific accuracy of the Bible in its astronomy, theology, etc., etc. He lacks nothing in self assertion and dogmatic assumption. As all theology is assumption, the more arrogant and dogmatic, the more consistent with its true nature. Koreshanity seems to be the only sect which now seriously attempts to reconcile the facts of nature with the incongruities and fallacies of the Christian Bible. It is positively true that the Bible contains contradictions and errors. If one is successfully demonstrated to be true, another is thereby demonstrated to be false. And how about the so-called prophecies about Christ, taken by the New Testament from the Old, that Thomas Paine long ago showed to be the most glaring impositions?

Koreshanity assumes the existence of a personal God. This is assumption without proof. This old idea had to be given up because, in the light of discovered facts, it could not be successfully defended. And more than that, there is not a particle of evidence of the existence of any kind of God. The universe is evidence of itself alone, and cannot possibly be evidence of a God. The terms used to express the attributes of such a created fancy of the imagination are self-contradictory. The idea of God originated in ignorance, and the word "God" has been used by all classes of people to express the sum of their ignorance. Then those who reverence and worship God, reverence and worship their own ignorance. If the Koreshans do this, they form no exception to this truism.

Koresh "knows" that biblical writers did not mean what

their language implies. " It [the Bible] is written in the language of universal symbolism and must be scientifically interpreted." Koresh "is its sole interpreter and expositor." Many people have been hounded and put to death for discovering facts contrary to the most easy and reasonable interpretation of the Bible, the way its defenders understood it to mean for thousands of years, and the way the writers undoubtedly meant to be understood. But this way of interpretation had been demonstrated to be false, and God was guilty of purposely keeping the people fooled for this immense period. But the traditions, legends, fables, guesses, errors, and imaginings of those ancient writers, which common sense teaches us require no other explanation than that they lived in an ignorant age, this dogmatist asserts to be accurate scientific truth. His scheme is another attempt to bolster up the Bible. But we may be sure that it will meet the fate of all other such attempts. Almost any humbug or fake can obtain a following— the supply seems equal to the demand. Those who have an inclination for the occult are generally the most credulous, and their support easier won.

Koresh knew that another cosmogony would have to be invented. All attempts to harmonize the Bible with science bad been signal failures. Even so great an intellect as Hon. W. E. Gladstone could not do it. But this know-it-all knows just what God intended in all things He is the "Messiah," Elijah, John the Baptist (Mat. xvii, 12, 13), the "God man" or the "man God." He is as great a fraud as Rev. John Alexander Dowie. He dogmatically asserts what cannot be proved. But in this he is not original—it is the way of the theologians. Those portions of the Bible having reference to science are now known to be fallacies and errors. Any pretended science with which they may agree is just as fallacious and erroneous.

Any person of ordinary intelligence and observation, unless deluded by some attractive vagary, knows that we do not live in a hollow earth; that we are on the outside instead of on the inside; that the curvature of the earth is convex instead of concave. He knows that all the space which Koreshanity says exists could not possibly contain the sun, moon, and planets. The disappearance of a ship's hull before the topsail can only be explained by the convexity of the earth. If the reverse was true, we could see the bulky hull before we could the topsail.

The argument that we live in a hollow earth, derived from a cell, is a great fallacy. Nature does not produce hollow cells. A single animal cell is a continuous mass of protoplasm throughout. The unicellular animal lives by what it procures from the outside. Our lives and energies are sustained by what we get external to us. If the analogy from a cell has any force, It proclaims that the earth is supported and increases by forces and materials derived from sources external to it.

Where is the personal God of Koreshanity? According to it, God must necessarily be on the inside of the hollow earth—the only space there is. Has anyone ever seen him? If the Koreshans can see him we can. Must we make the inference that Cyrus R. Teed claims to be God? "God Is personal and binne." "Koresh, the founder of the Koreshan System, and Victoria Gratia, Pre Eminent of the Koreshan Unity." I suppose If one wishes to see God he must go to Chicago. This theology is as true as any other. "He that believeth not shall be damned."

ELIJAH.

BY J. M. GILBERT

From *Free Thought Magazine*, September 1903

A lady, writing in the Semi-Weekly (Dallas) News, asks the question, "What relation existed between the old prophet Elijah and John the Baptist? Was there any? This, I think, furnished an interesting topic where it may be shown what an imposition and fraud Christianity is.

I once read a book entitled "The Millennial Kingdom," in which the author, William A. Redding, sought to prove that John the Baptist was Elijah. Malachi 4:5 says: "Behold I will send you Elijah before the great and dreadful day of the Lord." The first gospel makes Jesus say, when speaking of John the Baptist: "And if ye will receive it, this is Elias, which was for to come. But I say unto you, Elias has come already, and they knew him not, but have done unto him whatsoever they listed. Then the disciples understood that he spake to them of John the Baptist." But the fourth gospel makes John contradict this: "And they asked him What then? Art thou Elias? And he saith, I am not. Art thou that prophet? And he answered, No." If John was mistaken or spoke falsely here, how can we believe him on many other important declarations?

The first three gospels make John the Baptist to be Elijah in fulfillment of the prophecy of Malachi. How true this was we will soon see. The people were taught, and many believed, the end of the world would come during some of their lives. Elijah, who was to come before the "great and dreadful day of the Lord," had, according to the first gospels already appeared in the person of John the Baptist. John went preaching: "Repent ye: for the kingdom of heaven is at hand." John baptized Jesus. "From that time Jesus began to preach, and to say, Repent: for the kingdom of heaven is at hand." Jesus sent out the twelve and told them "And as you go, preach, saying, The kingdom of heaven is at hand."

Jesus taught that the day of judgment was close at hand. "The disciples came unto him, privately, saying, Tell us, when shall these things be? and what shall be the sign of thy coming, and of the end of the world?" He gave them signs (Matt. 24 c.) and said: "When ye see all these things, know that it is near, even at the doors." "Verily, I say unto you, There be some standing her, which shall not taste death, till they see the Son of Man coming in his kingdom." (Matt. 23:36; 24:34; 16:28.)

What were some of the signs? "The sun shall be turned into darkness, and the moon into blood, before the great and terrible day of the Lord come. Immediately after the tribulation of those days shall the sun be darkened, and the moon shall not give her light, and the stars shall fall from heaven, and the powers of the heavens be shaken." (Joel 2:31; Matt. 24 c.)

This darkness of the sun, and the moon failing to give her light, must have meant an eclipse. Metaphorically, the moon may be said to be turned into blood. Eclipses must have been periodical millions of years before the earth became inhabited, and thousands of years before the beginning of Christianity. No doubt some of them were recorded, or fresh in the memory and traditions of many people. An eclipse could not have been a sign of the end of the world, unless the very next one was meant. But hundreds of eclipses have taken place since and the end is not yet. The falling of the stars must have meant meteoric showers. These, like eclipses, have been periodical occurrences. The ignorant masses believed them to be falling stars. The shaking up of the heavens must have meant cyclones, earthquakes, and volcanic eruptions. Ignorant or hypocritical priests always represented such phenomena as the vengeance of an angry God. All these things were perfectly worthless as signs of the end of the world, but such was the wisdom of these inspired writers.

"And ye shall hear of wars and rumours of wars...For nation shall rise against nation and kingdom against kingdom; and there shall be famines, pestilences, and earthquakes in divers places." Has this not always been the case, in both ancient and modern times, before and since Christianity? Strife, war, and bloodshed have always been common among savage tribes and barbarous nations and still to-day among those claiming to be civilized. So have there been many famines and pestilences throughout all the ages of the world.

These things are also worthless as signs of the end of the world, but it is another illustration of the wisdom of inspired writers.

"And ye shall be hated of all nations for my name's sake." This could only point to a time, early in the first centuries, when the gospels were compiled, about the time Christianity became known as a separate cult. It is corroborated by the fact of their expecting the end of the world in a very few years. It was then that Christians were despised and persecuted on account of their egotism and intolerance, which caused them to be looked upon as dangerous enemies to the nation. The above language could not apply to any time after church and state became united Christianity has become fashionable and popular in several nations. The language could not apply to the future, unless Christians will admit that a great majority of people will eventually become too wise to believe in it. They will have to quit their boasting about an enormous increase in the spread of the gospel, and admit that it is on the decline.

"For there shall arise false Christs, and false prophets, and shall shew great signs and wonder; insomuch that, if it were possible, they shall deceive the very elect."

Hundreds of years before Christianity, Christs, Saviors and Sons of Gods were claimed to have existed, and multitudes believed in them. Many details in their history are identical with the history of Jesus. Such as claiming to be born of virgins, being born on Christmas day, working miracles and showing great signs and wonders. These furnish the originals from which the history of Jesus was derived. Most all of these ancient sons of God were myths, and were personifications of the sun. If one existed who claimed to be a son of God, he was a very much deluded person or an imposter. This warning was actually worthless, for it is the way of imposters to warn their deluded followers against others of their kind. If false Christs and false prophets could show great signs and wonders, how could such things prove Jesus to be a true one? Ever since man became observant enough of the phenomena surrounding him to have originated his superstitions, imposters have infested the world, and they will continue to do so as long as there is a place for supernatural religion in some dark corner of the brain of man. How could such things ever be signs of the end of the world? Here is another example of divine wisdom.

I think enough has been said to conclusively show that Jesus predicted a speedy end of the world. But his other teachings corroborate this:

"But when they persecute you in this city, flee to another: for verily I say unto you, Ye shall not have gone over the cities of Israel, till the son of man be come." How long do you suppose it would have taken twelve men to have gone over the cities of so small a country? They were to accomplish this in their lifetime, and some of them were to be still alive at the end of the world. They were told not to provide themselves with money or a change of clothing, but were to depend upon begging what little time the world was to endure. They were not to lay any treasures up on earth; not to take any thought for the morrow; to sell and distribute all they had. They felt certain that enough substance was already produced to last to the end, and that they could not possibly consume it all until all earthly things would be brought to a close. It would have been suicidal to practice any such advice as this, if the world was to endure thousands of years longer, and it would have been the advice of a fool.

We must conclude that Christ, if he actually existed, was very much mistaken and deluded person, or else an imposter; or that the writers erroneously, or falsely, reported his words. Rev. Theo. Parker said: "It is easy to show, if we have the exact words of Jesus, that he was mistaken in some points of the greatest magnitude; in the character of God; the existence of the devil; the eternal damnation of men; in the interpretation of the Old Testament; in the doctrine of demons, and in the end of the world within a few years." We must accept this dictum, or else say that gospels are false reports. We have seen that the first three gospels contradict the fourth. It can also be shown that they contradict one another. Rev. J. W. Chadwick says: "In the first three gospels we have one picture of Jesus, and in the fourth gospel another. If Jesus was the Jesus of Matthew and Mark and Luke, it is impossible that he could have been the Jesus of John."

The writer of the first gospel was guilty of imposing upon the ignorance and superstitious fears of the people by tabulating all the catastrophes and great phenomena in nature that he could think of, and representing that they were all soon to be ushered in as a final climax to the speedy end of the world. But as complete corroborative evidence of the fraud and imposition practiced by this writer it is only necessary to take one of the so-called prophecies of Christ:

"Behold, a virgin shall conceive, and bear a son, and shall call his name Immanuel." (Is. 7:14.) The writer of Matthew imposes this upon the world as a prophecy of Christ. (Matt. 1:22, 23.) But read in Isaiah from the first to the sixteenth verse inclusive. It becomes perfectly clear that two kings, Pekah and Rezin, were making war upon King Ahaz. The birth of the child was a sign to Ahaz that these two kinds should not prevail against him. The sign must precede the thing signified. The sign was the birth of a child, and the thing signified was that Ahaz was to be rid of these two kings before the child knew how to refuse the evil and choose the good. The time was limited for the fulfillment of this prophecy. It would have been a gross insult to Ahaz to have been told that, as a sign that these two kings should not prevail against him, a child would be born 700 years after. Thomas Paine says: "It may not be improper here to observe that the word translated a virgin in Isaiah doth not signify a virgin in Hebrew, but only a young woman. The tense is also falsified in the translation. Levi gives the Hebrew text of the 14th verse of the 7th chapter of Isaiah, and the translation in English with it, 'Behold, a young woman is with child, and beareth a son.' The expression, says he, is in the present tense. The translation agrees with the other circumstances related of the birth of this child, which was to be a sign to Ahaz. But as the true translation could not have been imposed upon the world as a prophecy of a child to be born 700 years afterwards, the Christian translators have falsified the original." But as a prophecy of that immediate time, as a sign to Ahaz that those kings should not prevail against him, it turned out to be false. They did prevail against him and he was taken captive. (II Chron. 28:5, 6.) Thomas Paine has said:

"They tell us that Jesus rose from the dead, and ascended into heaven. It is very easy to say so; a great lie is as easily told as a little one. But if he had done so, those would have been the only circumstances respecting him that would have differed from the common lot of man, and consequently the only case that would apply exclusively to him, as prophecy, would be some passages in the Old Testament that foretold such things of him. But there is not a passage in the Old Testament that speaks of a person, who, after being crucified, dead and buried, should rise from the dead, and ascend into heaven. Our prophecy mongers supply the silence the Old Testament guards upon such things, by telling us of passages they call prophecies, and that falsely so, about Joseph's dream, old clothes, broken bones, and such trifling stuff."

We will no longer be frightened by the malignant threats of

priestcraft or their Bible. We will no longer reverence or bow to them, or to their angry God, or slavishly do their wishes. The truth has made us mentally free from all such imposters and lies.

"When o'er mankind the church held sway,
In superstition's palmy day,
The arguments the priests adored
Were thumbscrews, fagots, fire and sword.
Now, when of these they are bereft.
The only weapons they have left,
Are threats of God behind the skies,
With personal abuse and lies,
Behind a wall of obscene Bibles
They skulk and sling their slanderous libels.
With hate they load their gospel guns
And poison shoot at freedom's sons.
But truth will silence soon their roar
And priests will be believed no more.
The persecuting, slandering clan
No more will dwarf the mind of man."

Homer, I. T. [Indian Territory; present-day Oklahoma]

THOSE "HOLY MEN OF GOD."

Their Ministerial Conduct Sanctioned by Scripture and Precedent.

BY J. M. GILBERT, M . D.

From *The Truth Seeker*, September 19, 1903

The one we have in mind now is the Rev. Mr. Wilkins, a Presbyterian preacher who lives at Ladonia. He helped to hold a revival at this place (Randolph, Tex.) last year. He seems to be guilty of "unministerial" conduct. But I think "ministerial" would be the more proper term, since more ministers are guilty than members of any other profession looked upon by the laity as being respectable. This holy man is reported to have been seen in Dallas in the Tenderloin district. Like the holy murderer, Moses, he looked this way and that way, and seeing no man he did like the pious Judah (Gen. xxxviii, 15, 16). He is also reported to have written a colored woman a note inviting her to be at his house at a certain time, as he would then be alone. He is said to have confessed to writing the note, but claimed he did it as a joke. He has been back here this summer, holding another revival. The church here was made aware of these charges against him, but they refused to investigate, and they let him preach. It strikes me that they were afraid that the charges might be true, and this proves that the churches will shield ministers in almost anything until they are forced to do something by the hue and cry from outsiders. They obtained several dupes at this revival, and this proves that a glib talker can pull the wool over their eyes, no matter what his character may be. This ought to show any one that what they call "getting religion" is of the earth, earthy, and that there is nothing supernatural about it. It is only a species of hypnotism, and the subjects are deluded into believing that they have religion.

But such conduct as mentioned above is characteristic of the men of God from the earliest times down to the present. There is a book published entitled "Crimes of Preachers." What the author says is so truthful and to the point that I think it good to quote some of it :

"It has been said by some apologists of the system of religion now in vogue In this country that the clerical delinquencies prove nothing against the system. In this they are mistaken. Of course. If Christianity had a foundation of fact these records would not prove that the fact is not there. What they do prove, however, is that the claim made for Christianity that it makes men moral is not true. For if the system is not sufficient to restrain its very teachers, how can we expect their pupils to profit by it? The point this book emphasizes—as an ex-Methodist minister, now a Rationalist, but always a moral man, forcibly puts it—is that religion, in and of itself, is not a moral force; that it is not one with morality; that it may and often does exist without morality, and that morality gains nothing by being associated with it. In proportion to their numbers, more ministers than members of any other profession commit crimes or yield to vice. A large proportion of these crimes are against women or with women. This perhaps is not strange when one considers the habit of pastoral visiting. When men are away from home attending to their duties in life the minister is loafing about, looking after the welfare of his flock pretendedly, but really making calls upon the women who most attract him…What the confessional is to the Roman Catholic church, such is the 'pastoral visit' to the Protestant church.

"In the past these brassy gentry, with solemn-visaged falsehood, have from every coward's castle in Christendom answered all the arguments, facts, and figures adduced by skeptics, by maligning the character of the reasoner or mathematician—especially if dead. 'Unworthy to blacken the shoes of their opponents, they blacken his character.' All this being more congenial to the taste of the ordinary follower of the meek and lowly Jesus than fair investigation and candid argument."

The author says that eminent writers on crime estimate that but one crime out of sixteen is detected and traced to the criminal; that not one-half of the published accounts of preachers' crimes have been seen, and that half of those which are ascertained are never published. "The churches endeavor to and do hide a great deal of the immorality of their ministers. The preachers who govern the ecclesiastical tribunals have a fellow feeling for one another."

The "Crimes of Preachers" gives the case of the Rev. Zachariah Parker, who was arrested at Dallas for embezzlement and had to give bond for $3,000. He passed himself off as a Baptist then. It also gives the case of the Rev. Zachariah Parker, Methodist, who was convicted at Paris, Tex., for "forgery and pension fraud; for eighteen years drew pension in name of widow of a former slave; the woman had been dead fifteen years." I knew this Zachariah Parker, and many who still live here knew him. He used to hold great revivals here, and he was looked upon almost as a god by the dear sisters. One of the sisters who frequented his meetings saw him on the train when they were taking him to prison, and he did not let on that he ever knew her.

This country has been well represented with immoral and criminal sky-pilots. Several years ago a Rev. Sherwood, an itinerant evangelist, came here and preached in his tabernacle and sold Bibles. The last I heard of him he was charged with stealing horses. The Rev. Murrell used to preach here for the Methodists. He deserted his family and eloped with another woman. The Rev. (Gosling) Edgar Manos used to preach here a few times. His speeches would put me in mind of a caged animal or of a maniac. He is reported to have had too intimate relations with a female, and had to leave the country.

The last we shall mention is the Rev. Fount Jones. This loud-mouthed blatherskite used to bray for the Baptists in their temple of ignorance at this place. He committed adultery with a married woman at Ector. This is a centre for piety (pus), and these sacred but obscene birds (carrion crows) congregate here from all the cardinal points of the compass to spew out the "carm" which they obtain from that reservoir of ignorance and filth of the dead past, the Bible.

Most of the Bible worthies were men and women of this character. Solomon had seven hundred wives and three hundred concubines. David was a liar, adulterer, polygamist, and a more brutal wretch never lived. God is represented as saying, "I have found David a man after mine own heart." What did the drunkard Lot do with his daughters in the cave? Abraham was a liar, adulterer, and polygamist. He married his own sister, became rich off her charms in Egypt by deceiving Pharaoh, and he almost deceived Abimelech in the same way. His lying son Isaac tried to deceive Abimelech In the same way. But Pharaoh and Abimelech were heathens, therefore truthful, honorable, and moral men. Isaac was the father of Jacob, a liar, cheat, and polygamist. Jacob's twelve sons were addicted to the same vice, and they were the founders of the twelve tribes of Israel, God's chosen people. Paul, the real founder of Christianity, used deception and boasted of it (2 Cor. xii, 16; I Cor. ix, 20, 22; Rom. iii, 7).

"The primitive Christians, accepting the Bible as an infallible authority, naturally regarded lying for God's glory not a vice, but a virtue." Did they not have the example of God who, according to the Bible, told the first lie (Gen. ii, 17; iii, 4), who broke his promises (Num. xiv, 30-34), who deceived and put lying spirits into the mouths of the prophets (Ezek. xiv, 9; 1 Kings xxii, 20-23; Jer. xv, 18)? Did they not have the example of Paul?

Mosheim, in his "Ecclesiastical History," says: "It was an established maxim with many Christians that it was pardonable in an advocate for religion to avail himself of fraud and deception, if it were likely they might conduce toward the attainment of any considerable good." Dean Milman, in his "History of Christianity," says: "It was admitted and avowed that to deceive into Christianity was so valuable a service as to hallow deceit itself," And Dr. Lardner says: "Christians of all sorts were guilty of this fraud." Take notice of the phrase, "Christians of all sorts," as we shall allude to it again. Scaliger says: "They distrusted the success of Christ's kingdom without the aid of lying." Bishop Fell says that in the first ages of the church the license of forging was very extensive. A distinguished French Protestant says: "For a good end they made no scruple to forge whole books." And this is how the gospels originated. They were written about the latter half of the second century by some unknown writers and the names of Matthew, Mark, Luke, and John falsely attached to them, and the church still perpetuates the falsehood that they were written by the men whose names they bear. Christians became so addicted to lying that it became second nature to them. The proof of this is to be seen in the innumerable lies told about Paine and Ingersoll and many other great men who had the courage to openly oppose their ignorant superstitions. In no other way could they perpetuate their system of falsehood and lies.

The above references and quotations were taken from Mr. John E . Remsburg's book, "The Bible." He proves that twenty crimes and vices are sanctioned by the Bible. And he says: "I expect the defenders of this book [the Bible] to complete the task I have here essayed. They will claim that the Bible is opposed to crime. They will, no doubt, cite numerous passages in confirmation of this claim. Let them do this. Then place the results of our labors side by side. This will show that the Bible abounds with teachings that conflict. This fact established, the dogma of its divinity must fall...So long as men's minds are confused and corrupted by these conflicting and demoralizing teachings, so long will immorality prevail. You cannot make men moral while they accept as their moral guide a book which sanctions every crime and presents as the best models of human excellence the most notorious villains. You cannot make them moral by teaching them that a lie is better for being called inspired; that vice becomes a virtue with age; that a dead rogue should be canonized and a live one killed."

The church has always claimed to be the greatest safeguard to good morals, but such a claim is absolutely false. Paul, writing to one of his churches, says: "It is reported commonly that there is fornication among you, and such fornication as is not so much as named among the gentiles" (1 Cor. v, 1). Mosheim, writing of a period two centuries later, says: "Many were sunk in luxury and voluptuousness, puffed up with vanity, arrogance, and ambition; possessed with a spirit of contention and discord, and addicted to many other vices." Salvian, a Christian clergyman of the fifth century, says: "With the exception of a few who flee from vice, what is almost every Christian congregation but a sink of vices? For you will find in the church scarcely one who is not either a drunkard, or a glutton, or an adulterer,...or a robber, or a man-slayer, and, worse than all, almost all these without limit." The Byzantine empire existed for a thousand years. During that time Christianity was supreme. Lecky says of this empire: "The universal verdict of history is that it constitutes, with scarcely an exception, the most thoroughly base and despicable form that civilization has yet assumed." Martin Luther testifies: "Under the papacy we were bad, but under the gospel we are seven—yea, more than seven—times worse." The above quotations were taken from Mr. Remsburg's pamphlet entitled "False Claims." Sir William Hamilton says that Luther, Melanchthon, and Bucer, and a dozen distinguished divines among the reformers "stood formally committed" to polygamy. "Luther, drawing his morality from the Bible, gave concubinage his indorsement. . . . In a letter to his confidential friend, Spalatin, he confessed to numerous adulteries" (Remsburg's "The Bible").

At this place last year a young Baptist preacher made the assertion that no one was without sin. He said that if the Bible taught any other doctrine it contradicted itself, and that if it contradicted itself he would stop preaching. He probably had in mind: "For there is no man that sinneth not. There is none righteous, no, not one" (1 Kings viii , 46; Rom. iii, 10). I wrote him a letter pointing out many contradictions, and among them I quoted: "Whosoever is born of God doth not commit sin;...he cannot sin, because he is born of God" (1 John iii, 9). I wrote him that if he was sincere he would have to quit preaching. His insincerity is proved beyond a doubt, for he is still preaching. Convince these sky-pilots of their error and they will still continue to preach the same old lie. A very appropriate motto for them would be the words of Isaiah: "We have made lies our refuge, and under falsehood have we hid ourselves." The above is a contradiction beyond a doubt, but I can harmonize it in the only possible way it can be done. "Whosoever is born of God" is not a human being. But all Christians are human beings, therefore no Christian is " born of God." All Christians are "of the devil" (1 John iii, 8). But Christians claim to be born of God. Do they tell the truth? If they do we will have to hold that what were once sins and crimes when committed by unbelievers are not sins and crimes when committed by Christians, and that Christians are not "men" and not "righteous." The mere exercising of belief completely changes the nature of all such acts. They have a special license to do anything, but anything they may do cannot possibly be sin, their belief has made black white and transformed a lie into truth. "And by him all that believe are justified from all things" (Acts xiii, 39). Christians can be anything untruthful, dishonest, immoral, and wicked. Like Paul, they can be "all things to all men." Those who still assert that a Christian cannot be thus and so do not know what they are talking about. Dr. Lardner knew that Christians could be "of all sorts." History testifies that they have been of all sorts. The sort of persons the world needs most must be something better than what it takes to constitute a full-fledged Christian. Luther obtained his morality from the Bible, and he said: " If men only believe enough in Christ they can commit adultery and murder a thousand times a day without periling their salvation." No wonder he said: "Under the papacy we were bad, but under the gospel we were seven—yea, more than seven—times worse." John Wesley said: "They [certain clergymen of England] are well pleased that their parishioners grow more diligent and honest...Nay, they are glad that they are brought to practice both justice and mercy; in a word, to be moral men. But the truth is, the Methodists know and teach that all this is nothing before God." Belief Is the only thing essential, and any fool can believe the way Christians do. When it comes to religion one must discard his reason to believe in Christianity. Those holy men that we have mentioned had a special biblical sanction and a specific command for their actions. " And thou shalt bestow that money for whatsoever thy soul lusteth after,...or for wine, or for strong drink, or for whatsoever thy soul desireth" (Deut.). Here Is a sanction for patronizing the saloon or the tenderloin district.

PRAYER.

BY J. M. GILBERT.

From *The Truth Seeker*, December 5, 1903

There may be prayers of doubtful termination, prayers against the inevitable, and prayers which always seem to be answered. In case of disease or injury it is always doubtful how it will terminate. Prayers at such times will be doubtful also, it depends upon the constitution of the patient and the manner of treatment. The prognosis in a majority of diseases is always favorable, the greatest percentage of cases recover. Prayers in their behalf will always appear to be answered. Prayers for our three assassinated presidents may have been doubtful at first, but finally they were prayers against the inevitable. Probably there was not a praying individual who did not utter a prayer for a Lincoln, a Garfield, or a McKinley. Their prayers were unheeded.

How aptly this illustrates the truth of the gospel. It promises that where two or three are gathered together in the name of Christ, anything they might ask would be granted. But here were not only two or three, but a whole nation asking for the same thing. Again, it says that all things are possible to him that believeth. Must we infer there was not a believer in the whole land? We are taught that faith like unto a grain of mustard seed will remove mountains. It is clearly meant that believers were to have more faith than a mere mustard seed, for were not all things to be possible with them? To say that they had such a small amount was equivalent to saying that they did not have any. When the faithful got sick they were not to send for doctors, but were to call in the elders, let them pray, anointing with oil, and the prayer of faith would heal the sick and the Lord would raise him up. But what necessity of oil when only faith is needed?

Probably the prayers were only a blind used for deception and the real efficacy for healing was in the oil. However that may be, Asa was held up as a shining example. He sent for a physician, and he slept with his fathers. But it matters not how much Asa is preached to them, the majority of Christians always send for a doctor. They never rely on faith or prayer. They have sense enough to know that prayers are worthless. They are infidels to that portion of the gospel. We are glad to have it so, and take pleasure in calling their attention to it. In recent years we have many examples of Christian Scientists relying wholly upon faith and refusing medical aid, and the papers report that many of them go where Asa went. The surviving ones who seem to be responsible for this fidelity to the gospel are indicted in the courts. And Christians claim this to be a Christian nation where it is a crime to be anything but a Christian in name only. Do not dare to practice all the precepts of Christ. If you do you are a criminal, and at the same time you would be a veritable fool. But be a hypocrite to be popular, you must claim to believe it all. To be strictly honest and truthful you will be classed along with those odious Infidels. "Anything but that! good Lord, deliver us! Let us be cowards, fools, hypocrites, and liars. Let your word be true even if we all have to turn liars to uphold it. Let us be fools for Christ's sake." I detest such a fake with my whole soul. We will only mention an instance or two of prayers against the inevitable. The Louisville tornado took place in 1890. The storm center was seen to gather in the southern portion of Wyoming. Notice was promptly given. They were warned that on Thursday night a hurricane would blow with a speed of fifty miles an hour. They had plenty of time for prayer. One church which was demolished killed the minister and his little son. Ten or eleven men who were playing cards in an adjoining building escaped without serious injury. In another place a saloon man and four of his patrons survived. What irony on mysterious providence! I do not say that these men should not have been saved, for such men are very often better than ministers. I speak of it in the light Christians try to throw around such things. In this tornado many were crushed under falling walls. Those who rushed to the scene could hear many cries for help but could not reach them all. There can be no doubt that many of those prayed to God, and their prayers were unheeded. After a storm starts it can be fairly predicted what route it will travel. Warnings are sent in advance to the villages, towns, and cities. There is always plenty of time for praying, and we know that hundreds drop on their knees when they learn that a hurricane is rushing towards them. But prayers are always powerless to change the course or to diminish the effects of the storm.

We have many records of where towns and cities have been built in the vicinities of volcanoes. The inhabitants are repeatedly warned by numerous rumblings. They have plenty of time to leave the dangerous locality. But still they remain. They say their prayers, attend mass, count their beads, and display their amulets and charms. It is all of no avail. The volcano bursts forth with great fury and few escape. At the Galveston disaster the people had warning. Of course there was plenty of time for praying, and we are certain thousands of prayers were said. After the hurricane began to blow and the waters made their rush there was still plenty of time for praying. We are told that a thousand years are as a day with the Lord. Then a minute would be as a century. Yet all praying was in vain. The island was submerged and devastated, thousands perished, and great havoc was wrought far inland.

A prayer is a sincere desire. In times of great peril every humane person desires the safety of all. A Rationalist, however, refuses to address any prayer to the supernatural, because there is no proof that the supernatural exists, and he knows that such prayers are never answered. An omniscient God, if such a being exists, would know the desire of all. They would not have to be spoken to be known. A spoken prayer is only the outward expression of the silent wish. Considered in this light, we can readily see that all people are praying continually, and we also know that the vast majority of wishes or desires are doomed to disappointment. If such a God exists, as claimed, it is the worst kind of foolishness, or downright idiocy, or damnable hypocrisy to pray to him.

A few years ago Sherman (Tex.) had a cyclone. About the same time, or soon after, a house or two were blown off their foundations. The majority of the people, all Christians, became abject cowards. They dug storm cellars. At the approach of every cloud above the horizon they would rush into those cellars and almost suffocate for want of breathing space. One day a druggist pointed out a passage In the Bible to a Methodist preacher and asked: "Do you think a person who believes that will go into a storm house?" The preacher replied: "Yes, if he believed that or any other passage be would go in during a storm." This was the preacher who said he was not called to preach, but did it because it was more comfortable than to labor. Sober-minded people know that they must make the effort themselves to get out of the way of the destructive forces of nature. They know that they must use human means and methods. They know that the great forces of nature will not turn out of their courses for the pious idler who prays, and that they will not leave him unharmed, any more than the meanest animal which exists. I once read an account, written by a woman, of where two wagon trains were making the trip to California in an early day. In one train the most of them were Freethinkers, in the other the people were very pious and would not travel on Sunday. The first train was attacked by Indians. But they did not resort to prayer, they used powder and lead and kept them away. As soon as the Indians discovered the other train they made an attack. These people had a trust in God: they fell on their knees and went to praying, and were massacred In consequence. Trusts in God in time of danger are suicidal, and in time of security they are worthless. Sensible people would as soon think of asking a God to put a roof on their houses to protect them from the rain and storm, or to ask him to weed their crops to protect them from future want, as to ask God to do anything whatever. Praying for one thing is just as rational as praying for another. People know that they must use their own judgment and the means at their disposal. When their own efforts fail, or the cooperative efforts of their companions, they know that all is done that can be done, and they must submit to the inevitable. "When man is powerless, heaven cannot save."

Not long ago many people in Kansas were praying against the floods. Not long since the people in Texas were praying against the pests which destroy the cotton crop. Since the summer revivals we have here two prayer meetings every week. Let us pause long enough to ask. Why do people pray? Let every one answer honestly. It is because many of them are simple minded and superstitious. With many it is merely a matter of form, ceremony, custom, or for hypocritical display. In this way many seek to hoodwink the unwary and unthinking. Those who pray the loudest and make the greatest pretensions to piety will bear to be watched. They are not always honest or truthful. Whenever we hear of a defaulter, an embezzler, or of the flight of a bank cashier with the bank funds, we naturally ask, What church did he belong to? We nearly always find them some Sunday-school superintendent, some deacon in the church, or some preacher. From the church to the jail, from the gallows to heaven, are well-traveled roads. Statistics of prisons and houses of ill fame show that the inmates are church members or nominal believers. You scarcely find an Atheist in prison.

Many who pray are perfectly aware that prayers are powerless to change the nature of things. They are like the man who returns thanks at meals. He very well knows that such a silly custom will not change the quantity or quality of the food upon the table. He also knows that he must work to produce it, or obtain it from those who do. He knows that it did not come by prayer and never will. The proper one to thank is either himself or some other human being, and not a God. If God rules the elements and sends the pests, as Christians profess to believe, he is all the time trying to destroy the substance which requires hard labor to produce. A thief comes and steals your horses, then thank him because he left your cow. To be a complete Christian you must not only thank him, but you must give him your cow.

There could be no law against theft in a strictly Christian country. But men become so habituated to superstitious rites that they do not wish to abolish them. But a desire to be as rational as possible ought to persuade them. They are vain, worthless, irrational, and idiotic.

Natural observation, experience, and common sense thrust this simple truth upon us. They teach us that prayers are ineffectual and vain. Every prayer with the name of God in it is a profanity; it is using that name in vain. Children learn most of their curse words in the Sunday school and church. They hear them more at such times than any other. Their elders are continually using them at such times, and they think what their elders do at such times is all right for them. Ministers are the profanest of men, but probably they do not believe in a God, and do not think there can be any harm in pronouncing the name of a myth. Their actions seem to prove that they do not believe in the being whose pretended word they preach, or else do not believe it is his word. We only have to read "Crimes of Preachers" to be convinced of that fact.

But maybe we are going too fast. In that word they have the promise that all sins will be forgiven those who believe. Ministers have a license to get up before an audience and use profanity, and their dupes think it perfectly proper, but it is a crime to do so before an audience anywhere else. There is a difference in localities and a difference In persons, that is all. One is a so called sacred place, made sacred by ignorance, and the preachers' calling held to be sacred by the same ignorance.

The other places are secular, and the person using the profane word is not a humbug and hypocrite, like the majority of orthodox preachers.

But some Christians are foolish enough to think that one day is more sacred than another, that a name pronounced by a person who affects piety is a holy word, but in one who does not it is profane. Nine times out of ten this latter person is the best of the two.

Prayers are on a par with many other ignorant superstitions—such as placing the horse shoe over the door, about the number thirteen, in the saying, "A whistling girl and a crowing hen always come to some bad end." Prayers are on a par with the negro with his rabbit's foot, with the counting of beads by good Catholics and the wearing of amulets and charms. All such as this is hoodooism, and prayers to any mysterious being must be classed in the same category. Each one of the things just mentioned have as much efficacy for good or evil as praying.

Once the superstitious natives believed that at every solar eclipse some great disaster was about to happen. Some terrible dragon was about to devour their god, the orb of day. They would grovel in the dust, mutilate themselves, beat on their tomtoms, and make all manner of noises and gesticulations. Their religious fakirs (priests) would utter harangues and incantations to drive away the demon. The eclipse always went away. Then would be a time of general rejoicing. The fakirs claimed the honor for the restored security against the imaginary evil. They did it with their incantations (prayers). They exacted tribute, just like the priests do to day. They praised religion and told how valuable they were as mediators between the rabble and the mysterious powers of the heavens.

Just so. The silly, the unthinking, the superstitious, and the hypocritical pray to-day. They pray in times of drought, floods, pestilences, and famine. After a time the drought is broken, the flood ceases, the pests die out, pestilence and famine cease their ravages. Naturally these things could not always last. But the prayers were answered, just like the savage's prayer which drove away the eclipse. They confound the doubter by citing these things as answers to prayers, just like the savage could have done in regard to the eclipse. These things offer a fruitful field to which pious tricksters and hypocrites turn to uphold their system of falsehood and deception.

From all this we infer that nature pays no attention to the complaints and prayers of men. She pursues her course regardless of the weal or woes of all the beings which inhabit the earth. She has no eyes to see, no ears to hear, and is without compassion. She is indifferent to the happiness or misery of all her creatures, from the lowest to the highest. Any kind of noise, sounding brass or tinkling cymbal, the rattling of dry bones, the sounding of trumpets, the hiss of the serpent, and the braying of those long-eared animals in and out of the pulpit, are with her just as effectual for either good or evil as those other noises (prayers) made with the vocal organs of human beings. It is high time for all sensible people to quit praying. We must depend upon our own efforts or obtain aid from our fellow man.

> The beams smile on, and heaven serene
> Still bends, although no prayer had been;
> And the breezes moan, and still they wave,
> When man is powerless, heaven cannot save."

FREE PRESS AND FREE SPEECH.

From *The Truth Seeker*, July 15, 1905

To the Editor of The Truth Seeker: I notice the question has been raised about admitting other than articles on theology to the paper. I agree with those who advocate "no press muzzling." I believe in free press and free speech to be practiced as well as talked about. Truth, then, will have a fair show in every line of thought. Those Freethinkers who advocate free press and free speech, and then protest about articles from the industrial and social radicals, seem to me to be a little inconsistent. It is the editor's prerogative to publish any article he sees fit. It is always to be understood that the editor does not indorse all that he publishes. Leave the editor free. Let him not discriminate against any phase of radical thought. Theology is not the only thing that is wrong. Ecclesiasticism is not the only thing that oppresses and creates burdens grievous to be borne.

There is a crying need for relief from the present industrial system. A great portion of the present code of conventional morality is fictitious. The false foundation has never yet been removed. Many Freethinkers are yet influenced by the theological taint when it comes to the social question. Many people can see the false god of the industrial system. They can see that the god and the devil of theology are myths. But they are yet superstitious, they still believe in a devil of conventional morality. They are willing for you to repudiate theology and its claims of duties to a god, but when you regulate your life naturally regardless of a fictitious conventional morality, they are as willing to condemn and commit you to social ostracism as a Puritan.

So, let us have more of Pentecost. His lectures are good. They are full of wholesome truths. He causes us to think on new lines hitherto hidden from us. It breaks the sluggish monotony of thoughts upon theology. Yours fraternally,

J. M. GILBERT.

AN EX-METHODIST FREETHINKER.

From *The Truth Seeker*, October 25, 1905

We had a Socialist speaking Saturday evening and night by Mr. Stanley J. Clark, state organizer for the party in Texas. He was once a Methodist preacher. He was to be here two years ago, and had obtained permission to use the school house. His appointment had been posted up for a week or more. Some Christian tried to persuade the trustees not to let him have the house, but was told that Mr. Clark had a right to use it. The Prohibitionists were at that time holding forth in the C. P. church. But they must have the school house that night. They were told they could use it if Mr. Clark did not come. Mr. Clark was unfortunately called away to see his sick child and did not get here.

Mr. Clark gave a lecture Sunday evening at the school house. This was the best thing that ever happened in this community. It was a Freethought lecture, a good thing to follow after all the revivals.

He said: "I do not talk to-day as a Socialist, but just as Clark. Hold me alone responsible. Some one has said: 'And ye shall know the truth, and the truth shall make you free.' It is because you have been following error so long that you are in so deplorable a condition. Your attention has been riveted to the skies while you have been kept in ignorance and subjection. You must turn your attention to this life and environments in order to eradicate the evils by which you are surrounded. When you make conditions right here so that every one can live a good life, it will then be time enough for spiritual things. The criminals and the depraved are caused by bad environments. I am weary of being told that we should be content with bad conditions here in order to inherit a mansion beyond the moon. We only need to know the truth and apply it to become free religiously, socially and economically. Truth is sacred wherever found, whether in the Bible or Ray's arithmetic. A lie branded holy is still a lie. Truth only needs to be stated. It does not require any defense. It does not demand followers. If God made man and so ordered all things, then God alone is responsible for the evils we endure. I pass it up to God. If God is everywhere, then I am in God, and am all right. The idea of God begins in the stomach. People change their ideas of God as they change their ways of living. Preachers exhort you to give to the Lord, but they do not tell you that the Lord's pocket book is in their own breeches. A religious thermometer is gauged by the pocket book—they drop back into the pews according to their dollars. Knock the profit out of religion and you knock the clapper out of every church bell in town. (One old man got enough and left). It is hard to teach an old dog new tricks. This is a scientific fact. The cells of the brain are generally so hardened that they will not admit new impressions. I defend the right of every man to his opinions. One life at a time is the right motto. The place to be happy is here and now. You have to create good environments to make a good and happy people. This life is our chief concern. Whether I shall live again does not concern me. I honestly say I do not know. You claim to know and know nothing. You have no better reasons to say you will live again than you have to say that the worm will live again that you tread upon."

 I cannot remember much of his speech, but I write the sense of what I do remember for publication if you think good. There were several out to hear that could not be induced to read anything of the kind. It will cause some to think who have not been in the habit. In that way it will do some good. Yours fraternally,

              J. M. GILBERT.

Randolph, Tex.

JUDAS ISCARIOT.

Contradictions and Pretended Prophecies Concerning the Alleged Betrayer of Jesus.

I.

From *The Truth Seeker*, November 11, 1905

"Then Judas, which betrayed him, when he saw that he was condemned, repented himself, and brought again the thirty pieces of silver to the chief priests and elders; saying, I have sinned in that I betrayed the innocent blood. And they said, What is that to us? See thou to that. And he cast down the pieces of silver in the temple and departed, and hanged himself. And the chief priests took the silver pieces, and said, It is not lawful to put them into the treasury, because it is the price of blood. And they took counsel, and bought with them the potter's field, to bury strangers in. Then was fulfilled that which was spoken by Jeremy the prophet, saying, And they took the thirty pieces of silver, the price of him that was valued, whom they of the children of Israel did value, and gave them for the potter's field as the Lord appointed unto me." (Matt. 27: 3-10.)

"Men and brethren, this prophecy must needs have been fulfilled, which the Holy Ghost by the mouth of David spoke concerning Judas, which was guide to them that took Jesus. For he was numbered with us and had obtained part of this ministry. Now this man purchased a field with the reward of iniquity; and falling headlong, he burst asunder in the midst, and all his bowels gushed out." (Acts I: 16-19.)

The contradictions are: Judas repented. His conscience did not seem to have troubled him in the least. Judas took the money back. He did not take it back.. He bought the field. The chief priests bought the field. Judas hung himself. He died accidentally through a fall. One of the above accounts is certainly false. Probably both are false, because both are made the subject of pretended prophecies. There is another contradiction. Satan entered into Judas before the passover. (Luke 22: 1-21.) Satan did not enter into him until the passover was finished. (John 13: 2-27.) We will now quote the other references about Judas Iscariot.

"Simon the Canaanite, and Judas Iscariot, who also betrayed him. And while he yet spake, lo, Judas, one of the twelve, came, and with him a great multitude with swords and staves, from the chief priests and elders of the people." (Matt. 10: 4; 26: 47.)

"And Judas Iscariot, which also betrayed him; and they went into a house. And Judas Iscariot, one of the twelve, went unto the chief priests to betray him unto them. And immediately, while he yet spoke, cometh Judas, one of the twelve, and with him a great multitude with swords and staves, from the chief priests and the scribes and the elders." (Mark 3: 19; 14: 10, 43.)

"And Judas the brother of James, and Judas Iscariot, which also was the traitor. Then entered Satan into Judas surnamed Iscariot, being of the number of the twelve. And while he yet spake, behold a multitude, and he that was called Judas, one of the twelve, went before them, and drew near unto Jesus to kiss him." (Luke 6: 16; 22: 3, 47.)

"He spake of Judas Iscariot, the son of Simon; for he it was that should betray him, being one of the twelve. And the supper being ended, the devil having now put into the heart of Judas Iscariot, Simon's son, to betray him. Judas then, having received a band of men and officers from the chief priests and Pharisees, cometh thither with lanterns and torches and weapons. And Judas also, which betrayed him, stood with them." (John 6: 71; 13: 2; 18: 3, 5.)

The New Testament contains numerous contradictions, but here all accounts agree in proving that it does contradict itself. Theologians make every possible effort to harmonize the contradictions, and here is one place the book harmonizes in proving the contradictions.. But such harmony as this they are not looking for.

I once made the assertion that the Bible contradicted itself. One person denied it and asked me to point out one. I pointed out this one about Judas. He could not then think of any way to escape the truth. When asked about it afterwards by another person he said there were two Judases, He could also have said there were several. But he meant to convey the falsehood that one of these contradictory accounts was about one Judas and the other account about another. But the person who asserts this is either very stupid or speaks falsely. But there is a great class of people too indolent to read or investigate for themselves. It is easier for them to take the word of their preacher, and the preacher's trade is to uphold pious falsehoods, a la Talmage, or a la Torrey. They eagerly accept as truth any old pious falsehood which favors religion, and peddle it around as gospel truth. In fact, they are all as true as the gospel. But the orthodox church would have been dead long ago had it not been for its stock of lies. They are its most valuable assets, and it guards this property with the most jealous care. But the person referred to at the beginning of this paragraph was intelligent. He had read the accounts. He must have been aware of misrepresenting. But he wished to shield the false dogmas of biblical infallibility and harmony. Many Christians think it is their duty to lie a little to uphold Christian truths? If there is only one contradiction in the Bible, away goes its infallibility and harmony. Thus two Christian truths are shown to be real falsehoods. Christianity is almost wholly composed of such truths. The writers of the New Testament are guilty of falsifying, as we hope to show later. Christians of to-day are largely patterns after the old. On ordinary matters they may be truthful, but when it comes to religion they have a New Testament license and example to lie.

We have heard it urged more than once that there were two

persons named Judas as a means to clear up the contradictions. It is not necessary, but we will try to briefly notice the other persons named Judas. Christians carelessly and unthinkingly accept such harmony, and if left unnoticed, they unwittingly think such assertions to be true. But they often repeat them after they know them to be false.

There is a Judas mentioned in Matt. 1: 2, 3. His name is given in the genealogy of Jesus, and he is said to have lived between Abraham and David. Matthew and Luke contradict each other here, "Judas the brother of James" is mentioned in Luke 6: 16, John 14: 22, Acts 1: 13. He is called "Jude," the brother of James, in Jude I. It is claimed that he wrote that epistle. Commentators say that Matthew (10: 3) calls him "Lebbaeus," and Mark (3: 18) as "Thaddaeus." But this is a mere assertion without authority. It is the way they so beautifully harmonize the Bible. But such harmony as this always goes with unthinking Christians. Judas the brother of James was one of the apostles. He composed one of the eleven (Acts 1: 13) when they met after Judas hung himself (Matt., 27: 5), or after he died through a fall (Acts 1: 18). Judas the brother of Jesus is mentioned in Matt. 13: 55 and Mark 6: 3. But he was not an apostle or "numbered with the twelve." "Judas of Galilee" is mentioned in Acts 5: 37. He perished about the time of the alleged birth of Jesus (Luke 1: 4-7; 2: 1). Another Judas is mentioned in Acts 9: 11. It is related that Paul took shelter at his house during his blindness. This 'was about two years after the crucifixion. A successor to Judas was immediately chosen at that time (Acts 1: 11-26). "Judas surnamed Barsabas" is mentioned in Acts 15: 22., It is said that he and Silas were chosen to accompany Paul and Barnabas to Antioch. "Joseph called Barsabas" and Matthias were candidates for the place left vacant by the death of Judas Iscariot. Matthias was chosen to fill the vacancy (Acts 1: 26). There is no person named Judas that will answer the purpose to harmonize the contradiction.

Matthew claims it as a prophecy as follows: "Then was fulfilled that which was spoken by Jeremy the prophet, saying, And they took the thirty pieces of silver, the price of him that was valued, whom they of the children of Israel did value, and gave them for the potter's field, as the Lord appointed me." But the New Testament refers to Zech 11: 12, 13 which reads as follows: "And I said unto them, if ye think good, give me my price; and if not, forbear. So they weighed for my price thirty pieces of silver. And the Lord said unto me, Cast it into the potter; a goodly price that I was prized at of them. And I took the thirty pieces of silver, and cast them to the potter in the house of the Lord." If this was by Zechariah, why did, the writer of Matthew say it was by "Jeremy the prophet?" Here is an inspired mistake, a good example of inspiration. But some uninspired person corrected the inspired writer.

Mr. E. Walters, a thorough Hebrew scholar, and author of "Searching the Scriptures for the Messiah," says there were two Zechariahs; that the first eight chapters were by one writer and the last six by another. Chambers' Encyclopedia says, "The prophecies of Zechariah may be divided into three parts. * * * Numerous biblical critics, both in Germany and England, consider the first part [chap. 1-8] only to be the work of Zechariah, and it cannot be denied that the internal evidence strongly favors this supposition, * * * while the remaining chapters are totally unconnected in subject with what precede. Whether these chapters are the work of one or two authors, has also been elaborately discussed, the evidence being, on the whole, in favor of the later view."

J. M. GILBERT.

JUDAS ISCARIOT.

Contradictions and Pretended Prophecies Concerning the Alleged Betrayer of Jesus.

II

From *The Truth Seeker*, November 18, 1905

Mr. John E. Remsburg, in his work entitled "The Bible," says that the twelve Minor Prophets comprised one book in the accepted Hebrew. So the inspired writer of Matthew had to guess. Mr. Remsburg says, "Zechariah is the work of at least three writers." He quotes Davidson as saying, "To Zechariah's authentic oracles were attached chapters ix-xiv, themselves made up of two parts (ix-xi, xii-xiv) belonging to different times and authors." (Canon, p. 33). The passage we are dealing with (Zech. xi, 12, 13) is from the spurious portion and was not written by Zechariah.

But this passage is not a prophecy at all. The transaction is spoken of in the past tense. The writer in Matthew falsified the text in substituting the word "they" for "I," and by adding other matter not belonging to it. He falsified the time. When he changed the "I" to "they" he was no doubt thinking of the chief priests. But he apparently forgot the chief priests when he added, "as the Lord appointed me." This last part of his sentence does not agree with the first portion. This plainly shows the fraud of trying to make the passage apply to the chief priests, who were of the third person plural, while the person in Zechariah was of the first person singular. Judas is not represented as speaking. He was no more appointed to buy a field than he was to hang himself. To make the last portion of Matthew's sentence agree with the first portion the words would have to be "as the Lord appointed them." If the chief priests were speaking, it would be "as the Lord appointed us." But they were spoken of, and were not the persons speaking, and the right word would be "them" instead of "me." To whom does the word "me" refer? It cannot refer to Judas or the chief priests. It cannot refer to the writer of Matthew, for he wrote long after the events to which the pretended prophecy refers. His identity is unknown. The church commits a fraud by teaching that this gospel was written by Matthew. The word "me" could only refer to the person who was speaking in Zechariah. The fraud of changing "I" into "they" is clearly seen.

The purchase of a field is mentioned in Matthew. There is no hint of a field in Zechariah. Matthew calls the money "the price of blood." In Zechariah it is called a "goodly price." There is no hint of blood or violence in Zechariah, and we must infer that the transaction was perfectly legal and right. If Christians wish to apply the "goodly price" to Jesus, they must think he was worth very little. They make him look like "thirty cents." But the words "goodly price" were spoken by the Lord himself. If Christianity is true, he must have felt very cheap in his own estimation. The plain inference is, these words do not have reference to the value of a life, especially not to the life of a God offered as a sacrifice for the salvation of the world. The pieces of silver were "cast into the potter in the house of the Lord" at the command of the Lord himself. But in Matthew the chief priests said this was not lawful. It is plain that the money in Zechariah did not represent "the price of blood," or else the New Testament lies about it.

After the person in Zechariah had completed the transaction, he said, "Then I cut asunder mine other staff, even bands, that I might break the brotherhood between Judah and Israel" (Zech., xi, 14). The Hebrew nation had been divided into two separate kingdoms named Judah and Israel They became united again about the time of Hezekiah's reign. They were now spoken of as a brotherhood under the two names. The words in

Zechariah undoubtedly refer to that time. It seems to me that any intelligent person ought to see the fraud imposed by the writer of the book of Matthew.

But Matthew names Jeremiah. Thomas Paine searched that book for the passage. He found Jer. xxxii, 6-15, as the nearest approach to it. It is there related that the word of the Lord came unto Jeremiah or person speaking, telling him his uncle's son would come to sell him a field. He. was told to buy the field. Jeremiah says that he bought the field for seventeen shekels of silver. The only thing in the passage in Zechariah agreeing to the case in Matthew is the number of the pieces of silver. The only thing in Jeremiah is the purchase of a field. The passage in Jeremiah is equally as well applicable as the passage in Zechariah. But neither of these passages is a prophecy of anything. They both related something already accomplished when they were written.

The book of Acts claims it to be a prophecy as follows: "Men and brethren, this scripture must needs have been fulfilled, which the Holy Ghost by the mouth of David spake before concerning Judas, which was a guide to them that took Jesus" (Acts i, 16). The passage referred to is Psalms xli, 9, and reads as follows: "Yea, mine own familiar friend, in whom I trusted, which did eat of my bread, hath lifted his heel against me." Is there the slightest of reasons for claiming these to be the words of the Holy Ghost? There is nothing in them that partakes of the nature of prophecy. Has not many a man been in the same position in which he could have used the same words? Ghost tales have been used to terrify us, but now we know that all ghosts are creatures of the imagination, whether they are believed to be holy or unholy. Did the Holy Ghost claim Judas as his own familiar friend in whom he trusted? The Holy Ghost was then sadly deceived. But Christians claim that the Holy Ghost knows all things. He must have known that Judas would be a traitor. Would he still have trusted him? Either these are not the words of the Holy Ghost, or else the Christian claim is false.

Do these words fit Jesus? Did he believe Judas to be one of his best friends and trust him? Then he did not know all things, and was not a God. He was as easily deceived as the average mortal. Did David ever know Judas, and did Judas ever eat of David's bread? To claim this as a prophecy is a misfit every way, and a gross falsehood.

But any one not rendered stupid by the false claims in the Bible, and those made for the Bible, can see that this psalm represents David as speaking of his own affairs. He complains and laments about how he had been treated by both enemies and friends, and says that even his most intimate friend had turned against him. David was the most cruel and corrupt person of that time. He was a thief, a robber, a despotic murderer, a traitor, an adulterer, and a polygamist. He had friends who were like him, but they could hardly be worse. One of these probably told on David, and it is of this that he complains. But the Bible declares David as a man after God's own heart. How is that for a book of good morals, and how are the churches and Sunday schools that uphold David as a good example? No wonder such a book as the "Crimes of Preachers" can be published. The nearer they are like David, the nearer they are men of God, men after God's own heart.

But just think of the great fraud practiced by the writer of Acts in making this into a prophecy to be fulfilled a thousand years in the future. And all the other passages in the New Testament which claim to be prophecies are no less fraudulent than this last one. In some of them the fraud is more easily seen. Thomas Paine said that when the passages, or mutilated parts of sentences, were restored to the Old Testament, and taken in connection with the context, they "give the lie to the New Testament." The truth of that declaration cannot be successfully refuted. We will now conclude by quoting a passage from Thomas Paine's "Examination of the Prophecies":

"They tell us that Jesus rose from the dead and ascended into heaven. It is easy to say so; a great lie is as easily told as a little one. But if he had done so, those would have been the only circumstances respecting him that would have differed from the common lot of man; and consequently the only case that would apply exclusively to him, as a prophecy, would some passage in the Old Testament that foretold such things of him. But there is not a passage in the Old Testament that speaks of a person who, after being crucified, dead, and buried, should rise from the dead, and ascend into heaven. Our prophecy mongers supply the silence the Old Testament guards upon such things, by telling us of passages they call prophecies, and falsely so, about Joseph's dream, old clothes, broken bones, and such trifling stuff."

J. M. GILBERT.

WHY CATER TO IGNORANCE?

From *The Truth Seeker*, March 10, 1906

Editor of The Truth Seeker: A few days ago we had a lecture by the Rev. M. A. Smith, deputy organizer of the Socialist party in Texas. He was a fair speaker and an earnest advocate. The Methodist preacher was out and received some hard hits. He exposed President Roosevelt's unfriendly attitude towards the laboring man. When 2,000 of the Russian people were shot down at the time they met to petition the Czar for relief, the President did not seem to know it—did not say a word. But when a grand duke was blown to pieces the President rushed to the office to cable a message of condolence—he was so sorry that an aristocrat had been killed. The many thousands of suffering poor were not worth considering. The speaker mentioned another instance where several counterfeiters had been sent to prison. The wealthy men who owned the business and did the scheming were pardoned, but the men hired to do the work were left in prison. These instances show how the President loves the workingman. He courts the favor of the Catholic church and aristocratic rulers. All the use church and government has for laboring men is to make dupes of them for their support. A genuine rebel against these despotic institutions seems to me to be the possessor of the truest manhood and the greatest lover of liberty and justice.

The speaker quoted the Bible and claimed Jesus as a Socialist. He has published a booklet entitled, "Jesus As a Social Reformer." He quoted, "In the sweat of thy face shalt thou eat bread." This belongs to the account of the mythical creation, the Garden of Eden, and the fall of man. These being myths the curse was a myth and never took place. Evolution is now accepted by the majority of intelligent people. Man evolved from a lower order of beings. The necessity to produce from the earth by tillage arose through a natural course of evolution on account of increased population and the failure of other means of subsistence, and was not because of a curse or command of God. And so with the other so-called curses. The serpent was to go on its belly and eat dust. But it is false to say that serpents live on dust. Their manner of locomotion came about through a natural course of evolution. And so with the earth bringing forth thorns and thistles. But if the Bible is the oldest book, as falsely claimed by fetich-worshippers, God was the first liar and the serpent the first truth teller. If this chapter teaches Socialism, then Socialism means an everlasting sorrow to mankind, for it says: "In sorrow shalt thou eat of it [the earth] all the days of thy life."

The speaker said that Jesus taught to take no thought of the morrow, not to lay up treasures. "Did he mean it? Certainly he did. It would be impossible under this system of government, but it would be possible under Socialism." Now, we believe Jesus to be a myth, as Adam was a myth. The gospel accounts of him are not history but fiction. But if such a man existed we may believe he meant what he said. He had no idea of Socialism. He was deluded into believing himself to be a God. He was ignorant and superstitious. He was intolerant and wanted to kill all who would not be ruled by him, and damn all who would not believe him. He came not to bring peace, but fire and sword, and to stir up strife, discord and hate. In this respect he was like other intolerant religious zealots. Our friend Maddock may object that these are not the words of Jesus. But the gospels are our only authority. Of course the gospels do not harmonize.

But why did Jesus teach to take no thought of the morrow and not to lay up treasures? He taught that the end of the world was at hand. That generation would not pass away, and some then living would not taste of death. It would only be a short time until the end of the world. It would not be necessary to produce any more. They already had enough to last until the end, and all that was necessary was to distribute the means of existence already stored up. After the end of the world they were to live miraculously. If he had not been a false prophet his words could have been obeyed. But it would have been suicidal if the world was to exist thousands of years longer.

But Socialists, and all reformers and revolutionists, disobey these commands. They are taking thought for the morrow in trying to make converts. These commands will be as impossible under Socialism as under any other system. It will always be necessary to lay up stores for future want, and any sensible person knows it.

Why run to the Bible? This book has been used to perpetuate ignorance and slavery. We enjoy what liberty we possess and a better life in spite of it. This book has been used to support all manner of evils and crimes. Mr. John E. Remsburg shows that it sanctions twenty crimes and vices. Intelligent Socialists know this. Why do they still cater to the ignorant prejudices in favor of the Book? Some who do this disbelieve the book as much as any one. I cannot see any good in it, but only a hindrance to true progress. They ought to try to free the minds of the people from the superstitious belief in the book. For as long as the minds of the people are enslaved it will be easy to enslave their bodies.

J. M. GILBERT.

Texas.

DOES A BELIEVER EXIST?

If One Is Anywhere to Be Found, Let Him Approach and Display the Sign.

BY J. M. GILBERT

From *The Truth Seeker*, October 10, 1908 & *Blue Grass Blade*, December 13 & 20, 1908

"And he said unto them: Go ye into all the world and preach the gospel to every creature. And he that believeth and is baptized shall be saved, but he that believeth not shall be damned. And these signs shall follow them that believe: In my name shall they cast out devils; they shall speak with new tongues; they shall take up serpents; and if they drink any deadly thing it shall not hurt them. They shall lay hands on the sick and they shall recover." —Mark 16:15, 16, 17, 18.

But Christians pretend that these words were not meant for this age, but only for the apostolic age. They know that they cannot show themselves to be believers, hence the necessity for the evasion. But they have no authority whatever for such an assumption. The gospel was to be preached to every creature of all the world, and the signs were to follow every one that believed. It was by the signs that any one was to know that he really believed. If one cannot give the signs he is not a believer. We have just as good (in fact, better) authority to say that the commands to preach the gospel do not apply to this age; that the promise to be saved through belief and baptism do not apply to this age; that the threat to be damned because of unbelief does not apply to this age; that not a particle of the New Testament applies to this age. If the signs do not apply to this age, then none of the commands, promises, and threats in regard to belief or unbelief apply to this age. We have better authority for saying these things than the Christian has for saying that belief is not the same now that it was 1800 years ago. They claim the same God and the same Christ that they had then. They say that God never changes. If belief could do miracles once, it could do it now.

What is our authority for saying that none of the New Testament applies to this age? It is conceded by the best authorities and apologists that Jesus taught that the world was to end in a very few years. Jesus said that some of those standing there should not taste of death until he would come into his kingdom and power. (See Mark 9:1). He taught them to take no thought for the morrow; to give to all that asked; to lay up nothing for future use. This advice would have been alright if the world was to end very soon. Jesus no doubt considered that there was already enough produced to last until the end. But if the world was to last for thousands of years longer, Jesus was a fool for giving such advice. Jesus sent his disciples out to preach, and told them that they would not be able to go over the cities of Israel until all those things would come to pass. It is clearly seen that Jesus was a false prophet, and that he was either a deluded person or else an imposter.

Prayer

It seems to any common observer that a real believer in a prayer-answering God does not exist. Many think that they believe, but they are practicing self-deception.

Consider the period of the last four years. The over abundance of rain that we have been having has been the ruin of the country. Crops could not be properly planted or properly cultivated. The rains washed away and drowned the crops; washed away the soil and cut the fields into ditches. This has been a calamity to thousands of people. Any one would have prevented it if they could. A believer could have done so by prayer. Over in James 5:17, 18, we read:

"Elias was a man subject to the passions as we are, and he

prayed earnestly that it might not rain; and it rained not on the earth by the space of three years and six months. And he prayed again, and the heaven gave rain, and the earth brought forth her fruit."

Did any one pray for less rain during the last few years? If any one did, it was clear that he was not a believer. We are told: "All things are possible to him that believeth."—Mark 9:23. "He that believeth on me, the works that I do shall he do also, and greater works than these shall he do."—John 14:12. "If ye abide in me, and my works abide in you, ye shall ask what ye will, and it shall be done unto you."—John 15:7. "All things whatsoever ye shall ask in prayer, believing, ye shall receive."—Matt. 21:22. But maybe these passages do not apply to this age. Then consistency demands that people quit making fools of themselves by praying.

But so much rain has not been the only evil. The boll worms and boll weevils have been destroying what was left from the floods. A believer could have prevented it all. But as it was not prevented, it is very good evidence that a believer does not exist. If such a one existed, he was guilty of criminal neglect and an enemy to the good of the community.

"Is any sick among you? Let him call for the elders of the church; and let them pray over him, anointing him with oil in the name of the Lord; the prayer of faith shall save the sick, and the Lord shall raise him up; and if he have committed sins, they shall be forgiven him."—James 5:14, 15.

If a believer existed, there would be no need of any one dying, or of being buried after dying. Christ is said to have healed the sick and to have raised the dead after they stunk. He said that a believer could do as great and greater works. If a believer existed there would be no need of doctors. One believer in a community would be amply sufficient to put doctors and undertakers out of business. When Christians send for a doctor, it shows that they do not believe. Remember the old warning: Asa sent for a physician, and he slept with his fathers.

Faith

What must be the amount of faith? "And Jesus said unto them, because of your unbelief: Verily I say unto you, if ye have faith as a grain of mustard seed ye shall say unto this mountain: Remove hence to yonder place, and it shall remove, and nothing shall be impossible unto you."

As all things are possible to a believer (Mark 9:23), he must necessarily possess as much faith as a grain of mustard seed. If he does not possess that much, he certainly cannot be a believer. If he possessed that much, there would be "nothing impossible" unto him. To say that one does not possess as much faith as a grain of mustard seed (which the New Testament says is the least of all seeds, but that is not true) is only one way of saying that he does not possess any faith at all and is not a believer.

How to Pray

The New Testament gives explicit instructions how to pray. But Christians pay no attention to it. They are told:

"And when thou prayest, thou shalt not be as the hypocrites are: for they love to pray standing in the synagogues, and on the corners of the streets, that they may be seen of men. Verily, I saw unto you, they have their reward. But when thou prayest, enter into thy closet, and when thou has shut the door, pray to thy father which is in secret, and thy father which seeth in secret shall reward thee openly."—Matt. 6:5, 6.

But nothing suits Christians better than to pray and agonize in public. The church is a public place the same as a synagogue. At a recent meeting they came out and preached and prayed at the Post office, at the drug store, and on the street corner. They are thus branded as a generation of hypocrites. "For a pretense they make long prayers" in the synagogues and on the streets, and wish to be counted holy for their much speaking. Jesus is said to have sent the multitudes away and prayed alone, except one time he was praying alone while his disciples were with him. Those who prayed in public Jesus called hypocrites.

A sensible person will not pray for rain or against rain. He will not pray against the boll worm or any other pest. But there is just as much sense in praying such prayers as any other kind of prayer. Is it not written "All things whatsoever ye shall ask in prayer," etc.? The sensible person knows that natural causes and forces cannot be changed by prayer. The natural forces are blind and take no more heed for the good of man than for the lowest worm that crawls beneath his feet. There is no intelligence behind them. If there was, some districts would not be withered by drouths and others drowned by floods. The pests would not destroy the rewards of honest toil. If God knows the want of man, he will grant them if it is his will to do so. So then prayer is useless.

God.

What is God? Is he a thing? If he is no thing (nothing), he does not exist. If he is a thing, and things cannot exist without being created, then God had to be created. This last God would have to be created by another God, and so on ad infinitum. The argument for a creation would prove the necessity for a multitude of gods, and there would be no end to it. Such an argument is reduced to absurdity, and is worthless to prove anything. If God can exist without being created, the universe and all it contains can exist without being created. The Bible says that all things are possible to a believer. Then let the believer create something new. Then we will believe him, his book and his god, and not until then. It is irrational to say that some things had to be created while another did not. We know that we have the universe. It is manifested to all our senses, while a God is not. The universe is infinite and includes everything and all space. It is a self-evident truth that two things cannot occupy the same space at the same time. If God existed, the universe could not exist. But the universe exists; therefore a God cannot exist. What is a person who prays to imagination?

The sun worshippers who prayed to the sun, and the heathens who bowed to idols or wood and stone, were more rational than those who pray to space, to nothing, to a figment of the imagination—to an assumed God that cannot be seen and heard and is not manifested to any of the senses. Prayer is the most irrational act that anyone could be guilty of.

To one not blinded by the musty cobwebs of reason-defying superstition, prayer is recognized as the vainest of vain things. It is seen to be of no more force than the baying of a dog at the moon, or the incantations of heathen savages to drive away eclipses. But Christians are all the time singing about the "old time ignorance" (religion) as good enough for them. A rock in one side of the sack to balance the pumpkin in the other side was good enough for the simpleton, because it was good enough for his father. The people of long ago used the old reap hook, the bull-tongue plow, the old hand-loom, and the old ox-cart because better ways had not yet been invented. What would you think of a man saying now, "These things were good enough for our fathers and they are good enough for me?" Our ancestors believed in the old superstitions such as witch-craft, etc., and believed the "old time religion" because they were no better informed. The truths of modern science had not yet reached them. Most of the orthodox preachers of today are doing their best to perpetuate the "old time religion" (ignorance) because their jobs depend upon it. They are the prime cause of the people remaining so long deluded.

—Randolph, Texas.

Charles H. Jones

"If a person's religious beliefs are based on truth, the more those beliefs are investigated the clearer will the truth appear. The wonders and truths of electricity and of all other sciences show more and more clearly the more they are investigated. Are religious beliefs an exception to that universal law or rule? Cannot religious beliefs and doctrines stand investigation?"

CHARLES H. JONES was born in Cass County, Missouri on October 20, 1861. His father was Lycurgus Jones, a Kentucky-born farmer. His mother, Martha A. (Younger) Jones, was born in Missouri. Three maternal uncles, Cole, Jim and Bob Younger, were outlaws who robbed banks and trains in league with equally notorious outlaw brothers Frank and Jesse James

Jones had one sister and three brothers, two of which may have been named in honor of his outlaw uncles.

In 1881, the Lycurgus Jones family moved to Denison, Texas, where father and sons, unlike their notorious relatives in Missouri, were respectable citizens who operated a furniture business on Main Street. Following the death of his father, and after brothers Coleman and Robert moved to Indian Territory, the Denison store began operating under Charles' name only.

On July 30, 1902, Charles H. Jones married Minnie M. Marsh, a teacher and principal in the Denison schools and an instructor at North Texas Normal College in Denton. She was also an occasional writer and orator.

In 1910 Jones left the furniture business to sell real estate and make loans.

At some point in his life, Jones became an atheist. Between 1916 and 1918, he wrote twenty-four short articles criticizing religion, which were printed as paid advertisements in two local newspapers. Jones also kept a close watch on news of a religious nature and attended church services from time-to-time, apparently to listen to sermons that he would later rebut in print.

Jones was a well-read materialist who based his opinions on the fact that none of the claims made by Christianity could be proven. He was also apparently very familiar with the Scriptures. In his articles he often pointed out Bible verses that were contradictory or seemed to make no sense.

Jones died of pneumonia on March 14, 1924 while vacation with his wife and daughter in Dallas He was buried at Denison's Fairview Cemetery.

From 1960 to the present time, the Mr. and Mrs. Chas. H. Jones Trust Fund, a legacy from the Jones estate, has provided continued financial support to the Denison Public Library.

ONE WORLD AT A TIME IS ENOUGH

From the *Denison Daily Herald*, October 9, 1916

If we had fewer religious dissertations about another world and hereafter and more practical lectures from able educators, scientists, physicians and experts upon the practical, every-day affairs of this world, mankind would know far more of nature's laws and be far happier than now. Knowledge of nature's laws and living in accordance with them is all that can save mankind from the only hell there is, the hell of unhappiness here and now.

More and more does the world want to hear from men who think and men who know most about the every-day affairs of the people. Those who cite the creeds of the dead do not furnish the information that will do them the most good.

The superstition of today is the inveterate belief that this world exists only for some other coming world.

Religion whose end and aim is not happiness in this world is a cruel superstition, for it tends to undervaluation and neglect of this life by fixing people's minds upon a supposed future life. One world at a time is enough.

AS TO BELIEF OR DISBELIEF IN THE INSPIRATION OF THE BIBLE

From the *Denison Daily Herald*, October 21, 1916

A Rev. Mr. Bulgin of Oregon, in speaking of the Jonah and the While story said that, "If the Bible said a 'chigger' swallowed Jonah he would believe it." There are tens of thousands just like Mr. Bulgin.

It certainly is strange, if not pathetic, that so many persons are afraid to examine their religious beliefs. They think it is alright to study all sides of everyday business questions and to decide according to what appears to be the most reasonable. Do they act this way about their religious beliefs? The majority certainly do not. They are afraid to, afraid of public opinion and afraid of disturbing their religious beliefs.

This fear of investigating one's religious beliefs explains why we have "Holy Rollers." If the "Holy Rollers" would investigate a little more, they might quit rolling.

Ask those persons if they want to know the truth whatever it may be. Invariably they say, "Yes." Ask them if a jury should decide a case in court when it has heard the evidence of only one side. They will answer, "Certainly not." Then ask them if they have ever read even one able book that gives the arguments against their most important religious doctrines. Almost invariably they say that they have not. Ask them to read one of those books and immediately you will witness a fine exhibition of dodging.

Now isn't it funny, or strange, or pathetic, that grown persons will act that way, that they will thus let prejudice and fear prevent their examining their religious beliefs? If a person is born with brains, that is proof that they should be used the same as being born with eyes proves that eyes should be used.

If a person's religious beliefs are based on truth, the more those beliefs are investigated the clearer will the truth appear. The wonders and truths of electricity and of all other sciences show more and more clearly the more they are investigated. Are religious beliefs an exception to that universal law or rule? Cannot religious beliefs and doctrines stand investigation? Do not assume that what you believe has been proved. Believers in the Mohammedan religion, and earlyday [sic] Christian believers in witches said the same, no doubt.

Here is a quotation of a most important passage from St. Mark, Chapter XVI—17, 18:

"And these signs shall follow them that believe; In my name shall they cast out devils; they shall speak with new tongues;

"They shall take up serpents; and if they drink any deadly thing, it shall not hurt them; they shall lay hands on the sick, and they shall recover."

Note that this power was to be given not to the Apostles only, but to "them that believe." If there is one person in Denison who believes what is quoted foregoing, let him set a day to exhibit the power said to be given to "them that believe." Let him advertise it far and wide and invite the sceptical [sic] to bring a few rattlesnakes and a large dose of Arsenic. By handling the snakes and swallowing the Arsenic without injury to himself, he can start a movement that cannot fail to convert the whole world in a short time. It is strange that the Apostles failed to accomplish more if they possessed these powers. Every "believer" could convert thousands himself, and ever convert could convert others until shortly the whole world would be converted. Since the Bible itself says, "And these signs shall follow them that believe" surely no person can justly say that it is shocking or foolish to state exactly what the Bible says.

Mankind cannot advance in civilization except through knowing the truth.

THE REV. J. E. AUBREY'S SERMON ANSWERED BY CHAS. H. JONES [1]

From the *Denison Daily Herald*, November 10, 1916

On beginning this article I thank Mr. Aubrey for his courteous treatment, Sunday evening, while delivering his sermon, "Christianity Tested by Results," in answer to my published article, "Belief or Disbelief in the Inspiration of the Bible." Too many persons mistake abuse for argument and immediately proceed to question the sincerity of those who disagree with them about the Bible. They assume for themselves the right to hold views or beliefs, but often are inclined to deny that right to others.

If what a person believes is true, he should not fear to submit it to discussion, but should welcome discussion, for Truth will show clearer the more it is examined. Truth, and Truth only, is what I want, and if I understand myself, no one else shall be readier than I to admit error when convinced of error. Nobody will attempt to maintain that the race can hope to advance in civilization if it builds on what is not true—on the false.

Most of my good friends are Christians, and I have only good-will towards them and all other sincere and well-disposed Christians. I do not fall out with them because we do not agree as to the inspiration of the Bible. No two persons have the same mind, nor the same experience or knowledge. It stands to reason that they will reach different conclusions about various things, and why not about religion? It would be more than amazing if they did not. That they do hold different views about religion is seen daily. Belief is the result of evidence. It cannot be had, or changed, except through evidence. It cannot be commanded. It cannot be put on and off like one's coat.

Christians take the peculiar stand that one must believe the Bible to be inspired, no matter how silly the particular person's views may be about belief and inspiration. No doubt there are thousands who cannot give a lucid reason why they believe. It staggers me that the beliefs of the even the "Holy Rollers" about the Bible seems to be more acceptable to Christians, than are the eminently sane views of Herbert Spencer or Edison, both of whom are pronounced Skeptics. A recently converted Hottentot's belief in Christianity is accepted as superior to the opinions of Spencer and Edison. Such views call for an inspired psychologist to explain them.

Mr. Aubrey spoke rapidly for more than an hour. He made numerous statements which seemed to please the large audience that was present. One cannot answer here, in one article, the various statements made, and so, before starting to answer them, it may be well to explain a little as to what views are actually held by so-called Skeptics.

Many Christians seem to think that Skeptics would destroy the Bible and all morality. Such a view is so amazingly absurd that one feels ridiculous in explaining that nothing is further from the truth. Every Christian is a Skeptic toward other religions than his own. If we speak of Buddhists, Christians are Skeptics, and Buddhists are skeptical concerning Christianity. To determine who the Skeptic is we have to find out first what religion is spoken of. Those persons in this country whom Christians call Skeptics are pretty generally about like other people, except in this, they deny inspiration of the Bible and also the consolation of belief in hell. Otherwise their ideas of morality and their conduct will average as high as Christian's average, though Skeptics do not depend on any Supernatural Power for guidance.

On the contrary they depend for guidance upon the lessons taught by history, and experience, reason, and common sense, to the extent of their opportunities and ability. They do not supplicate the skies for help. They look to themselves and their surroundings here and now for results. One world at a time is enough for anybody to manage. Skeptics would not destroy the Bible if they could, but would keep it and use it, not as God's Word, but just as they would use any other book. They would select and use the good and true to be found in it. They would let alone and would pass by the obscene in it, the cruel, the vindictive and the teachings of slavery and polygamy and the many passages which no person will read in public or to his children.

Are these parts inspired? IF they are not inspired, why did a Divine Being leave them mixed with what is said to be Divine and thus cause continuous confusion and argument? Why mix accounts of cruelties and wrongs perpetrated on others by God Himself (according to the Bible) for children to read and believe to be the actual word and acts of God? Certainly only the inspired (?) are able to see any goodness in that.

To my mind those cruel, vindictive, obscene things in the Old Bible said to have been taught and practiced by God Himself, and by His chosen people, is positive proof that the Bible is not a real God's word, but is the work entirely of men, of many men, in early days, who perhaps did the best they knew how. There is nothing to the Bible that man could not have written. If this is so, it is needless to assume that God had anything to do with it. Let ministers point out one passage that could not have been written by some man.

The idea of hell was born of spirit of revenge and hate, and it should be banished from the minds of civilized people. One of my motives is to help free the minds of tender, loving mothers and fathers and children from fear of that hideous nightmare. In my next article I shall take up some one or more of the statements made by Mr. Aubrey.

THE REV. J. E. AUBREY'S SERMON ANSWERED BY CHAS. H. JONES [2]

From the *Denison Daily Herald*, November 11, 1916

Mr. Aubrey said that, to his mind, the strongest proof that the Bible is God's word is, that it satisfies man's faith and higher aspirations and longings through its promise of immortality to man. I cannot give his exact words from memory, but I aim to give his exact meaning.

He said man had sought far wide for that which would satisfy his longings, but that he had never found satisfaction until he found it in the Bible promise of immortality. He said something exists to satisfy every desire of the body, therefore it must be that something exists to satisfy the longings of the soul, and that something is immortality, which is promised in the Bible. This, he says, proves the Bible to be God's word.

There is a wide difference between a promise and the reality of what is promised. To make homely illustration—the grocery man, to his frequent sorrow, knows the wide difference between cash and a promise. A promise of immortality does not prove immortality.

As to one's longings, good people everywhere "intensely desire that poverty, pain, crime, war and death may cease all over the earth. They long for youth, for perfect health, and that the ravages of old age may not overtake them. These longings have not and do not prove their fulfillment.

There are in existence today Bibles of other religions that promise immortality. Christians deny that these Bibles are God's work. If the promise of immortality proves one Bible, it proves all Bibles that promise immortality, and so, the immortality argument destroys itself.

Excavators in Egypt have found and deciphered the writings of people who lived thousands of years before Christ, before the time our Bible says the world was created. Those Egyptians had a book called "The Book of the Dead." In that book were highly moral teachings. They believed intensely in immortality. But for lack of space I would quote several of their teachings. The promises of immortality in the Egyptian "Book of the Dead" proves, according to Mr. Aubrey, that it is God's word, though the Egyptians lived thousands of years before the Christian Bible was written.

Does the Bible throughout teach immortality? It does not. It is contradictory. In 1 Timothy, VI Chapter Paul the inspired prophet contradicts himself. He speaks of "eternal life," then in verses 15, 16, or the same chapter in speaking of Christ he says, "the King of kings, and Lord of lords; who only hath immortality—" If only Christ has immortality, then man does not have it.

Job denies immortality (VII-21). "As the cloud is consumed and vanisheth away; so shall he that goeth down to the grave shall come up no more."

Christians speak of the comfort that belief in immortality gives. They of course have in mind the thought of eternal happiness for themselves and those they love. I ask them what about the other side of their belief? What about immortal anguish for the majority of the race? "for many be called, but few chosen" (Matt. XX, 16). Is immortal anguish a satisfaction to longing souls?

No real God ever inspired such teaching as that. The idea of immortality did not originate with the Bible or any other book.

In the words of the eloquent Ingersoll, "The idea of immortality, like the great sea, has ebbed and flowed in the human heart, beating its countless waves of hope and joy against the shores of time, and was not born of a book, or of any religion, nor of any creed; it was born of human affection, and will continue to ebb and flow beneath the clouds and mists of doubt and darkness as long love kisses the lips of death. It is the rainbow of hope shining upon the tears of grief. We love, therefore we wish to live, and the foundation of the idea of immortality is human affection and human love, and I have a thousand times more confidence in the affections of the human heart, in the deep and splendid feelings of the human soul than I have in any book that ever was or ever can be written by mortal man."

THE REV. J. E AUBREY'S SERMON ANSWERED BY CHAS. H. JONES [3]

From the *Denison Daily Herald*, November 13, 1916

Mr. Aubrey said that because of the Jews' belief in God they had held together as a people, and had progressed continuously through the centuries as no other people had who did not believe in God. He said that proved the Bible to be God's Word.

Of course Mr. Aubrey means the Christians' Bible and the Christians' God, for he and other Christians do not believe in the Bibles and gods of other religions. In other words, Christians are Skeptics as to other bibles and gods than their own.

It is generally known that Jews deny that Christ ever came to earth, and it follows that they do not accept Christianity. This being so, it is odd that any Christian minister should point to Jews as proof of Christianity. According to the Bible, the Jews considered Christ an imposter and blasphemer and they crucified Him.

According to the Bible the Jews were God's chosen people. If their belief in God was correct, how is it that those correct views failed to lead them to accept God's Son, Christ? The coming of Christ was a calamity to the Jews, since they did not accept Him, and, therefore are all lost. Did not God foresee what would happen to His chosen people? Did not His work fail there as to the Jews? If it failed, was His work perfect, and if imperfect, who is responsible for it? Failure is proof of imperfection. It does not answer to say that the Jews were given the chance to accept Christ. From the beginning God must have foreseen how it would turn out. If the Jews were mistaken in rejecting Christ when they saw Him, is not that proof that they do not know a God (Christ) when they see Him, and may they not therefore, be mistaken as their own God?

If the Jews' belief in God proves God, why does not their disbelief of Christ disprove Christ? Their belief ought to be as good one way as the other. If that is not reasonable, nothing is.

Mr. Aubrey says that Jews are progressive now, and I believe that every unprejudiced person will agree with him as to that. But if their belief in God caused their progress before Christ, why is it their progress did not stop when they denied and continue to deny God's Son, Christ? No doubt God would just as lief that the Jews should deny Him as that they should deny his Son.

Long before Christ, and while believing in God, the Jews were long in bondage in Egypt, and they were continually harassed by other nations at other times. Though they later denied Christ and continue to deny Him, they appear to be in better condition today and fully as progressive as ever.

Belief in a thing is not proof that that thing exists. Belief in witches does not prove witches. If belief proved a thing to be true, then the beliefs of Buddhists, and dozens of other religious beliefs would all be proved to be true.

Christians deny that other religious beliefs are true. They say that only their belief is true, and then the Protestants and the Roman Catholics deny that each other teaches the correct Christian belief. It certainly is might puzzling to an uninspired person, and yet both Protestants and Roman Catholics must be right for each one says it is, and then the Protestants, including the Mormon Christians, disagree over points which they say are necessary to salvation.

If the Christian Sign-board (the Bible) points in every direction, who can pick the right road, and would a really inspired book point in every direction as is shown to be the case by the different beliefs of the different churches?

I believe it is best to know the truth.

THE REV. J. E. AUBREY'S SERMON ANSWERED BY CHAS. H. JONES [4]

From the *Denison Daily Herald*, November 18, 1916

Christian ministers, and Christians generally, are fond of saying to the Skeptic, "What do you propose to give us in place of the Bible if you take it away?" I have no doubt but that Mohammedans and other religions ask the very same thing of the skeptics who deny that their Bibles and religions are of God.

Such a question is no argument, and it proves nothing except that every religion has the habit of claiming that all good in the world is due to it. We have all argued with those who claim everything.

What are some of the good things which make us a great people? Soil and climate come first. Did the Bible furnish them? All knowledge of the sciences as of electricity, of steam, of medicine, of geology, of soils, of astronomy and all the rest. Did the Bible furnish any light on these subjects? Does anybody go to the Bible to get information on any one of these subjects. Not that anybody has heard of.

I came near overlooking some of the Bible astronomy recorded in the first chapter of Genesis. There God created light and darkness and grass and herbs a good while before He made the sun, moon and stars. He separated the light and darkness, one from the other, just as one would separate black beans from white beans in a bag. He worked hard for six days (and rested on the seventh—tired like any other person) making the earth, but on the third or fourth day, He, by a wave of the hand (so to speak), created the rest of the universe, for "He made the stars also." (Gen. I-16).

I think one would be entirely safe in saying that if the Esquimaux in the Arctic regions were to have the Bible a million years it would not cause them to equal the people of the United

States or Europe. The climate of the Arctic regions is against such advancement of human beings. Evidently soil and climate come first in race development and not the Bible. Association of human beings under favorable conditions develops moral conduct and rules of moral conduct. Climate, soil, and human association, one with another, together with acquired knowledge of nature (the sciences) are what makes our Nation great.

God did not care much for knowledge. He planted only one tree of knowledge in the Garden of Eden. I do not recall that Christ ever said one word in favor of education. The apostle, Paul, scorned science. He called it "science falsely so-called" (I Tim. VI-20). Evidently the scientists of Paul's time did not believe what Paul taught. Since they were there when Paul was, we can gather the opinions of the scientists from Paul's remark. That ought to mean considerable to us.

Moral conduct, and rules of moral conduct, are developed from the association of human beings with one another. Society could not exist if that were not true. When a savage, or any ancient who lived before the Bible, planted and cultivated a field of corn or a garden, he knew that that corn or garden was his and that the fellow who sat on the fence and talked while he worked had no right to gather the corn or eat his onions without his consent. It is thus that moral conduct is developed in all relations.

A book of moral rules could not be understood until human beings had through experience, developed some knowledge of conduct itself. They could then better understand written rules, but not before, there the Bible did not by its written rules originate moral conduct. There are various Nations today that, as a whole, deny the Bible, and yet without it they have developed many fine rules of moral conduct. The Egyptians had done this thousands of years before the time the Bible said the earth was created. This proves that morality and moral rules result from the association of people, one with another, and that moral conduct of necessity comes originally before the written rules, before the Bible.

If the Skeptic keeps what is best in the Mohammedan's teaching (but not as God's word), and takes out the false, what does the Mohammedan want in place of the false? If you pull the weeds out of a man's garden, what does the man want in place of the weeds? If the skeptic proposes to keep and use all that is true to nature, and therefore useful, in the Bible, the same as in any other book, and remove the false, including the fear of that hideous nightmare, hell, that does not in the least destroy any proper and true incentive to moral conduct. Fear of a hot hereafter is a very crude incentive for civilized people. The skeptic's answer is that he would put whatever is true, in the place of whatever is false in the Bible as elsewhere. His idea is that the greatest happiness of the individual and of the race can be secured only by learning the truth and living according to it.

THE REVEREND AUBREY'S SERMON ANSWERED BY CHAS. H. JONES [5]

From the *Denison Daily Herald*, November 20, 1916

Mr. Aubrey said the Bible contains or expresses God's will to man. He said we could not justly judge the Bible if we picked out parts, or passages, and analyzed or criticized them by themselves. We must take it as a whole, and judge it as a whole, he said, and if taken that way it would show itself to be God's word.

Another Denison minister said practically the same thing a few weeks earlier in The Herald. This seems to be the view of most ministers.

Let us see if the ministers are right, whether we take it as a whole or whether we take it part by part.

When your child studies arithmetic, does it study it as a whole, or does it have to study it a part at a time? At first it has to study numbers. That is a part. Then it studies addition, then subtraction, then multiplication, then division and so on. Each of these is a part of arithmetic, and it is the only way a child can study it. When the child has mastered these parts, then and then only, is it able to consider arithmetic as a whole. It finds that every part of arithmetic fits in perfectly with every other part. There is no conflict of one part with another. They all fit together like brick[s] in a wall.

How about the Bible?

One cannot study the Bible unless he studies the parts, the words, the verses, the chapters. Having studied these, he can then consider the whole, but not before. Do all the parts of the Bible agree with one another as one has a right to expect if an All-wise God wrote it, or inspired the writers of it?

Would not any ordinary human parent leave perfectly clear directions for his children if their salvation depended on it? Then would God do less for His children? Was God able to leave perfectly clear directions to them, and was He able to see that those directions should reach His children without alteration? It is absurd to argue that God could not do that. If He could not, then He is not all-powerful, and if not all-powerful He is not God.

The different parts of the Bible do not agree throughout. There are scores and scores of contradictions in it. No well-informed minister will deny that. If there is a minister who denies that, let him call publicly for the proofs and the proofs will be forthcoming with chapter and verse. The ministers are invited to call for proofs.

If the Bible contains scores and scores of contradictions, which it does, is not that positive proof that it was written and compiled by men? It certainly is. I ask the ministers to point out God's will in the Bible. If they attempt it, will they not have to pick out parts, that is, do exactly the things that they argue against doing? But the churches do not agree as to God's meaning, even on points which they say are necessary to salvation, Roman Catholics and Protestants for instance, or Protestants themselves, Universalists, Unitarians, Mormons, Holy Rollers. As to baptism, the Methodists insist that sprinkling will do. The Baptists and Disciples insist that one must go down "into the water and come up out of the water."

Ministers pretty generally try to avoid all this by saying when the Bible was being translated into our language, the translators made mistakes, and some of them wrote their own views into the Bible, that is, there are many interpolations in the Bible. That certainly puts the matter in bad shape indeed. God permitted His directions to become so mixed that the general public cannot tell which was written by Him.

Of course that demands ministers to explain, then the people's salvation depends on the ministers' explanations, and the ministers do not agree. It is too bad, and still Christians say the Bible is inspired.

Instead of teaching something that no one knows anything about, let us spend our time, energy and money in teaching something that somebody knows is true, something useful for here and now. The future will take care of itself. As civilized people, let us be ashamed of teaching the savage doctrine to mothers and father that poor, weak, fallible human beings will be sent to eternal trouble by a loving God.

WHAT CHRISTIANS SAY ABOUT SKEPTICS

From the *Denison Daily Herald*, November 14, 1916

The Bible and Christians teach that the skeptic with his family and his friends who believe like him as to the Bible, will all be sent to eternal trouble when they die. When the skeptic says he does not believe that a loving God would do that, and he starts to give his reasons why he does not believe it, Christians are amazed and horrified and say he is trying to destroy all morality.

It is all right for Christians to teach hell for skeptics, but it is all wrong for skeptics to argue that they are not going to be so harshly treated. Human beings and Christian beliefs are queer things.

Ministers talk a great deal about the consolation of their belief. They expect to be saved, and their belief is a consolation to them even if "many be called and few chosen."

Christians are better than their religious beliefs. No Christian father or mother would send his or her son or daughter to eternal trouble because the son or daughter could not swallow the Adam and Eve store, or the Jonah and Whale story, or the great freshet story, that is, the Noah and his Ark (with one window) story.

One new minister lately said he believed the Bible from lid to lid. He is like the Rev. Mr. Bulgin who said that, "if the Bible said a chigger swallowed Jonah, he would believe it."

Ancient people who believed in cats and crocodiles used their reason the same way. However, I do not deny them the right to use their reason the best they know how provided they will permit me the same right.

IS IT A FACT THAT CHRISTIANITY IS THE HOPE OF THE NATION?

From the *Denison Daily Herald*, December 8, 1916

A popular Denison minister lately advertised and preached that "Christianity is the Hope of the Nation." He quoted Charles W. Eliot, President Emeritus of Harvard University as holding that view.

I do not think that Dr. Elliot meant that Christianity, as taught by the churches today, is the "hope of the Nation." I shall show this clearly by quotations from his reported addresses, and by other unmistakable proofs.

Dr. Eliot is a Unitarian. Unitarians deny that Christ was God, or the son of God, as taught by the churches. They do not believe that the Bible was or is inspired. They deny the Garden of Eden and "fall of man" story. They deny the miraculous conception and resurrection of Christ that man might be saved from the supposed "fall." They believe that Christ was a great and good human being, a man whose teachings, if followed, would finally life man to the highest of which man is capable.

In that sense, Dr. Eliot may believe that Christianity is the hope of the Nation, but that sense, if accepted, destroys the fundamental teachings of the Christian churches generally.

If there was no garden of Eden and no "fall of man," then Christ did not die to save man from that supposed "fall of man." Unitarians believe I some sort of a really loving God, and they have more respect for Him than to think that He created a hell and imposed death on an innocent son for the benefit of the guilty. If Christians admit disbelief in the Garden of Eden and "fall of man" story, and disbelief in the miraculous conception and resurrection of Jesus, and disbelief in the consolation of hell, then they may claim that Dr. Eliot stands with them. But such is not the case, sad to say.

I give a number of Dr. Eliot's published views concerning the churches and their teachings today, following:

"The creeds of the evangelical churches are, as a rule, built on the "fall of man" as described in the story of the "Garden of Eden," the absolute correctness or trustworthiness of the story itself being assumed on the ground that its author was inspired by God himself. The conduct attributed to God in that story would be wholly unworthy of any man whose standards of conduct accorded with the average sentiments about right and wrong of civilized people today."

In speaking of Christ's death as believed in and taught by the churches, he says, "In these days, the whole conception of one being—human or divine—suffering, though innocent, for the sins of another, or of innumerable others, is revolting to the universal sense of justice and fair dealing. No family, no school and no court would venture to punish the innocent, when the guilty were known, in order that the guilty might escape punishment. Any human father would be outraged by the suggestion that he had ever dealt or could so deal with his children; and yet every member of the great Christian churches is supposed to believe that God deals in that way with the human race; and that the victim offered up for the redemption of the human race was, in a peculiar sense, the son of God."

He said further:—Since the latter years of the eighteenth century it has become more and more difficult to impose belief on educated people, and intelligent men have steadily lost faith in mysticism and symbolism and have come to rely more and more on the careful ascertainment of facts the human reason and the natural sentiments of reverence and love. They have also come to prefer for themselves and their families liberty, independence and public order founded upon agreed-upon law, to obedience, submission and order founded on discipline administered to the many by the few. With these new tendencies of the human spirit the great Christian churches are not in full accord."

Speaking of the war he says, "Every ruler concerned with the present war calls upon God to give victory to his arms—and is giving thanks for victories for its (his) side which are cruel defeats for the other."

In speaking of the sciences, he said: "For the last one hundred and fifty years it has been natural and physical science which has been the main contributor to the increasing welfare of mankind. Science has won its way in spite of the opposition of the principal Christian churches; and the opposition did not cease until within the memory of man now living; indeed, it still breaks out from time to time."

He said further, "The condition of Europe at this moment is the last and most convincing demonstration that the great churches of Christendom have lost their power to keep man from sin, to guide him on an upward path, and to make him happy."

These quotations are only a small part of what Dr. Eliot said. They speak for themselves. Do they indicate that he thinks that "Christianity," as taught by the various churches today, "is the hope of the Nation?"

I will now quote from the Confession of Faith, or from the Catechism, of one of the principal churches, as to what the churches teach. It is this:

"The souls of the wicked are cast into hell, where they remain in torment and utter darkness, reserved to the judgment of the great day. At the last day the righteous shall come into everlasting life, but the wicked shall be cast into eternal torment and punished with everlasting destruction. The wicked shall be cast into hell, to be punished with unspeakable torment, both of body and soul, with the devils and his angels forever."

See also Matthew 25:41—Depart from me, ye cursed, into everlasting fire, prepared for the devil and his angels."

In my opinion there is not in Denison a father or mother who would not, on Judgment day, show a kinder and a more loving and forgiving spirit than the spirit exhibited in the last two quotations foregoing.

The fact is, the race has improved, and our ideas today of right and wrong are superior to the ideas of the early day writers who wrote the Bible. They most likely did the best they knew how.

IS THE BIBLE INSPIRED CONCERNING WOMEN?

From the *Denison Herald*, December 12, 1916

A woman with both eyes shut can see that a man wrote the first three chapters of Genesis. All the blame for all the trouble in the world was there laid on woman, in the Garden of Eden story.

Adam said (Genesis 3:12), "The woman whom thou gavest to be with me, she gave me of the tree, and I did eat." According to the bible, that is where all our trouble started—woman caused the "fall of man."

No one can well say that Adam's conduct towards the woman was as manly as it might have been, but we must not judge him too harshly. We should bear in mind that Adam had only lately been created out of ordinary "dust," and that he had had no "bringing up." Then too, Adam must have been created with a weak will, for he "fell for it" at the first temptation. Adam could most justly inquire why his Maker created him with a weak will and a strong appetite for apples, and then planted an apple tree full of juicy apples close by and forbade his touching them. We can justly ask that same question ourselves, why Adam was created with a weak will and then tempted?

Let us consider Adam's conduct a little further. Most men nowadays have better manners than Adam exhibited, also a higher sense of right and wrong. Even a "Street Gamin" would be gallant enough to try to shield the woman a little bit, and at least, he would have admitted that he shared in the guilt of purloining those apples.

The eating of those apples by Adam has given millions of Christian women indigestion, and no cure can safely be promised them unless they revise the bible and leave the Garden of Eden story out.

But to continue—there are in Genesis two entirely different and contradictory accounts of how and when woman was created.

In Genesis 1:27, on the sixth day, "God created man in his own image—male and female created he them."

In Genesis 2:20-23 God brought every "beast of the field, and every fowl of the air—unto Adam to see what he would call them."

Evidently Adam must have been something of a conundrum to his Creator, since his Creator did not know beforehand what names Adam would give, for He had the animals brought "to see" what Adam would call them. Since Adam had never had any experience with names—no uncles, no aunts, no neighbors, no children with names, the naming of all the animals must have been a poser. No wonder God shifted the job on him and wanted "to see" how it would work.

And so, all the cattle, fowl, and every beast of the field were brought before Adam to be named, "but for Adam there was not found an helpmeet for him." Evidently, while naming the animals, Adam was to look for a helpmeet among them.

Adam proving to be somewhat particular, no helpmeet was found for him among the "cattle, fowl or beasts," and so, he was put into a deep sleep (Gen. 2:21-22-23), and God removed one of his ribs and made a woman of it.

Concerning this account of the creation of woman a certain writer said "But how God ever got a woman out of a man's rib surpasses our comprehension. It looks as though it would be impossible to make a woman out of a whole man, let along [sic] out of one old bone. Woman was not made in anybody's image, only her own, and we are glad of it. That is good enough for us."

The idea that an All-wise and All-powerful Creator of the universe inspired the childish Adam and Eve story is too much—it is amazing. On that story rests the "fall of man." Christ's coming and his resurrection rests on that "fall of man," for, if man did not "fall," then Christ's death was a mistake, for He did not need to die to save man from that "fall."

Instead of censuring the views here expressed, just ask yourself if they are reasonable, if they are true. If you think they are not, then you are asked to answer them and point out wherein they are not reasonable. That is the way to upset the unreasonable.

If any minister thinks he can give to the public a satisfactory explanation as to the two contradictory accounts of the creation of woman, no doubt the public will be pleased to read it.

IS CHRISTIANITY OPPOSED TO FREE SPEECH?

From the *Denison Daily Herald,* December 22, 1916 and
Denison Morning Gazette, December 26, 1916

History proves unmistakably that when any one branch of the church is in power, it will suppress other churches and beliefs that disagree with its own beliefs.

In various publications throughout the country there is today a war of violent abuse going on between Protestants and Roman Catholics because of their differences in belief as to what the Bible teaches.

If belief in the Bible invariably produces division and bitterness between well meaning and sincere people because of their differences of belief as to what the Bible teaches, is it reasonable to think that the Bible is God's word?

If one branch of Christians when in power would suppress other Christians, what chance for free speech would outsiders have?

I believe that forty-nine out of fifty church members do not, as individuals, consciously aim to suppress free speech. That their attitude, due to their belief, does tend to suppress free speech, they no doubt would deny. But let us point to the proofs which everyone can see, when his attention is directed to them.

Is it not a fact that practically every business man, professional or public man, dodges expression of his honest views if those views disagree with the beliefs of the churches? Why do they dodge? Because experience has taught them to fear the disapproval which injuriously affects their business or professional work, and endangers their making a living.

Why is it that no one church would consent to allow any other church to be in control of the government? Simply because every church fears suppression from every other. Their own attitude proves what I say. Free speech will always be suppressed when any Christian sect controls the government.

Does this strife and division among the people arise over differences of about moral conduct? It does not. It arises over doctrinal differences, each insisting that it alone teaches what the Bible teaches. There are something like 188 different Christian sects. Each teaches that the Bible means something different from what the other sects teach. That is unmistakable proof that an All-wise God did not inspire the Bible, for an All-wise God could and would have made His meaning clear to all. All would agree instead of disagreeing. But this disagreement does prove that different men at different times wrote different parts of the Bible, and those different writings were put together at different times by different church councils, as the history of the Bible says they did.

Christianity cannot live peacefully with other beliefs. If Christ was intolerant, His teachings naturally lead to intolerance. Christ said (Mark 16:16) "—he that believeth not shall be damned."

Though Christians disagree as to what the Bible teaches, they are almost a unit in saying that outsiders must believe that its teachings are the perfect word of God, else those outsiders will go to an insane hell and take others with them. If it is alright for God to damn them eternally after they are dead, it must be right to suppress them for the benefit of others while they are alive. Was there ever in the world a more ridiculous, a more inhuman belief than the belief in hell?

It is my wish that every man hold up his head and insist on his right to express his honest opinions.

Victor Hugo said, "There shall be no slavery of the mind." Ingersoll said, "Only those are traitors in the great realm of thought who abandon reason and appeal to force."

THAT TALKING SNAKE IN THE GARDEN OF EDEN STORY

From the *Denison Daily Herald*, January 2, 1917

We have all joked about the big fish stories, but that story about the talking snake in the Garden of Eden beats the big fish stories all hollow, except the Jonah and Whale story.

The odd thing about this is that many people see the joke in the fish stories but fail to see anything funny in the talking-snake story. Instead of seeing anything funny, they are as solemn as a funeral about it.

If those persons were to read such a childish story in the Bible of some other religion, they would laugh at it, and at the idea that the Creator of the Universe busied Himself with such childish doings as in the Garden of Eden story.

Our great museums would be delighted to have a specimen of that talking snake, and so would our sideshows. It was a talking snake, remember, and before God cursed it, (Gen. 3:14), it must have stood upright like a man when it walked, instead of crawling on its stomach as it now does, for, in cursing it God said "upon thy belly thou shalt go, and dust shalt thou eat all the days of thy life."

It appears that the snake did not travel on its "belly" until after God cursed it. Did not God know beforehand that the snake would tempt Eve and cause the "fall of man?" Furthermore, snakes do not eat dust all their days as God said they would. A mistake certainly was made there.

Wider knowledge and a more scientific outlook nowadays has given the people more and more of that Missouri habit we hear about. They say "show me" when somebody says that once upon a time there was a talking snake.

Those talking snakes must all died off immediately for the science of snakeolgy knows nothing of them although the Bible account gives us to understand distinctly that such snakes were to follow.

We wonder what language that snake spoke. It talked to Eve, you know. Did it speak English, Greek, Latin or Hebrew, or did it have snake dialect which Eve understood off hand? Eve must have been somewhat different from the women of today, else that snake would never have got close enough to her to hold a conversation.

One thing can be said in favor of that talking snake. It told the truth as to what would happen. God said to Adam, (Gen. 2:17), "for in the day that thou eatest thereof (the apple) thou shalt surely die." The snake said, Gen. 3:4, "Ye shall not surely die." Strange to say, the snake was right about it, for Adam and Eve did not "surely die" the day they ate the apple for they were driven from the Garden and they reared a family outside, (Cain and Abel), and according to the Bible the human race started right there. And right at the start Cain raised "Cain," but that is another story.

Ministers say these childish stories are symbolical, that is, they illustrate a "hidden meaning." That makes matters just as bad or worse. Why "Hidden Meaning?" Of course that takes ministers to explain, but if the masses of the people cannot understand what the Bible says unless ministers explain it, then the peoples' salvation depends upon the ministers explaining the Bible correctly, but then the ministers themselves disagree as to what the Bible teaches.

Now, is that childish Adam and Eve story true or not true? If not true, is it not best, for people to know the truth? Can it ever be best to teach what is not true? If not true, why consume peoples' time and money teaching it and fuddling their brains over it. Teach something that is useful, something that somebody knows is true. They will be better off for it. My aim is to help that along though many mistakenly think I would destroy morality. They are badly mistaken. Uprooting weeds from a man's mind benefits him.

If that serpent story is childish and not true, then there was no "fall of man," and God did not sacrifice an innocent Son, Christ, to save man from a "fall" that never happened.

IF THE BIBLE IS TRUE, THE PERSONS DESCRIBED FOLLOWING ARE ETERNALLY LOST

From the *Denison Daily Herald*, January 15, 1917

Christians say that the Bible is God's word and that those who do not believe it is His word will go to everlasting torment. They say this because the Bible teaches that such is the case. Christians do not consider this to be a cheerful subject, but how can they expect to avoid it so long as they continue to believe and teach that the large majority of the human race goes to eternal trouble?

If the Bible is true and Christians are right, the persons described following are all doomed to spend eternity in the Christian's hell, which was created by a "Loving Father."

(1) Millions of Christians in every generation who believe in the Bible but do not live up to its requirements will go to the Christians' hell.
(2) Hundreds of millions of people who believe in other religions and deny that the Christians' Bible is God's word will go to the Christians' hell.
(3) Multiplied millions who never heard of the Bible or never heard enough to know what it teaches, they will go to the Christians' hell. See (John 3:36)—"he that believeth not the Son shall not see life; but the wrath of God abideth on him." There are numerous similar passages. This is why missionaries are sent to teach "the heathen" to "believe." They think it necessary to their salvation.
(4) All Unitarian Christians must go to the Christians' hell, for Unitarians do not believe in the inspiration of the Bible, nor that Christ is God's Son, in the sense that the churches teach.

(5) Millions of persons in so-called Christian countries who have been told that the Bible is God's word, but who are unable to believe it when they discover scores of contradictions in it, and when they read of the cruelties, slavery, war, obscenities, human sacrifices, polygamy, and other immoral things that the God of the Bible commanded and upheld. Verses and chapters can be given proving this. These millions will go to the Christians' hell, if the Bible is true.

(6) All famous scientists, and inventors like Edison, who believe in evolution and thereby deny the Adam and Eve story, the "fall of man," the talking snake, and that woman was manufactured from one of Adam's ribs. All these great men will go the Christians' hell.

(7) All Hebrews who believe in the Jewish religion, that their fathers taught them, will go the Christians' hell forever and ever, because Jews do not believe that Christ ever came to earth.

(8) And worse still. One of the Christian churches that has the greatest number of members teaches that all little babies that die before being baptized will be banished from heaven and from the presence of God, forever and forever. These tender little babies will be banished to some sort of a "limbo" which is not heaven, nor the red-hot hell, but it is banishment from heaven, all because of Adams' "fall" in the Garden of Eden.

(9) All older children, especially those who have reached the age of supposed accountability, who have not joined the church and been baptized, or have not yet med the requirements of the respective churches, all these, dying, will go to the Christians' hell if the Bible is true and Christian beliefs founded upon it are true. When we remember that comparatively few children from fifteen or

sixteen years old downward belong to church, we begin to see how many millions of these are eternally lost.

(10) Protestants say the Bible of the Roman Catholic is not the true Bible. (You know, the Roman Catholic Bible contains several books not in the Protestant Bible, and besides, the two Bibles do not read exactly alike.) Protestants say that Roman Catholics do not teach the true Christianity. If Protestants are right, I leave it to thm to say where Roman Catholics will spend eternity.

(11) Roman Catholics say practically the same things about Protestants that Protestants say about them. Each says the other is wrong. I leave it to them to say where Protestants will land, in the everlasting hereafter.

I could go on naming others that will spend eternity in the Christians' hell if Christians are right and the Bible is true concerning hell, but it is too horrible. No good and loving God would create an everlasting hell for His children. No human parent would do it. It is one of the greatest wrongs of the age to load the tender, sensitive minds of children, and the minds of loving mothers and fathers with the fears of a hideously inhuman hell. It is a wrong motive for right conduct. Belief in it divides well meaning people. Speed the day when anybody will be ashamed of believing that any poor, imperfect human being, no matter how bad, deserves eternal torture without opportunity ever to do better.

Personal letter from Mr. P. C. Preston

The Pipeano Company
The Pipeano
An organ made and played in connection
With and from the piano keyboard

Percy Preston Patents

Denison, Texas,
311 W. Woodard St.
Jan. 15, 1917

Mr. ?. =. Jones,
Denison, Texas.

Dear Mr. Jones:-

May I say these few words with only the best of feeling and a desire to be a blessing.

"If the bible is true Mr. C. H. Jones will spend eternity in hell because of his treatment (rejection) of Jesus Christ and many will be there with him who will say to you, "I would not be here except for your teaching and example.

And that hell was made for the "Devil and his angles [sic] by the "Loving Father" and not for the saved, but that those who refuse the mercies of God must go there in justice to Himselfe [sic] and those he has promised to protect.

It is often said that "A man can find what he looks for."

I would be glad to talk with you if it would not be intruding, but not for the sake of argument. I have an experience which you have evidently missed.

Yours very truly,

P. C. Preston [signature]

Personal letter to Mr. P. C. Preston

Denison, Tex. Jan. 16/17

Mr. P. C. Preston,
        Denison, Tex.

Mr. Preston,

I have your letter concerning my articles in the newspapers. I am sure you are sincere in your expressed views as to the bible. I know that I am sincere in what I write about it. Anybody can see that my views bring me neither profit nor popularity, as most of my good friends are Christians.

These Christian friends do not seem able to see that I have a moral motive in writing these articles. If there is a good God I defend his reputation from the belief that He would create a place of eternal torture for poor, weak, imperfect human beings whom He brought into the world, if it is true that He created everything, and that human beings are the result of His creation.

Neither you nor your wife, having brought children into the world by your own choice, would create an everlasting hell for them, no matter how bad they might be. I believe you will admit that is so, and if it is, you are kinder than the bible teaches that its God is.

Bear one thing in mind—if there is a good God and He were known to me, I would worship Him, but the supposed God of the Old Testament who practiced all sorts of cruelties, I do not believe in.

That belief in a cruel hell causes division among well meaning people, and as I said in my article, "It is the greatest wrong of the age to load the minds of sensitive children and of loving fathers and mothers with the fear of a hideously inhuman hell."

If Christians were willing to submit their beliefs to the test of reason and argument, and would read books presenting the other side of the matter instead of closing their minds to such, they would get their eyes opened in so many ways.

Do Christians answer the reasons that Sceptics offer? They do not, but instead they usually begin by censuring the Sceptic instead of trying to answer.

I consider that to be nothing else than childish.

Suppose a man were to try a case in court and instead of answering the arguments he should at once begin to call the other side names? Would that be an answer? Would it be sensible? The truth is what I want, no matter where it leads to.

Of course any "inner witness" that any Christian thinks he may have had cannot be any evidence to those who never had such "inner witness."

If what I said in my article is not true, as to all those that will be lost (if the bible is true), I stand ready to change my opinion when anybody shows I am mistaken. So far, nobody has been able to do that.

(2)

Let Christians answer the arguments if they can. That is the reasonable course. Not one in fifty knows the history as to how the bible was formed.

Christians say and continually teach that the Sceptic with his wife, his family, and all his friends will go to an everlasting hell and will take others with them. (That is when they believe as he, the Sceptic, does)

When the Sceptic says he does not believe a good God would be so harsh and starts to give his views in defense of himself, his family and his friends, Christians immediately say he is doing a great wrong.

Christian belief cannot live in peace with other beliefs.

I believe in the right of free speech for every shade of honest opinion whether it agrees with own opinions or not.

I write to help preserve free speech.

I want people to spend their time learning something that somebody knows to be true.

I do not fall out with my friends because we disagree on this subject. I am always willing to discuss it with them in a friendly spirit, but unless they are able to disprove my good reasoning the arguments I make, I cannot see any prospect of their convincing me or anybody else.

Very truly yours,
Chas. H. Jones

P.S. If you wish to know some of the grounds on which Sceptics base their arguments, I shall be pleased to lend you a small book.
CHJ

IS THE SKEPTIC HONEST CONCERNING THE BIBLE?

From the *Denison Daily Herald*, January 17, 1917 and *Denison Gazette*, January 18, 1917

No person can fairly say that there are not a great many able men who deny that the bible was inspired by God, or that it is God's word. Can there be anybody so prejudiced as to say that these men do not express their honest opinions about the bible?

The Skeptic does not increase his popularity by expressing such opinions. He does not increase his patronage, or support, if he is a professional man or a politician. If he is an author, he can expect only a limited sale of his books. What does he get out of it in any way except the satisfaction that comes from the thought that he is helping to uproot some of the errors that bar the progress of man?

There is one particularly objectionable thing that some few persons say about Skeptics without any justifiable grounds for saying it. It is that the Skeptic denies hell because he wants to live an immoral life and, therefore, he does not want to believe there is such a place. Of all weak assertions or arguments, that is about the weakest.

If there is a hell, and if the Skeptic really believes there is, a child can see that his arguing against it would not destroy it or put it out of existence. Cannot the Skeptic see that as well as anybody? Then, what satisfaction or relief can a Skeptic expect to gain for himself, here or hereafter, by arguing against it while believing there is such an insane, inhuman place?

Since all men have different minds and are differently informed about nearly everything, it is but natural that they have different views and different beliefs about almost everything, and especially as to the hereafter which no one really knows anything about.

Persons have their beliefs about the hereafter, but believing it is not knowing. Other religions have beliefs, and so, belief is not proof. Some think they have experienced an "inner witness" proving a Hereafter but that is no proof to those who never had such a "witness."

However, Skeptics do not deny those persons their right to hold such opinions, nor their right to express them, and Skeptics hold that they, themselves, are entitled to equal right to express their opinions.

When men assume the right of free speech for themselves concerning their own, or other religions or beliefs, but deny the honesty of those who disagree with them and tell them to "keep silent," they thus prove themselves intolerant and that they would suppress the free speech of those who disagree with them if they could. Fortunately for the progress [of] the race, public opinion stands up more and more for the right of free speech and of fair play in these matters.

Instead of censuring, let those who disagree with the Skeptic consider his arguments and his reasons, and answer them if he can. That is the point. Answer the arguments. Truth is what is wanted.

THE REV. W. D. DARNALL RIDICULES EVOLUTION AND "A MODERN INFIDEL" [AND] APPROVES OF A HELL

From the *Denison Daily Herald*, January 22, 1917

Note: This article was written for & delivered (a copy) to the *Church News* but the ministers would not let it be printed.

In the Church News of January 20, the Rev. W. D. Darnall says a modern infidel is one who tries to prove that some of his ancestors were "billy goats, apes or monkeys," and he asks to be shown the animals connecting the infidel with those named. That is Mr. Darnall's manner and method of answering the evolutionist. There is no argument or reasoning in it.

Every person should welcome investigation and discussion, and should keep an open mind for truth from any source. Vast accumulations of evidence exist in proof of evolution, and many of the very greatest minds accept it as true, as I shall show. Since Mr. Darnall denies evolution, why did not he offer some reason against it? The person who has good reasons on his side is generally glad to produce them

What Does Evolution Teach?
Evolution teaches that all life everywhere originated from natural causes, from the combined forces that exist in nature, and that it (life) started in an extremely simple form of life. During vast periods of time that simple form of life varied and branched, and progressed, and produced all forms of life that we know anything about, including man.

What Are the Proofs of Evolution?
In the space here one can point to only a few out of the vast accumulation of facts which prove that evolution is true.

The strata, or layers of the earth's surface form leaves of rock in which are recorded the proofs of animals and plants for millions of years.

Those fossil remains of the lower forms life found in the stratas of rock rise higher and higher "with no sharp lines between, but insensible shading from first to last." These rock records of animal and plant life, through the ages cannot be counterfeited. They cannot be denied. Geologists are able to estimate the approximate ages of these earth leaves or strata, and their estimates run into multiplied millions of years. If one will read a standard work of geology, one can see how those estimates are made and their reasonableness. In the great museums of the country one see thousands of these fossil remains of animals and plants. One can find many in the rocks around Denison. There are numerous other methods of proving evolution true, but I cannot use room here to state them. Read a good work on geology.

Man has existed hundreds of thousands of years according to eminent authorities. Skulls of prehistoric men have been found showing inferior brain development in earlier men. There are today many savage tribes representing man in lower stages of development. Man has rudimentary organs which have nearly disappeared from disuse, owing to ages of change in manner and conditioning. The appendix is one.

Breeding of stock for improvement proves that such change and development can and does take place. There is overwhelming proof of evolution for whoever will examine the evidence.

The development of man has been so gradual that a thousand lives would probably not give time to note the shades of change and progress. He who asks to be shown a half man and half monkey knows very little about evolution.

Since Mr. Darnall ridicules evolution, it must be that he does not know that nearly all, if not all, of the great universities teach it. Darwin, Huxley, Herbert Spencer, Haeckel, and score of the greatest men the world has known accepted it. To make the proof more striking, I will quote from the "Biblical World"—as follows:

"In a symposium based on the question, 'Does Modern Science Still Believe in Evolution?' thirteen savants of America reply in the affirmative to the Biblical World. The query was sent out by Dean Shailer Matthew, of the University of Chicago, publisher of the magazine.

"In an editorial preceding the interview he says the queries were sent out so that believers in the Christian religion might know whether they must reckon with evolution in framing their beliefs.

"The scientist[s] who declared that the Darwinian theory is accepted still are: here followed the names of thirteen professors in the various sciences, teachers in various great universities in the United States.

The evidence is overwhelming in proof of evolution. The earth has existed millions of years. Man has existed hundreds of thousands and perhaps millions of years.

The bible says everything was created perfect less than 6000 years ago. See the time "4004 years before Christ" printed on the margin of the first chapter of Genesis, in any large, older bible. Six thousand years ago as compared with the real age of the earth is about as near right as to say that a bucket of water equals the Atlantic ocean.

The famous scientists, Huxley, said: "Thoughtful men, once escaped from the binding influence of traditional prejudice, will find in the lowly stock whence man has sprung, the best evidence of the splendor of his capacities; and will discern in his long progress through the past a reasonable ground of faith in his attainment of a nobler future."

THE CHURCH NEWS EDITOR AND COMMITTEE REFUSE SPACE FOR AN ANSWER FROM CHAS. H. JONES

From the *Denison Daily Herald*, February 3, 1917 and *Denison Gazette*, February 5, 1917

The Church News of January 20 published an article from the Rev. W. D. Darnall in which he called on the "Evolutionary Infidel" to point out the animals connecting the infidel with the "billy goat, ape, or monkey."

As Church News published Mr. Darnall's article, it seemed but fair that it should consent to publish an answer to Mr. Darnall.

I registered a letter to the Rev. Jas. E. Morris, editor of Church News, requesting space to answer Mr. Darnall. What I got for my pains was "a plenty." The Reverends J. E. Aubrey, Jas. E. Morris and Geo. W. Sherman sent me a joint note in which they refused me space "for pay or otherwise," and in addition to that they said that I was not "sincere," and that my letter "was not sent in good faith." They then published their note. I answered the gentlemen as follows:

Denison, Tex., Jan. 30, '17
The Reverends Jas. E. Morris
J. E. Aubrey
Geo. W. Sherman
Denison, Texas.

Dear Sirs:

I have your joint note of Jan. 26, '17, in which you decline to allow me space in the Church News to answer "paid or otherwise," the article by the Rev. W. D. Darnall, in the Church News of January 20.

The reasons you give for declining, are, as stated by you, as follows:

"These things together with the manner in which you sent your request (registered) convinces us you were not sincere, and that your letter was not sent in good faith."

To get at what you mean by "these things," and the whole ground on which you question my "sincerity" and "good faith," I will state what your joint note states. It is as follows:

(1) That I registered my letter of request to Mr. Morris. My answer to that is that I wanted to know positively whether or not Mr. Morris got my letter, so there would be no uncertainty concerning his attitude toward my request. Wherein is lack of sincerity or of good faith shown in that?

(2) That I said I did not expect that my article would be published. My answer to that is that I expected refusal, but I thought I would make the request, nevertheless. I wanted to put the article in Church News and I stood ready to write the article. Because I doubted that I should be allowed to put the article in, wherein does that exhibit lack of faith or of sincerity on my part? And particularly so, since my expectations have been fulfilled.

(3) That I published in the Herald [(]Jan. 22) an answer to Mr. Darnall before I heard from Mr. Morris, in answer to my letter of request.

My answer to that is, that my requesting space to answer in Church News in no way cancelled my right to publish answers sooner or later in the other papers. If I had published an answer in another paper, even before, or at any time after writing Mr. Morris, that could not cancel my right to ask, nor my wish, to answer in Church News where Mr. Darnall published his article. Notwithstanding that, I did wait from Saturday morning, Jan. 20, until after morning mail time the following Monday, Jan. 22, that is, into the third day after writing Mr. Morris.

If Mr. Morris did not have time to attend to it, that was a detail which I knew nothing about, and besides, it had no bearing, and has no bearing on my right to print my answer in the Herald while waiting to hear from Mr. Morris. I stood ready to furnish the article to Church News.

In what respect is want of "good faith" or "sincerity" shown there?

And what has any of this to do with the truth or falsity of my arguments concerning evolution?

You did not have a shadow of ground for questioning my sincerity or my good faith. Your assumption was wholly gratuitous.

One fact, among others, appears clear to me, and that is after you read my article in the Herald you were not willing for those arguments to be read by the Church News readers.

I send a copy of this to each member of your committee.

Very truly,
CHAS. H. JONES

In the foregoing letter I failed to note that these gentlemen said that "your signature does not appear at the bottom of your letter." They would make it appear that I wrote anonymously. I did not. I signed my name by typewriter to the letter, just as a great many men sign their ordinary letters.

Too many people resort to the dodge of questioning the sincerity of the man with, whose opinions they disagree.

CHAS. H. JONES

DARWIN THE EVOLUTIONIST DID NOT TURN TO THE BIBLE AND CHRIST

From the *Denison Daily Herald*, February 13, 1917

A minister in his sermon on Infidelity last Sunday night stated in substance that the eminent evolutionist, Charles Darwin, who wrote the "Origin of Species," regretted late in life that he ever expressed the evolutionary views contained in that book. He stated further that Darwin, while bed-ridden and presumably near the end of his life, frequently had his hand on the open Bible, "which he was always studying" and that he called the Epistles to the Hebrews, "The Royal Book," and that he spoke "on the holiness of God," and that he asked a visitor to come and talk to his servants and neighbors on "Christ Jesus and His Salvation." Also that Darwin said in speaking of his book, "I was a young man with unformed ideas."

I happen to have the history of just how that story started. I shall show that it is not true.

The story originated from a "Lady Hope," whom nobody seems to know, unless it be the editor of a religious paper, The Watchman-Examiner, who published the story without proof of its truthfulness.

The story was promptly denied, and "Lady Hope" was called upon for proofs, and, as stated by the editor, "Lady Hope" refuses to discuss the subject at more length. She gave the excuse that she did not want to distress the family of "the great and good man whom I so ardently admired." It is reported, however, that she said "she could tell more." This showed "great regard," indeed. She refused to supply proofs, let it be remembered. Her excuse was a foxy one.

If "Lady Hope" had told the truth, the indications are unmistakable that she would have considered it a great feather in her cap to prove that the world famous Agnostic, Darwin, had turned to the Bible and Christ.

The flimsiness of that story by "Lady Hope" disproves itself, but I will not stop at that. I will furnish complete and unmistakable proof that it is not true, and that proof is a letter from Darwin's son, Francis Darwin. I quote the letter as published in the religious paper, the Watchman-Examiner, as reported—as follows:

Brookthorpe, Gloucester, Eng.
Nov. 7, 1918
The Editor the Watchman-Examiner, New York

Sirs, I have on extract from your journal of Aug. 19, 1918, entitled "Darwin and Christianity," by Lady Hope.

This account of an interview with my father cannot possibly be a statement of fact. Neither I nor my sister have any knowledge of Lady Hope's visit to Down.

It is not true (as Lady Hope states) that my father was bedridden, for some time before his death. His supposed reference to the chief scientific work of his life is quite incredible. Nor are these the only points which convince me that, whoever Lady Hope may have visited, it was not Charles Darwin.

Moreover, it is impossible that he should have become ardently and openly Christian without the knowledge of his family. He was an Agnostic, as is proved by his autobiography (Life and Letters, 1, 313), written in 1876. If he had subsequently changed his views on religion, he would—with his well-known love of truth—have said so in some additional autobiographical notes written in May 1881, a year before his death. But no such statement exists.

As you have been misled into publishing the article in question, I trust you will make public denial of its authenticity.

Faithfully yours,
FRANCIS DARWIN

I judge that ought to settle in Denison the story of Darwin's turning to "Christ and the Bible."

And now as to "Lady Hope's" statement that Darwin said in speaking of his book, "I was a young man with unformed ideas." Let us see how much truth is in that.

It can be disproved by every person in Denison who can read. Go to the Century Dictionary and find a short biography of Charles Darwin. Darwin was born in 1809. He published his book, "Origin of Species," in 1859. He was fifty years old when he published it. How about the "I was a young man with unformed ideas"? He published his "The Descent of Man" in 1871 when he was sixty-two years old. How about the story, "I was a young man with unformed ideas"? The titles of the books, without reading them, show that Darwin was an evolutionist and an Agnostic and therefore did not believe the Bible was God's word.

Darwin was a great and noble man. For fifty years he patiently investigated the problems of nature for the benefit of mankind. His life, work and views are expressed in his books which show beyond the shadow of a doubt that he was an evolutionist and an Agnostic. No eminent scientist but will say that is true. Does not a noble man's life work mean anything, unless he believes in Christianity, like "Lady Hope"? If he only pretended to be an Agnostic all his life, and admitted he was a Christian only when he was ready to die, that would be to prove that Darwin was a scoundrel all his life. The person who would imply that of the great Darwin should hide himself.

Is such life and work as Darwin's to be questioned on the flimsy basis of an unknown "Lady Hope" story?

HOW THE INFIDEL MAY CONVERT HIMSELF

From the *Denison Herald*—February 16, 1917

Last Sunday evening in a sermon on infidelity, a minister told how an Infidel may covert himself. It was a very plain recipe. It was as follows: He said for the Infidel to give up his secret sin, and then get down on his knees and pray to God thus: "O God, if there is a God," etc., etc. On his doing this, God would reveal Himself to the Infidel and thus convert him.

Now as to the secret-sin part, I am convinced there are a good many pretty decent Infidels in Denison whose truthfulness, honesty and general morality are not surpassed by those who accept the Bible, but for the purpose of this article I will select two famous men, now living, who are well-known Infidels. They are the great inventor, Edison, and the great nature-writer, John Burroughs.

Will any man question the honesty and sincerity of these two great men, or say that they are addicted to some secret sin? It would take a queer specimen of a man to do it.

These men not being guilty of some secret sin, then, according to the minster's recipe, all that remains for them to do to be converted is for them to get down on their knees and pray as directed, "O God, if there be a God," etc. and God will reveal Himself and they will be converted.

Just here comes the hitch. Unfortunately for the minister's recipe, the Bible teaches the contrary. The Bible gives us distinctly to understand that faith and belief are necessary before answer to prayer may be expected.

I will quote a few passages from the Bible to prove this.

(Hebrew 11:6)—"But without faith it is impossible to please God."

(Matthew 21:21-22) —"Verily I saw unto you: If ye have faith, and doubt not, yet shall not only do this," etc.

"Whatsoever ye shall ask in prayer, believing, ye shall receive."

(James 5:15) —"And the prayer of faith shall save the sick."

There are numerous similar passages showing that faith, or belief, must go with prayer, according to the Bible.

Now, as these men not only lack faith in the Bible as being God's word but positively disbelieve it, it follows that the minister's recipe won't work.

Edison has done more good for mankind that perhaps any other man that ever lived, and still, if what the minister says is true, Edison and the gentle, pure and noble John Burroughs must go to eternal trouble because they do not believe in an insane, inhuman hell.

Who is there than can believe such teaching or doctrine as that?

I believe that Denison Christians are generally well-disposed and kind-hearted.

When the well-meaning non-Christian neighbor at last falls into eternal sleep, I do not believe there is a single Christian in Denison who would be so unkind and unforgiving as to send him to everlasting trouble, if the decision were left to the Christians.

Is God less kind than the Denison Christian?

THAT JONAH AND THE WHALE STORY, OR, JONAH AND HIS SUBMARINE HOTEL

From the *Denison Gazette*, February 19, 1917

We all know the story of Jonah and his submarine hotel, or his trip to sea in a fish.

In a sermon last Sunday evening, a visiting minister said that Jonah's conveyance was not a whale, but was a "monster fish," or "sea monster," I forget just which. Anyway he did not question that Jonah made the little side trip, or "inside" trip, as told, in the Bible. This recalls the Rev. Mr. Bulgin, who said, "If the Lord ordered a chigger to swallow Jonah, I would believe it."

But let us "search the scripture" and see whether Jonah's conveyance was a "sea monster," or "monster fish," instead of a whale.

(Jonah 1:17) "Now the Lord had prepared a great fish to swallow up Jonah. And Jonah was in the belly of the fish three days and three nights."

(Jonah 2:10) "And the Lord spake unto the fish, and it vomited out Jonah upon the dry land."

(Matthew 12:40) "For as Jonah was three days and three nights in the whale's belly; so shall the Son of Man be three days and three nights in the heart of the earth."

In none of these passages is the word "sea monster," or "monster fish" used.

The quotation given from Matthew is said to be Jesus' own words. As Jesus says it was a whale, it is to be presumed that He knew what kind of fish He was talking about.

Having (I think) settled that point (that it was a whale), I proceed to ask—Is the Jonah and the whale story true?

When food is taken into the stomach, the stomach juices immediately begin dissolving it, and in three or four hours the food passes from the stomach into the intestines. One wonders how Jonah managed to dodge those stomach acids, or juices, for three days and three nights, and also one wonders if the whale did not have a whale of a case of whale indigestion.

(Jonah 2:16) "And the Lord spake unto the fish, and it vomited Jonah upon the dry land." Necessarily it must have been a low, flat shore. The water near such shores is usually low and the shore itself damp some distance out. For a whale to vomit Jonah on dry land must have been "some job."

But in what language did the Lord speak to the fish—in Latin, English, Choctaw, Eskimo, or just "fishy" language? And does a fish understand language, and where did it learn it?

But the worst is yet to come. Experts say, so I have read, that a whale's throat is so small and so constructed that eatables the size of a saucer, or plate, would choke it to death, and, therefore, it could not possibly swallow a man. Hence the need of changing the whale to a "sea monster," or "monster fish." But remember, Jesus said it was a whale.

The Jonah and whale story did not originate with the Bible. God had nothing to do with it. It is not a true story. It is a Solar, or Sun Myth, or legend, and was known to many nations of antiquity, and the bible writers built the Jonah and whale story on the older stores, or from them. An eminent German divine and professor of theology, and other critics can be quoted in support of this statement.

If this Jonah and whale story is only a myth, and is therefore not true, and there was no "Jonas three days and three nights in the whale's belly," then, the Bible writers were mistaken.

If they were mistaken, it necessarily follows that Jesus was mistaken when He said in (Matt. 12:40) "For as Jonas was three days and three nights in the whale's belly; so shall the Son of Man be three days and three nights in the heart of the earth."

I have quoted what the Bible says. Is the story true, or is it not? That is the question. The truth is what we ought to want, and nothing but the truth.

EDISON, THE GREAT INVENTOR, SAYS, THE CHRISTIAN GODS ARE MYTH

From the *Denison Daily Herald*, March 5, 1917

The Church News of March 2 quotes the Christian Herald as saying, "Mr. Edison does not hesitate to declare his belief in the existence of God as seen in nature, and in providence.

And that Mr. Edison said, "Too many people have a microscopic idea of the Creator. If they would only study his wonderful works as shown in nature herself, they would have a much broader idea of the Great Engineer and his divine power. Indeed, I can almost prove his existence by chemistry."

Mr. Edison believes in a Supreme Intelligence, and so did the famous infidel, Thomas Paine, but their beliefs were and are founded on nature and the laws of nature, and both reject the Bible and the God of the Bible.

Christians say the Bible is God's Word and the foundation of their belief, and that it sets forth God's will.

Mr. Edison calls that "a microscopic idea of the Creator," and he advises people to study nature for proof of God.

Evidently, Mr. Edison does not believe the Bible is God's Word, else would not refer to it as "a microscopic idea of the Creator," for that is where Christians get their ideas of the Creator.

According to the report, the Christian Herald writer said, "The true man of science finds what the verse of the Bible declares, that, "In the beginning God created the heaven and the earth," Gen.1:1.

The Christian Herald writer assumes that Edison has "found the God, who in the Bible, "Created the heaven and the earth." Since Edison only "believes" in a Supreme Intelligence, and since he rejects the Bible account of God, the Christian Herald writer's assumption is without foundation.

A report of Mr. Edison's views shows for itself. In an interview published in the Columbian Magazine for January, 1911, Mr. Edison stated his conviction that the gods of the churches are myths, and that Jesus Christ never laid claim to divinity.

"Gods? Gods?" Mr. Edison queried, "A Supreme Being sitting on a throne and commending human beings to eternal peace or condemning them to everlasting punishment, for what they have achieved or failed to do upon this earth? The thought to me seems as abhorrent as fallacious."

That quotation from Edison describes the God of the Bible, and gives Mr. Edison's opinion. Evidently he does not believe in an everlasting hell for the majority of mankind.

Mr. Edison may have had in mind the thirty-first chapter of Numbers, which reads as follows: "And the Lord spake unto Moses, saying, Avenge the children of Israel of the Midianites," etc. In this chapter some of which is unprintable, the Lord directs Moses to make war on the Midianites, to destroy and burn their cities, take everything they have, kill all the men and male children and part of the women, but to "keep alive for yourselves" the rest of the women and female children. These to be distributed to the captains and to the priests. "The Lord's tribute was thirty and two persons." (Numbers XXXI:45.)

When these cruel and inhuman practices are referred to, Christians say, "Yes, but that was done by the Lord in Old Bible times." They say we now have a new dispensation, but not a new God.

It seems to be sufficient to ask if it was ever right for any God at time to issue such commands to Moses as you will read in Numbers, chapter 31?

"BEING ON THE SAFE SIDE,: AS TO BELIEF IN THE BIBLE, IS A CHILDISH REASON BORN OF FEAR

From the *Denison Herald*—March 24, 1917 and *Denison Gazette*—March 26, 1917

Many Christians say to the infidel, "If I believe in the Bible and you do not, I have this advantage: If the Bible is true I gain everything, and you are lost; if the Bible is not true, I lose nothing, and I am still as well off as you are."

That argument looks good until it is examined, then it looks puny.

Instead of permitting his views to be governed by fear, a grown man should hold up his head and insist upon his right to use his reason on any subject. If his religion will not stand investigation, so much the worse for his religion.

Christians who are governed by the "safe side" views are afraid of hell, and afraid of trusting their own judgment. Fearing hell, they fear to investigate the evidence against their belief. Could a man succeed in any business if he acted that way about it?

This fear of investigating one's religion is the reason why people accept as true the absurd Adam and Eve and snake story, and the Deluge story, which says that Noah put from two to seven of all the different kinds of animals and bugs and snakes in the world into a boat that had only one little window in it 22 inches square (Gen. 6:16).Evidently Noah was a crank on ventilation.

Those who accept such absurd stories so as to be on the "safe side," would accept Mohammedanism to be on the "safe side," or any other religion, if they had been born where those religions are taught. No doubt the people in those countries teach that the safe thing to do is to accept their religion.

If a person would make sure of being safe, he should believe in all of the different religions, for it might be that some other religion than his own is the right one.

Suppose we consider only Christian beliefs. To be safe, Protestants should accept Catholicism, and Catholics should accept Protestantism. Baptists should accept sprinkling, and Methodists should accept immersion. Then there are the Mormons and Holiness and scores of other Christian beliefs. There are Predestinarians who teach that God from the beginning of the world predestined certain men, women and children yet unborn to an eternal, insane hell through no fault of their own, no matter how good citizens they might prove to be. There are in the United States about 170 different and differing Christian bodies, each teaching that the Bible means something different, and each teaching that it alone teaches what the Bible teachers. Since only one of them can by any possibility be right, the man who would be on the "safe side" is in something of a pickle to know just which one is the right one. He risks 169 chances of losing to one chance of guessing right as to which side is the safe side. He needs to be a mighty lucky guesser, and he should make sure of having his rabbit-foot in his handiest pocket when he goes to guess.

If the Christian is mistaken in his belief, has he not lost something? Has he not, and does he not continually spend both time and money supporting what is not true? Is not this done at the expense of time and money that would or should be spent in studying and learning and furthering useful information which somebody knows is true, something useful here and now?

Truth and truth only is what every person should want. Truth cannot become known except through investigation. If a man's belief won't stand investigation, his belief is not founded on truth.

No good God will damn a man for honestly investigating and for honestly judging the best he can according to the brains he has. Would God damn the results of his creation?

No savage would ever progress beyond his savage parents, if, in order to be on "safe side" he refused, through fear, to think beyond what his parents thought.

ARE PRAYERS ANSWERED? NOBODY CAN PROVE THAT THEY ARE

From the *Denison Herald*—May 28, 1917 and *Denison Gazette*—May 29, 1917

If prayers are answered, why is it that somebody has not stopped this European war? There have been set aside special days in this country for public and private prayers that the war should stop, and millions have prayed, and still the war goes on just as if no prayer had ever been made.

If prayers for so good a purpose are not answered, what is the use of praying for anything?

The Bible tells people to pray, and it certainly leads people to expect answer to prayer, else why should it tell them to pray? Here are a few quotations from the Bible:

(James 5: 15 to 18) "And the prayer of faith shall save the sick. The effectual fervent prayer of a righteous man availeth much. Elias was a man subject to the passions as we are, and he prayed earnestly that it might not rain; and it rained not on the earth by the space of three years and six months. And he prayed again, and the heavens gave rain, and the earth brought forth her fruit."

If nature (rains) can be controlled by prayer, then surely wars can be controlled by prayer. Wars are carried on by men, and men are certainly more easily controlled than nature is. Considering the unspeakable misery this war is causing millions of men, women, and children, it would be a great and good act to stop it, and if prayer ever deserved to be answered, this one certainly does.

But the war goes on regardless of prayers. What ails the prayers? Is it possible that there is not a righteous Christian on earth to do effective praying?

What about the prayers of the Ministers, and of the Pope, and those who say they are already saved, and others that are sanctified? Are none of these sufficiently righteous to pray an EFFECTIVE prayer?

May it not be that the Bible is mistaken in saying that prayer is answered? In fact, is it not proved every day that it is mistaken? If it is mistaken, then it must be that God had nothing to do with writing or inspiring it, and it is only man-made, for surely God would not allow mistakes to be in his book. Being All-powerful He COULD prevent mistakes being in it, and being All-loving He WOULD prevent it.

As the Germans pray for victory against the English, and the English pray for victory against the Germans, only God knows how He could answer to the satisfaction of both.

Is God unchangeable? Does He know what is best and will He do what is best? If so, then, prayers do not turn him aside from what He is going to do, and they are therefore unnecessary and useless. Prayers imply a changeable God.

Some Christians say, "Such things are beyond man to understand," and that "God's ways are not our ways." If that is the case, then what are our brains for, and why write a book and put in it things which we are not expected to understand? If these things will bear investigation, what is the idea in concealing their meaning from us?

Many people take much religious credit to themselves because they pray, when the fact is, it is the easiest course to take, and the most useless. It is like begging—asking something for nothing. It costs time and energy and trouble to go and do something really useful for a person. As one writer said in substance, "Ploughing is better than praying." That is, work, or doing, is better than agitating the atmosphere with supplications.

Though people pray for victory in war they do not expect to get any help that way. Instead, they place their faith in rapid-fire guns and long-range cannon.

Would not the Germans have a walk-over if the British and French should lay aside their guns and cannon and depend on prayer for victory?

Christians pray just like believers in other and entirely different religions pray and just like some ancient peoples prayed to stone and wooden images before the Bible was ever thought of, and the prayers of one accomplishes just as little as the other. Just think of the billions of prayers sent up monthly. Is it not odd that in all these prayers no one can show that a single one was ever answered? and still they keep on praying.

It would be interesting to know how many people really expect or believe that their prayers will produce any results.

"Prayer is an intimation of what you want, and not of what you will get."

ARE PRAYERS FOR GOOD CROPS A WASTE OF BREATH?

From the *Denison Herald*—May 6, 1918

We are asked to go to church to pray for good crops—that "God would bless the labors of the husbandman and grant such seasonable weather that we may gather in the fruits of the earth, and ever rejoice in thy goodness."

The wish to benefit the people is commendable, but the method proposed to insure good crops (by praying) is too uncertain—it is too easy to be true. If true, would it not be a soft snap for the lazy man?

Would you rent your farm to a man who should tell you that he intended to cultivate it largely by praying? Well, I guess not.

If such a prayer were to be answered from "on high," let us see what that power would need to attend to, to make good crops.

In Grayson county he would need to inject considerable ginger and much information into a lot of the farmers, and unroot many acres of Johnson grass. He would need to get ride of the pink boll worm in South Texas, grasshoppers in Kansas, chinch bugs in Missouri, drouths, floods and I. W. W.'s in various parts of the country, and many of the neighbor's chickens in Denison.

Johnson grass and cockle burrs will grow luxuriantly without prayer, in fact, in spite of prayer, but many a man has failed to raise good wheat and corn by the liberal use of both prayer and hard work.

If good crops can be produced by prayer, or by a combination of prayer and work, there should never be a crop failure, and no person on earth need ever go hungry. A reasonable question arises, Why is it that someone has not produced good crops continuously by prayer, during the hundred or thousand years, or longer?

Without work, prayer is dead, except perhaps the psychological effect upon the one who prays and those who may hear the prayer. On the other hand, intelligent work will produce good crops, regardless of prayer, if the season and soil are right.

Here are two verses by "H. P. C." on prayer:

"If there is aught that you desire,
   Say a prayer.
Great or small that you require,
   Say a prayer.
If you are weak and would be bold,
If you are hot and would be cold,
If you have sought in vain for gold,
   Say a prayer.

If you are up against it right,
   Say a prayer.
If you have no funds in sight,
   Say a prayer.
When drought causes you vexation,
Don't waste time on irrigation,
For gentle rain make supplication,
   With a prayer."

As to the moral effect of prayer, the asking for something for nothing. It is productive of far better morality to teach children known facts, one of which is that success and happiness as far as possible, can be secured only by honorable intelligent work. Prayer is begging.

To pray for good crops so we can fight the Kaiser better is a very round-about way of securing victory. Why not pray for immediate victory of the allies and save hundreds of thousands of lives, thereby, or better still, why did not somebody pray before the war started, that there be no war? Would not that have been infinitely better if prayers are answered? And, also, a fine opportunity to prove the existence and the goodness of the Power prayed to?

Such work as that could be far better for poor humans beings than is "numbering the hairs of our heads" or "watching sparrows fall."

Prayer indicates what you want, but it is no sign that you will get it.

WILL ONE-MINUTE DAILY PRAYERS ENABLE US TO WHIP THE KAISER?

From the *Denison Herald*—June 28, 1918

The Dallas Pastors have started a new stunt to whip the Kaiser. That stunt is to pray one minute daily at eleven o'clock for victory. These prayers are to be started by the ringing of fire bells and church bells, and by the stopping of street cars for a minute. All this is a reminder to pray.

It seems that the Pastors are not satisfied with what the Lord has done, and is doing about this war, and they want to call His attention to that fact daily, at eleven o'clock.

The Pastors seem to think that if a good many people will daily remind the Lord of His neglect, and will be Him and pull at Him to do better, He, the Lord, will finally give in and will help on our, the Allies side.

But the Germans are praying just as hard or harder for their side, and if we are to judge by what the Kaiser says, he, the Kaiser, and God are working together like brothers.

We want to see the Kaiser beaten into the dust for the suffering he has caused the world, and we are all putting up our money to that end, and it is money, food, guns and soldiers that will whip him, and not prayers.

To save time and trouble, the Dallas Pastors should hire talking machines and set them saying prayers over and over, day and night. If anything will attract attention, it is these talking machines going day and night. No doubt the Lord can hear talking machine prayers as well as he can hear whispered prayers.

The question is, does the Lord of the Bible want this war stopped? If He does, why has He not stopped it, or better still, why did He ever let it start?

If He cannot stop it, He is not All-Powerful. If he can stop it and will not, He then permits the stunting and starving of millions of children, and the killing of millions of boys and men, by this war which He could have prevented if He would.

Having permitted the war to go this far, do you think these one-minute prayers, or any other kind of prayers will turn Him from His course?

So far the only relief the wounded soldiers and starving children have received has come from human beings right here on this earth—from the Red Cross and other human organizations run exclusively by human beings. And so far, the Lord has sat still and done nothing. Will these one-minute prayers rouse the Lord to His duty at this late day?

The skin covered Tom-Toms of certain tribes are beaten to drive off evil, and these Tom-Toms gave a psychological effect on those who use them. Prayers have psychological effect on those who pray, and on some who hear the prayers, but prayers bring no support from the skies—support that can be proved to have come from the skies—not a single case. We await proofs but do not expect them.

The sooner we learn to depend wholly on our own efforts, and to the efforts of others in this world, the sooner we shall get out of life the happiness there is in for us.

Thomas Volney Munson

"Faith glories in its invented spooks, yet it is frightened to death (in reason) by them. Reason grows fat and happy on fact and truth, and hence has no ghosts to fear."

THOMAS VOLNEY MUNSON was born at Fulton County, Illinois on September 26, 1843. His parents were William and Maria (nee Linley) Munson. He had two brothers and three sisters.

Munson's parents were members of the Disciples of Christ, who raised all their children in that denomination.

In 1861 Munson enrolled in business school in Chicago, and then taught school back home for a year before enrolling at the Kentucky Agricultural and Mechanical College at Lexington, where he first had doubts about the religious beliefs he had been taught as a child.

After reading Darwin's *On the Origin of Species* (1859), and also *The Variation of Animals and Plants under Domestication* (1868), he gave up the Christian faith entirely.

On June 21, 1870, less than two weeks being graduated with a Bachelor's degree, Munson was married to Ellen Scott Bell.

In 1873 Munson and his wife bought property near Lincoln, Nebraska. In 1876, the couple moved to Texas, where Munson's brothers had helped to found Denison four years earlier.

From 1876 to 1887 the Munson family resided on a small farm where the budding botanist started the nursery business that sustained him and his family throughout his long life. He also won the first of many awards, and socialized with his fellow "infidels," a minority in a town filled with churches. Among those with similar views were brothers Theo and Ben, and *Sunday Gazetteer* publisher B. C. Murray,

In 1880, Munson was one of the founders of the Denison Liberal League. In 1884, a year after earning a Master's degree from his alma mater in Kentucky, he wrote the first of several freethought articles that were published in J. D. Shaw's *Independent Pulpit*. In 1887 Munson and his family moved into the house he named "Vinita."

In 1889 Munson was awarded a gold medal by the French government for saving the French wine industry from certain ruin by sending pest-resistant grafts from his Texas vines. The following year, after founding the Denison Philosophical Society, he was elected treasurer of the Liberal Association of Texas, a position he held for at least three terms.

In 1906, B. C. Murray published Munson's small anti-religious tract, *The New Revelation*, in which he openly wrote of his atheism. On January 21, 1913, Munson died. He was buried at Denison's Fairview Cemetery, following a completely non-religious funeral.

EVOLUTION.

CHAPTER I.

From the Denison *Sunday Gazetteer*, December 16, 1883

As there seems to be a general interest awakened on the topic of evolution, and few comprehend what is meant by the term, I present the subject in a new and familiar form, so that even the boys and girls may easily understand it, and not learn to regard evolution as some horrible ism which is going to drag us all down to hell, but only a name for the most harmonious system of classification of all facts known to man, including all religions and philosophies as well as all objects in nature. It will be seen by this view that evolution is not warring with Christianity or any other religion. I shall endeavor to show that all religions are the product of evolution, and are unavoidable, and all perform a good or evil office according to the standpoint from which they are viewed. If evolution be true, it *must* show that all religions—no matter how much at variance with each other—are necessary, natural products. Hence the evolutionist who condemns Christianity, and still more, if he condemns his own fellows for believing it, also condemns evolution and himself in the same judgement. It will be seen that Christians, Mohammedans, Confucians, Mormons are all right and good in their place. But let us to the argument.

First, we assume what all admit to be true, so far was the combined observation of mankind has discovered, that matter is infinite in extent, duration, motion and diversibility, and by which properties alone we know it. That absolutely we know nothing of the final or ultimate essence of matter. By infinite is meant entirely beyond the farthest reach of man's perception.

Matter in quality or kind is found to consist of "simple elements" chemically speaking, of which some sixty-six have been discovered, with a probability of more yet to be found, and indications in some cases that yet a further analysis may be made, reducing the so-called "simple elements" still lower, and consequently to a list of few in number, with argument, by analogy, possibly to one ultimate form of material corpuscle, and that all the more complex forms arise from the different groupings of these corpuscles, just as bricks can be laid together in numerous forms, yet ultimately all of one size and shape. However, beyond the sixty-six known elements this further simplification is not positive knowledge; but only theory built upon a few observations seeming to point in that direction.

The "simple elements" are known and classified according to their difference in density, elasticity, compressibility, color, taste, feel, odor, attractions and repulsions, either singly or in combination with one another. In ordinary temperatures some are solids, such as gold, iron, silver, carbon; some liquids, as mercury; some gasses, as oxygen, nitrogen, hydrogen, chlorine, bromine, etc.

The constant motion of matter throws its different elements and their combinations into different relationships and gives rise to new and constantly changing combinations. We term these combinations individuals, especially, when so organized as to maintain themselves a greater or lesser extent of time in their general contour against outside or antagonistic bodies or forces, and to have the power to throw off a portion of themselves, which will go on and build up to a full size on the same plan as the parent, such as a quartz crystal, always with angles with the same degree of divergence, or as a plant or animal. The more complex and numerous the properties or phenomena of any combination, and the greater the power of maintaining that combination against outside motion, the more completely do we consider it individualized, no matter how much or how little space it occupies. The principles of this individualization of matter we include under the term evolution.

It does not follow from this that any such thing as creation, in the popular sense that something was brought into existence out of nothing by the edict of a force or being separate and above matter must be necessary.

On the contrary the essence of matter with its inherent properties, always existed, and cannot absolutely become more or less in quantity. A change of position or form is constantly going on in everything everywhere, slowly or rapidly, and each new position exhibits also a correspondingly varying property or force. Thus we see a body by rapid movements causes the latent forces or motions of heat, light, electricity of different varieties to become apparent. Where we find certain crystalline structures built up of certain elements, such as carbon and its various chemical combinations, the diamond with its peculiar unvarying angles, appears, or some other peculiar crystal comes forth, according to the elements entering into the individual structure. Its form always and invariably comes according to the material and dynamical properties existing in the subject and its surroundings, and has no need of an outside creator. So we see a certain organized combination of oxygen, nitrogen, carbon, hydrogen, iron, potassium, sodium, etc., gives rise to an individual form we term a plant, which can add to itself or other matter, throw off parts of itself in seeds, buds, or cells possessed of the same organizing force to build up new individuals of a similar character, within due limits. Thus we go on and on till we come up to the peculiar and complex conscious life force, which is no exception to the rule of the crude mineral or the blossoming plant. Just as certain elements of matter are given or withheld, so will the feeling be full and happy, or depressed and miserable.

Give a proper amount of nitrogen and the muscles will be firm, strong and elastic. Take it away from among the food altogether, and the muscles soon shrivel to mere threads and life departs or becomes latent. Give lime in the accustomed inherent channel of the food, and the bones are large and firm. Take away lime and the bones become mere gristle, while the other parts may remain about normal. Give the accustomed Phosphorous in its legitimate channel and the brain is active and thoughtful in its proper exercise. Take it away and the brain becomes dwarfed, thought ceases, and a mere idiot or plant-like animal, which has to be fed with a spoon is the result, if life does not become latent entirely. Give too much or too little of the various foods containing the "organic elements," and abnormal or bloated growth occurs, with all the concomitant feverish or excited life characteristics or a starved, feeble action results. Hence, we conclude there is not, never was nor can ever be such a thing as miraculous creation. Mind neither creates matter, nor matter mind. Whenever, in the regular order of things a certain combination of elements occurs in quality and quantity then a certain peculiar individual appears, crystal, plant or animal, conscious or unconscious. But as the particular combinations never identically occupy the same position and cannot, so no two individuals are identically the same in every point and cannot be any more than a circle can remain such and be a square at the same. time. So no two diamonds are alike in everything, no two plants are identically the same; no two persons look exactly alike or think exactly alike; no two communities can be organized just alike; no two religions can be developed exactly alike, nor can anyone remain forever the same and united. Just here is where Christ disclosed himself to be only a man after all his boasted claims of being equal with God. He prayed fervently to his Father, that is to God, to himself if he were God, that his followers would always be one and united. If any prayer in all the universe should, from a Christian standpoint, have been answered, that one ought to have been. But it was not, and ever in Christ's own day dissensions among his own followers arose, and ever since they have grown wider and wider, and have run into thousands of hair-splitting sub-divisions, thus giving the lie to Christ—God himself; for in another place he declares that even his followers could have whatever they desired, through prayer, even to the moving of mountains, if they only asked in faith.

But according to the law of evolution these divisions in opinion are a necessity, and ever sect is good and right in its place.

Selfishness has for ages made the stronger religions or sects try to put down the weaker by scaring them through the gate of faith with the flaming torch of hell! But all to no avail. Evolution and involution pursued the even tenor of their way until to-day men are learning the laws of universal courtesy in matters of opinion, each to have and enjoy his own as he must, and not intrude it as a doctrine of faith on others.

Thus we can be more happy than otherwise by endeavoring to make others happy in their own ways and opinions, so long as they do not make them offensive or tyrannical.

What I write or speak is by no means meant or in any way desired to weaken or unhinge any faith or opinion, for if I were mean enough to do so I am thoroughly convince by all my powers of observation of controversy that it would tend rather to the contrary. I only try to follow the scriptural injunction, to give a reason for the faith (opinion) within me, as my personal defence, when needlessly attacked by the Jones, Smith & Co. party, who want everybody else to believe just as they do. "By your works you shall be judged."

In my second chapter I shall pursue the path of evolution into its moral development of society.

                      Sincerely,
                      T. V. MUNSON

EVOLUTION.

CHAPTER II.

From the Denison *Sunday Gazetteer*, December 23, 1883

MORAL DEVELOPMENT OF SOCIETY.

I. The individual. Each atom of matter is surrounded on all sides by other atoms, singly or in groups, and is attracted or repelled from position to position. In some positions it is very unstable, and seems almost nervously anxious to secure a more quiet or stable situation; as, for instance, if a light needle is laid gently upon water it will not sink, especially if oiled, although specifically heavier than water, yet it quivers and moves about at every jar or slight wave. The cohesion of the particles of water, though weak among themselves, is just sufficient under the needle to hold it up, or to outweigh another force—gravitation—in the needle, pulling it down, but once press the needle below the surface until the cohesion of the water is on all sides of the needle, and it at once settles down to the bottom of the glass. If it were in the deepest sea, its progress downward would become slower and slower, till a point would be reached where the density of the water—specific—gravity, by the pressure from above, would become equal with the steel in the needle, and there would be another stopping point. Or suppose while the needle lies upon the water in the glass, a magnet is brought near, so that the point of the needle is toward it. The needle will at once rush to the magnet, and yet will not be quiet, for the same force along its other parts also wants to get nearer the attaching body, and around the needle comes till it lies quietly alongside of the magnet, and in fact becomes a part of the magnet itself. So to make a powerful magnet, it is only necessary to place side by side a number of small magnets. This peculiar force seems in many respects close akin to the life-force, as it will impart of propagate its itself from one piece of steel to another, just as the life force is propagated from one mass of albumenous or protoplasmic matter, like white of egg, to another. Professor Faraday found that all kinds of matter had magnetism in them, but in different degrees. So we see almost all kinds of matter constitute food for one kind of plant or animal or another. Thus we see matter of certain relationship to other matter draws it to itself; forming a community of atoms, of steel, gold, iron, or a still more complex community of communities, as water, albumen, oil, alcohol, starch, sugar, or more complex still, as plant or animal tissue, when we have wood or flesh; or still further, when a very complex tissue of bone, flesh, blood and brain in certain delicately poised proportions give rise to motion, feeling, perception, and conscious conception by comparison of retaining impressions, and we have a very complex individual, which will perceive, reject or repel offensive, and attract and appropriate agreeable mater, thus becoming able to preserve its individuality, as a community of various matters, for a much longer period than the same collection of matter could possibly do if it had acquired no centralizing force, or had lost it by disorganization. The compound powerful magnet would be no magnet at all if it were not carefully organized successively, north pole to south pole, all the way through, So the man or the animal ceases when the rule of its organization becomes broken, as when bone instead of muscle is deposited in the heart, ossification of the heart and death ensure. Water secreted in the pericardium instead of the lubricating serum, causes dropsy of the heart. Thus the thousand and one ills of life come, by the wrong matter, or improper amounts getting into the wrong place.

 The study and rectification of these things give us anatomy, physiology and hygiene, individual, personal morality; and to accomplish it most thoroughly, it has been found necessary for certain persons in every community to make a specialty of it, and become doctors. Did the bodily physician realize more earnestly that the beauty, strength and happiness of the social body, both physical and mental, depends more largely upon him, or should than upon any other member of the community, we should salary him better still, and have less use for the quack with nostrums, and the still more zealous, spiritually theorizing pope, priest and preacher, dealing out their nanseons deadly doses of dirt and nonsense. Instead of the preacher, the doctor should occupy the church with his demonstrations in anatomy, physiology and hygiene, accompanied with lectures on personal morality and happiness. No common school course should be wanting in a thorough training in the rules of health. Theories of every kind should be prohibited. Let each draw up his own theories to suite the working of his own mind.

SOCIETY

So much for the moral development of the individual. Let us follow him in his relation with others of his kind. Each individual is surrounded on all sides by other individuals in various stages of development; it is constantly affected and modified by them, so that there can be no individual which can maintain itself for any length of time identically, as it was previous to that period. The little pulling babe, Volney Munson, long since passed out of its individuality into the lubberly boy; that into a gawky young man, full of sentimentality, religion and love for the girls. Thence babies and business came. Prayer didn't bring pancakes, nor church-going clothes, bread or home, but many a doubt and wrangle between members and churches of other creeds. Business required knowledge of earth, water and air to make it successful, so life could be sustained by converting the crude elements into the necessities, so that support had not to be begged or beaten from others. This knowledge revealed many undesirable facts not made by man, in direct opposition to the fundamental declarations of his former creed, the Bible. ?No one could or did demonstrate the Bible to be as it claimed, but the facts of nature stood boldly up from day to day, and forever demonstrated beyond all cavil to everyone who looks at them. Then faith became useless, and per force to-day T. V. Munson is an infidel, in the full and true sense of the term. That is, he has no faith, or blindly-assented-to rule of doctrine, only a common sense way of finding out things. He is not the only one known who has traveled a similar path. Moses, though petted and pampered by the Egyptians, became disgusted at the slavery imposed upon the Israelites and led them away through trials and tribulations, finally into a happy land of freedom. But his idea of freedom and reformation was far from the broad, universal freedom of to-day. While it was wrong for Jews to be slaves, yet to him it was right for the Jews even, to hold slaves of the most abject type, captured from among the heathen, and until within the present century his ideas of freedom held good. He established a most tyrannical and galling religion, but still a long step in advance of the polytheistical religions mostly prevailing up to his time. And his monotheistic religion still is largely adhered to, but his Deity is growing dimmer and less jealous and revengeful all the time.

Christ in boyhood was apt, and at thirty, though he dared not to rebel openly against the burdensome circumcision, burnt offerings and tyrannical rulings of the priesthood, he staid among them and argued daily in the synagogues against their narrow, unphilanthropic practices, and in three years became so bold and advanced a reformed that his age could not keep up with him. And charges of Infidelity and blasphemy were brought against him: "Physician heal thyself." In his extremity he called in all his powers of patience, magic and acute logic, learned in his sojourn for eighteen years among the seers of Arabia, and finally claimed to be God; and at the last moment cried in despair: "My God, my God, why has thou forsaken me?" A strange speech, truly, for God to utter.

But he left a noble impulse. He was a great and good

reformer. He was the Volney, the Voltaire, the Renan, the Paine, the Ingersoll, the Spencer of his age.

Paul became an Infidel, and joined the Christians. He had a broad intellect and saw farther than many other Christians of his day. He was a learned Jew and respected his old friends too much to fall into abusing them for their blindness, so preached universal salvation, and several of the churches which he established, Antioch, among others, always taught a liberal doctrine, similar to Universalism of to-day. Yet when the storms raged about Paul's ship, he never thought of steam and screw propellers for safety, but fell to praying. His ship got considerably broken up, but finally outweathered the gale, as thousands have done, filled with none but cursing seamen. Yet he claimed the victory through the efficacy of prayer. However, his prayer at least failed to soften the heart or stay the cruelty of the tyrant Nero, who put an end to his useful life. In his zeal as a Jew he calmly witnessed Stephen's murder, and then suffered the death of a martyr for the same cause Stephen defended. Then Constantine evolved from a heathen into a sort of Christian, gave birth to the cruel old Roman Catholic church, which has ever since claimed that the common people have no right sense enough to read aright the Bible, without the select, specially called priest of God.

When these priests became so wonderfully endowed by God that they had the right to sell indulgences and pardons, the honest old Dutch Luther arose in disgust from among the laity and defied the Pope, established the "Brotherhood" or United Brethren, and gave an immense impetus to populist education. Its seeds permeated all Europe, and reaching the astute, proud, zealous Frenchman, Calvin, evolved still another branch, the great limb in the tree of ecclesiastical evolution, Presbyterianism. Calvin took a very short step in evolution. Through his egotism he defied the Pope, yet to appease his fiery zeal and blind faith he calmly burned the great and good Servetus, to his own eternal shame. Since his time the limb has budded and branched so often under lesser lights that it is hard to tell where that strict old Sabbatarian Presbyterianism may not spread to. Alexander Campbell, not fully satisfied with a mere sprinkle as sufficient to constitute a scriptural burial, left Presbyterianism and hybridized with the Baptists, who went clear under backwards, and were surely buried. But their total depravity began to crop out, and he could exactly feel that he was totally depraved, for if he was then there was no salvation at all, as a thing totally rotten or lost, cannot be restored. So the results of the hybridity in this good and great scholar, was to abandon all written creeds but the Bible. They (his followers) however, have his well memorized creed, or views of scripture, in their minds, all the same. It is remarkable in this "Christian church" as to the great number of infidels it is turning out—a good sign of rapid advancement. With the Ingersolls, Presbyterianism did not have to go so far as to hybridize to make an infidel. She turned Bob out beautifully by quite an unusual sport, just as the great Golden Pocklington grapes came at a bound from a single seed of the Black Concord. So John Wesley, on hearing the reading of a single passage on conversion from Luther's writings, sprung to shouting, and instead of being a Lutheran, after that he was a Methodist. Since his time there has been much method in the camp meetings and shoutings of all Methodists. Yet we have Northern and Southern Methodists, Episcopal Methodists, and scores of others. At various times many of the twigs of all the different branches have shown unmistaken infidel fruit, and to-day there seems to be a superabundant crop of these twigs all over the tree. The Liberal Leagues, not fully free from the sectarian impulse to fight somebody, have established a veritable sect called Free Thinkers. They have a creed, and already the rough bark and moss begins to appear on their backs. Their free thought is no more free than was Christ's or Paul's or Calvin's. Organized theoretic thought never can be wholly free.

So I could continue to point out the branches and twigs of this conglomerate Jewish, Gentile, Christian, Roman, Protestant and infidel religious tree, till we would be lost in a maze of leaves and babel of words. This is enough. I need not mention the much older and larger religious trees of Asia, with their tops filled with dead and dying limbs of ignorance and superstitions.

Like all other departments of nature, they all are forever dividing and sub-dividing, involving and evolving according to regular physical and mental laws. All are agreed on one thing, and that is to work for the good of humanity. Humanity is the great moral magnet destined to draw all mankind more closely together. Opposition only occurs when the wrong poles of the smaller sectarian magnets are presented to each other. Education, especially in the science of human nature, will enable us to place the right poles together. We are all brother in this great human forest. Hence I conclude, an absolute, eternal individuality is impossible. Hence in actual knowledge there can be no eternal, unchangeable personality. All individuality is transient, relative, only a part of some other. Hence an individual cannot be omnipresent. Hence God being omnipresent, cannot be an individual, and at best this term a can only be another name for the aggregate of all force, the concomitant attribute of matter, equally incomprehensible in the absolute, and irrelevant to man's welfare.

In chapter III I shall present my views of the law of necessity moral development.

T. V. MUNSON

EVOLUTION.

CHAPTER III.—SOCIETY

(Continued.)

From the Denison *Sunday Gazetteer*, December 30, 1883

Say some men of Faith and Fear: "Why, if I believed as you do, I would turn to stealing, robbing, killing, and all manner of crime, for I should have no fear of future punishment." What a dreadful compliment, the person uttering such sentiments passes unconsciously upon his own inherent tastes; upon the impulses implanted by his father and mother in his very blood corpuscles! Acknowledges himself a base thief and murderer at heart, and is only restrained by the flames of hell he sees in the distance of superstitious faith. In an issue of a few weeks ago, the Gatesville Advance, under the caption "The Infidel," said among a half column of similar false, illiberal vituperations, that "the infidel" (one who cannot believe his peculiar superstition) "is so because he wants to fit to his character a religion that will serve him." "In a greater increased portion would the wicked rejoice could all vestige of a belief in future rewards and punishments be destroyed." I quote these things as great curiosities of the nineteenth century. They would have been proper enough 500 or 1,000 years ago in the countries carrying on the Crusades, but to-day they only distort a derisive smile from every well educated person. To say such things is to call Goethe, and Humboldt, and Shakespeare, and Lyell, and Schiller, and Volney, and Voltaire and Bacon, and Renan, and Hume, and Buckle, and Huxley, and Darwin, and Tyndal, and Liebig, and Franklin, and Jefferson, and Washington and Paine, and Lincoln, and Ingersoll, and Beecher, and Newman, in fact, nearly every leading scientist, besides hundreds of the brightest and purest lights in, or once in, the churches, thieves, robbers and murderers.

Thousands of the best specimens humanity ever produced stand as solemn, grand, beautiful monuments against such false malignant charges. But this merely as a prelude to "The Law of Necessity in Moral Development." Admit change in form and position, be it ever so small at a time; and infinite time to work in, with successive changes every moment in everything, as we see it, and infinite ariation in kind and extent necessarily follows not only in material but also in the resulting phenomena, including moral attributes. All these changes necessarily take a certain course, and can have no other, ever with a creative act, if it were possible, from an outside force separate from matter and its attributes, without breaking the equilibrium of all nature and producing universal chaos; for when the equilibrium is broken at one point, adjoining parts would have to seek to adjust that disturbance, and consequently leave their present office unfilled. Thus on from atom to atom would this creative contagion run till every atom of the universe was readjusted or destroyed. So that every new creative act, if it affect anything, would be equivalent to a new creation of the whole. Let the most critical logical rules be applied here before condemning it as illogical. If there is any virtue in reason, logic, mind, brain at all, it is when its laws or regular sequences are unbroken.

A rigid cylinder on foot in diameter and one foot or more in length, in order to pass into a rigid circular hole one foot in diameter, must go in lengthwise of the cylinder's axis; or in order to occupy the most of a given space with honey or other substance in separate cells, the cells must be hexagonal. The bee first starts with an irregular, circular-like cell, and as she approaches the limits of extent each cell takes on the hexagonal form.

If a mass of leaden balls of uniform size, density and compressibility, be pressed solidly together till no spaces remain between, each ball which lay entirely within the mass, will have become a dodecahedron, which has every side and angles of that figure. So with all other forms, though we may not so readily comprehend their peculiar environment, yet we can see each visible circumstance has left its impress, and there is nothing in reason preventing the conclusion that its entire make-up likewise depends upon natural surroundings. The environment is composed of inside or subjective forces obtained during its previous existence, called "inherited properties," and outside, or objective influences. The environment itself is also constantly varying, either slowly or rapidly, so that an individual remains absolutely the same only for an infinitely short duration. "Why, then, have we a continued consciousness of our past individuality?" asks the creationist. Simply because we retain former impressions for a considerable time. The continuity is not suddenly broken. We retain our personal consciousness of the past hour far more vividly than that of a year or more ago; and in the grown-up person, the first years of infancy have been entirely obliterated past all the powers of memory to recall; and when we compare our photograph of forty with ourselves in the long shirt of driveling infancy, we have to stretch the imagination immensely to discover any resemblance. Nothing could more beautifully illustrate and demonstrate evolution than a series of photographs of ourselves taken annual from birth onward. It would also be a precious keepsake for everyone, by which fashion, association, education, would each show their evolving turns.

Then, I conclude, the law of necessity must rule. The bee must make hexagonal cells to do where work to best advantage, yet she does not always do so; valleys must lay between hills; a triangle must contain the sum of two right angles; the angles of a regular hexagon must contain sixty degrees; a circle cannot be a square at the same time; an individual must be what its environment or circumstances of existence make it. The circumstances of enterprise and economy will always lead to better financial success than indolence and wastefulness. He who puts his money into a lottery ticket, and then idly waits for a great prize, will most generally find that his neighbor, who invested the money in his own well-learned business and worked it hard, has secured immensely the largest prize. Some invest in faro, some in gilt concerts, some in marriage associations, some in mutual savings banks, some store their hard earnings in a dusty trunk in the cellar or attic for thieves and mice to gnaw, some sink their money, themselves and families in whiskey; while the industrious, frugal man of public enterprise, invests and reinvests in a business which honorably gives him subsistence and a surplus to pay into the public treasury, his share of general community expenses.

Finally, in want, the "chance man" lays hold upon the "regular sequence man" and calls him a monopolist; result: the rock-pile or "pen," where the "chance man" finds a chance sure enough to learn the rudiments of good citizenship. Pain is but a guardian angel, the pathway to pleasure.

Conscious individuality implies both pain and pleasure; the former when the individual is being destroyed, the latter when he is being built up. This pain and pleasure beget a fear of death and a love of life, an effort to avoid pain and perpetuate pleasure, in a word, to self-preservation. This is the first and deepest impulse of all-conscious beings, unless they see or feel sure they think they see inevitable and perpetual torture or grinding misery ahead so long as they may live—a long drawn, agonizing death—when the same impulse prompts to suicide. The shortest and easiest known route is then preferred. In this case, too, the weakest die and the fittest live. But in society self-preservation depends largely upon the rules of action of the community, and hence wise selfishness looks farther than to mere individual action, and the insane, would-be self-destroyer, if detected in time, is restrained, nursed and doctored till life has its attractions again, if possible, when this impulse will preserve its life as usual.

So it is with any other impulse. When it becomes distorted and destructive to society in its action, society, the whole, of which the individual is only a part, lays hold upon that part and restrains it or prunes it off altogether. But this broad kind of selfishness does not belong to all conscious life. It has come up by degrees. The eyeless oyster and stone-stemmed polyp care naught for their fellows, nor could they aid if they wished. But give them specialized touch, taste, smell, hearing and sight, with their accompanying nervous collecting and recording apparatus, the nerves and brain, and we have an individual which will not only shrink from pain and hug pleasure directly, but one which can locate the sources of pain and pleasure, can remember not to go to the one again and will seek the other oftener, so that as it senses for acquirement of knowledge enlarge, impressions multiply, and finally reach that point that when a new impression is made, some old one, quiet on the tablet of memory, is at once aroused into new action. This brings comparison of the new with the old, and the new is accordingly classified in the library of the mind for future reference, and this we call reason. But what myriads upon myriads of generations lie between the sluggish snail with its dull knobs, half seeing, half feeling the region over, only half inch ahead of it, and the eagle's piercing glance, which sweeps the horizon of many miles, and the area within, and picks his game and course with the utmost ease, and in his well-learned cycloidal swoop, can unerringly seize a falling fish let loose by his beaten slave, the fish-hawk. How still greater the long, long ages between the reason of a fly that is happy in pure, personal selfishness, caring nor seeming to perceive naught of its comrade's pains or death, though they may lie dead and dying on every hand, and the mind of a Garfield, which could be in sympathy and communion with all mankind and nature everywhere. But there is an unbroken chain all the way from the lifeless clay, once individualized, but long cycles ago laid in its silent tombs of the stratified geological, dateless, countless time through the pulsating Amœba or Eozon Canadensis all along up to a Cavier, a Newton or a Shakespeare.

Let us away with that philosophy which cries "blind instinct" to all the acts of animal life except that of man. Any individual or community of individuals of men may repeat an act so often that it will become automatic, and their progeny have a tendency to repeat that act without thinking or learning how. This may be termed instinct in its incipient form. But let it go one from generation to generation and it becomes as much an instinct as that possessed by any animal. The infant instinctively nurses as much as does the kitten or young rat.

First—The most simple form of selfishness is known by importunity. The bleating lamb, the crying babe, the sick, crippled beggar. It is too frail to labor, too devoid of cunning to steal, simple want, without ability to supply. A call for help may save it. This it can do, and of necessity it cries. The only remedy is to lovingly give it what it needs, that it may gain strength to take of itself. Among mankind, when this principle is applied in its broadest sense, it is termed philanthropy.

Second—The fox cannot openly catch birds or other needful prey; the ignorant, greedy man cannot gain subsistence by honorable competition. Lacking knowledge of and care for the rights of others, they steal, which requires slyness. They try to obtain their object, unperceived, if of a timid nature, and thus become liars. The thief is always a liar. If bold, they murder, even in broad day, but the object is the same—to secure the labor of others. It is the most universal form of selfishness, and to counteract it, almost the entire civil code is used. Although possessed by so many in some form or other, yet is universally detested. Education is its best prevention.

Third—The results of the reformation of the second form of selfishness brings us to the third, which shows favor that favor may be returned. This is the basis of all true commerce—social or financial. It knows its own rights, and in order to preserve them respects the rights of others. It sacrifices nobly in emergencies to acquire fame, or wealth, or greater social enjoyment. If purely for the latter, it is called nobleness. It never asks unless it intends to give in return. It is just to others, because it likes justice bestowed upon it. It is kind to others, for kindness makes its own heart. It is honest, for it dislikes to be cheated itself. It is truthful, for it knows how falsehood in others may blast itself. It is no tale-teller, for if its own failings were published it would have a bad character. It loves, for it is in ecstasies when beloved. Of all passions, love comes most spontaneously, most instinctively, as it began farthest back in the development of our sympathies. I speak of parental, maternal, paternal and family ties. Educate them, purify them. Let all the dross of lust be refined away into an intelligent, reasoning impulse, which will give us healthier, handsomer, brighter, more loveable children, and thus reclaim the Garden of Eden and make a heaven of home.

Seeing that useful knowledge, the temperate use of all our faculties, the diligent employment of our time in securing an honorable competence, the respect for the feelings and rights of others, the observance of personal cleanliness and order, lead to health, competence, peace, long life and honor in the minds of others; but that, on the other hand, ignorance, intemperance, fraud, indolence and disrespect of others leads to disease, poverty, disgrace and premature death; we observe the former and increase, or the latter and perish.

THE TIES OF HUMAN BROTHERHOOD

A paragraph most pregnant with suggestion as to the industrial progress of this world since the opening of this century is the following, from the New York Tribune: "How science has multiplied the ties of human brotherhood! A sharp word spoken by a statesman in Europe, indicating the possibility of a war between France and China, comes under the sea by wire and lifts the price of wheat in Chicago a cent a bushel. If American farmers could get all the advance, the word spoken in Paris would be worth $4,000,000 to them. And some dignitary with a long queue, away on the other side of the globe under feet, may take a step any day that shall affect all the industries of this nation." What a wonderful extension of environment is space has there been within the memory of people now living! The former independence of each other that characterized nations is giving way to an interdependence that will in time acquire a permanency that cannot be ruptured without great injury to them. As Herbert Spencer has so well shown, the growth of this will in time make war prohibited in the custom of all civilized nations.

If in any of these writings I have wounded a feeling anywhere, it was unintentional, and ask all who may have felt that I was desirous of forcing my opinion upon anyone, or wished others to abandon theirs, only in case they should find for themselves others which made them better and happier, to take this as a testimonial that no such intention was entertained.

Thanking you, Mr. Editor, for your patient indulgence, and you, my readers, for the respect you have shown in wading through these long papers. I bid you a Happy New Year and long rest from religious discussions. Respectfully,

T. V. MUNSON

"WHAT IS GOD?"—A NAME, NOTHING MORE.

From *The Independent Pulpit*, October 1884

Written for the Independent Pulpit

Friend Geo. D. Powell:

Your thoughts on "What is God!" in INDEPENDENT PULPIT No. 7, so well correspond with my own that I wish to congratulate you upon the solution of the problem, which, when once done, seems so simple. The issue of personality is illogical in its very essence. To have personality implies *individuality*, and individuality implies a part of the whole, hence we would have an *omnipresent part!* Absurd. Still further, the old theory required a head to all evil—the Devil. But before anything else, God was. Then logically, for there to be a Devil, he must somehow come out of God. But the Devil is *totally depraved*, as God is absolutely pure and good. Hence, total depravity came out of total purity! Another absurdity. So that, to a logical, thinking, honest mind, be it in or out of "church," the personal God must be abandoned, just as it was in the writer's case after being a zealous Christian for many years. What then? Simply, *"there is no God"* (I can stand it to be called a fool), as claimed in the Bible. But there is *force*—not a force as an independent entity—everywhere in connection with matter—not separate or independent of it—differentiated in keeping and harmony with matter. Absolutely, the ultimate nature or essence, both of matter and its ultimate force, has not been discovered, and we are warranted in the conclusion, never will be, as it is infinite, while brain and observation are finite. But we know the essence of both, *in part*, and as our power to acquire knowledge grows, we learn more and more of the essence or properties of both. For instance, once some men thought a certain kind of stone could be found which would convert everything it touched into gold. On the contrary, it has been found that the amount of gold, either simple or in combination, remains absolutely the same forever. That it can neither be made or destroyed absolutely. Also the "thunderbolt of God" has been found to be a peculiar form of force, made active, and at times apparent to the eye, by putting matter, or rather, bodies or collections of certain forms of matter, into motion while surrounded by other forms of matter, through which the force or motion was not easily transmitted. By still further investigation, it has been found that what we see or feel is not an entity at all—only a *motion*. That light, heat, electricity, life, are only modes of motion whose wave lengths have in many cases been measured. That this motion goes back to matter for its source. So here we are at the fountain of all, the great, mysterious, infinite—*matter*. In the absolute, either in essence, or extent of time or space, *incomprehensible*, but in *part*, as the knower is part, *known*. Then I am a *gnostic, in what be known*, and *an agnostic in the unknown*. Neither one nor the other altogether. "How can matter know?" Not discovered. We see; it does. We could as well ask "how can matter thunder or vibrate?" Here we must be content to remain, but we can be happy in knowing we are a part. We change with its interchanges, but in the whole it is one and the same, mysterious, incomprehensible, eternal, infinite, knowing nothing, caring for noting, hearing and answering no prayers, beside it there is nothing to know or care for. Knowing is an attribute of an individual, as knowledge comes by comparison, and to compare there must be other individuals in the field of observation, finite with the finite observation. There can be but one infinite, and must be an infinite number finites to make it. We may call the whole, God, or Universe, or Infinite Matter, or Spirit, it matters not. They all are simply expressions to indicate the great unknown whole, whose existence simply we feel sure of because we know some of the parts. But for the sake of clearness, let God be retained to apply to those fancies of the superstitions of old, which were always possessed of personality and consequently individually, thought truly only human fancies. Then we are not to live for Gods, but for men and women, to make them as noble and happy as possible, and this is best accomplished by beginning with one' self. The greatest—God as well as man—is he who thinks, and acts and feels the best.

T. V. MUNSON

SPIRITUALISTIC RELIGION.

From *The Independent Pulpit*, November 1884

Written for the Independent Pulpit

In No. 7 of the INDEPENDENT PULPIT, your correspondent, "T. Y. K.," tries to mix up Liberalism and Spiritualism, and asserts, "we will give you a religion founded on reason and experiment, that will remove all your doubts and fears." Now, this is just the person I long have wanted to see. Let him go forth like a true scientist, and substantiate his assertions by experiment and demonstration, just as Lyell did in geology, demonstrating that the earth is millions of years old, instead of about 6000, according to "Revelation," just as Darwin demonstrated that change, ever so small, and infinite time to work in, gives infinite development, and thus demonstrates evolution—now acknowledged by all familiar with the facts of science; just as Prof. Marsh, in his enormous museum, has demonstrated by actual samples in many species and genera, that evolution is true, especially noticeable in the genus of the horse, where, with skeletons of extinct and living specimens, he clearly proves to every one who can see bones, that the ancient horses had three toes, two of which gradually became shorter and shorter, through countless ages and generations, till now all there is left of the two side toes is the horny button on the inside of the leg. What else than evolution can account reasonably for that button? Just as the laws of falling bodies were demonstrated by Newton and Kepler, including the revolution of the earth around the sun, in opposition to the former *belief* that the earth was flat and stood still; just as every great truth of science has been demonstrated, and can be demonstrated again and again by any one who will take the time and means always at hand, not confined to the "ifs" and "ands" and dark conditions of ignorant mediums. "T. Y. K." can immortalize himself or herself (as the case may be) by giving to the world such demonstrations. I am a being with a "spirit" just as much as "T. Y. K." or any "medium," and according to logical reasoning, possess all spiritual attributes a well as they, and should as readily have the power to make spiritual experiments and see spiritual demonstration as they. Christianity, which "T. Y. K." condemns, is the grandest and most utilitarian form of spiritualism ever promulgated. So, when "T. Y. K." *demonstrates* Spiritualism, and teaches the scientific principles of it, so every other being possessed of a "spirit" can understand them and demonstrate Spiritualism for himself, then will he stand along with Humboldt, Goethe, Haeckel, Spencer and Draper as an acknowledged, true scientist, and a benefactor to his race, and then can all become intelligent Christians.

I write this with no desire to get into a war of words, as my works in the practical development of my chosen calling—horticulture—will permit me only to make this criticism of our "Liberal" papers. Most of them admit into their columns a lot of Spiritualistic twaddle, without challenging the truth of the vague assertions, thus giving a quasi endorsement to modern Spiritualism, while at the same time they furiously assail a more ancient and grander Spiritualism by far. It takes no prophetic genius to foretell that the ancient Spiritualism, so palpably crumbling to pieces on every hand before our very eyes, with its corrosions of hydra-headed sectarianism, doubly segmented by the acute, penetrating acids of scientific experiment and demonstration, that the "death rattle" is already in its throat, its huge chest now and then spasmodically heaves to secure a fresh breath—*a revised translation*, or some other means to relieve it from its horrible nightmare of death. Evolution sternly and severely says: "Of ignorance you were born, served well the purposes of ignorance, but ignorance itself must die, and its child, superstition, cannot survive. But life and love and joy remain to be still further developed by observing the laws *intelligent selection,* not trusting blindly to the superstitious cure or blessing, in answer to a raving prayer or the slow and wandering choice of "natural selection." Let this dastard hybrid, modern "Spiritualism," either give genuine scientific demonstration, or die the death of error.

T. V. MUNSON

Denison, Texas

AN INTERESTING CORRESPONDENCE.

From *The Independent Pulpit*, May 1886

Mr. T. V. Munson—Dear Sir:

I wonder whether you have ever thought since of that bright Monday morning chat we had, for it has been a source of much pleasure to me to think what a blessing I received, being justified by faith.

Romans 3-28, 5 1. I. Corinthians, 6-11.

But on the other hand my joy was hushed when I heard you say what you did. To think that a man in the Nineteenth century of Christianity should deny that Christ was the Son of God!

Don't persuade yourself to believe that any longer. Stop short; go back to where you were when you were that young man and get your faith, for without faith we can do nothing.

You will agree with me that the mind has power over the material, or that success, for which we all labor, is from the mind, from which arises every thought and action that is carried on by the physical being.

Well, now, sometimes in our aimings we forget the physical and it is overcome with evil.

Now, you are a man with a good deal of energy, and, perhaps, neglect yourself in your pursuits of business, and some day it will happen thus to you. If it ever happens thus you will think of this letter, and read Matt. 12-37; to see where you stand in the sight of God.

I wish I could tell you of what a glorious hope of Heaven I have, but it is a pleasure in which the mind revels that cannot be explained.

Mr. Munson, make one more effort to gain that heaven not made with hands, and enjoy this life and the one to come. Hoping to hear from you, that I may assist you in return for many favors. I remain yours,

Very respectfully,
G. E. H—*

* *
*

Mr. G. E. H—:

DEAR SIR: —Yours of 26th is received. I am glad to hear you are contently at home again, and unspeakably happy in your faith and hope. I have not the slightest desire to disturb your felicity. No, I had not forgotten you. Had frequently thought of your queer appeals for a situation, "for Christ's sake." When I remember how Christ taught to "take no heed for the morrow, what ye shall drink, or wherewithal ye shall be clothed," who so rigidly taught to despise earthly goods, and to leave all and follow him, to keep apart from unbelievers, your appeal to an unbeliever to give you a situation to make money struck me quite forcibly, and amused me not a little.

But I do not sneer; I believe you to be an excellent young man, who has yet to learn much concerning thought and the right of individual opinion. I once was very much in your position. I know I have been unflinchingly honest as to my convictions, but have not shut my eyes to fact.

Now, I may something that will shock you, yet I tell the plain simple truth. Christ was a young, enthusiastic man when he died—only 33. He had acquired but little accurate knowledge and traveled but little, and that in a very ignorant and superstitious country. From all we can learn of him he was naturally of an enquiring turn, very empathetic and sympathetic, but withal a *man*, and one who taught many impractical things— things which the world, nor small congregations, even individuals have never and can never perform. He taught that if faith were as a grain of mustard-seed one could remove mountains, could have anything desired if only asked for in faith. I for many of my best years tested the utter falsity of this doctrine. I know I had faith if any person ever had; I asked no unreasonable things. I asked them in the still quiet of night in my chamber—if there is any virtue in quietness and darkness. I asked in the depths of nature's forests—"God's first temple." I repeated and implored, but never was there any reply save the mocking echo of my own voice—"Oh, God, my dear Father! for the sake of Jesus, Thy Son, who died for me, please do this for me. Thy humble child, that I may increase in faith and good works."

I was careful to ask not foolishly for unnecessary of unnatural things, nothing like moving mountains. Ten years of my most robust manhood, daily spent testing this declaration of Christ, and observing all Christendom doing the same with no other effect than the waste of time and utter destruction of faith in Christ and his promises, all the time being under the teachings of the ablest "light" in the church. I became an Infidel. Who is to blame? "The Devil," you say. Well, in all my life I never have had the satisfaction of seeing the gentleman. If he can so easily and completely thwart the purposes of God, it is about time for God to resign—that shocks you I know; but I can't help it. It is a just judgment—if God is insufficient let him stand aside.

The proposition that God, an all-wise, omniscient, perfectly pure and loving being, who, before the universe of matter was, or even angels, brought forth from himself everything and called it good, brought along with that creation the devil and hell, absolute depravity, we have the logical absurdity of absolute depravity coming from absolute purity. God had much better remained quiet and never created anything, then all this pain, misery, unbelief, devils and hells would never have existed. No one is to blame for it but God. It is impossible for me ever to believe again such nonsensical nonsense. Neither do I wish to disturb those who do.

"Where ignorance is bliss, 'tis folly to be wise.' I have now, however, general conclusions as to the existence and action of nature, which please me far better than my former views.

Doubtless, I have erroneous views of some things, unquestionably; but nothing save the acquirement of more facts will eliminate these—not Christ. I am older, considerably than was Christ, have traveled more, studied all these problems more, read more, discovered more than did Christ; know much more of the earth, of mankind—he knew nothing of married life, of railroads, or railroad strikers, of steam, electricity, the sciences, or astronomy—and hence with common sense and observation ought to be better able than he to judge of these things, without putting it on a boasting or egotistical basis at all, as Christians are likely to charge, and long with it, also, blasphemy, that terrible word. Well, let me tell you my young friend, when you have passed as much experience in life as I have, been as near death, and God, and the devil, and hell and heaven as I, then neither will hell, death nor the grave scare you much. Yes, I may think of you better when death comes, and I may not; that will depend upon circumstances. One thing sure: it will not scare me much. You will have to make a different appeal from that to make me faithful. Show me God, and the devil, Christ at God's right hand in heaven 1500 furlongs square; the devil and all his angels in hell, writhing and gnashing their teeth. Pray God to do this in a letter to me, or any other reasonable way, and have your prayer answered, and you will save a true, noble soul from hell. I want no foolishness. I mean business, and here is a chance for you to demonstrate according to the promise of Christ.

But you will never do it. God cannot do it. None of things will I ever see, only in imagination.

I do hope you will always remain an upright man, drop your old opinions when you acquire facts which give you foundation for better ones. Seek to discover truth wherever it may be found, which will increase the happiness of your fellow-beings. I enjoy a very large acquaintance of excellent, educated, progressive men in all parts of the United States. Among them I find a large element who have arrived at the same general standpoint with myself, but like their faces their opinions differ; yet they enjoy each other all the more for that, knowing it to be a law of nature that no two things are ever exactly alike.

I shall be pleased to see you stand some day prominently before your countrymen in horticulture—the pursuit you have chosen. It is a noble one, if intelligently and liberally followed. But let me caution you against one thing. Do not allow your mind to dwell too long upon one subject, religion, especially, as it tends to insanity.

The great future has nothing in it for the honest, useful man to fear. He has used all his powers to the best of his ability in the bounds of temperance, and that breeds no fear here nor hereafter. No one is responsible to another for coming into life, neither in going out. If there is a heaven in the future for us, none will enjoy it better than I, or be happier to shake hands with you, and all good men there. Of one thing I feel sure, if of anything of which I know nothing, there will be no eternal hell, as such is inimical to eternal goodness.

With best wishes for your health and prosperity, I trust you will not allow this letter to trouble you now, or when you come to die. Be a man and think, rather than be scared to death by faith.

Sincerely,
T. V. MUNSON.

---

*This is only an extract from a letter which was not written for publication.

A BROADER PHILOSOPHY NECESSARY.

NOMINAL LIBERALS NOT TRULY LIBERAL—THE BIBLE AND ALL RELIGIONS THE RESULT OF EVOLUTION, AND GOOD IN THEIR AGE AND PLACE, BUT EVIL OTHERWISE.

From *The Independent Pulpit*, July 1886

Written for The Independent Pulpit

If we accept the theory of Evolution, with its reverse side, Involution, which, by thinkers general of every school, is now admitted to be demonstrated, we are then bound by that principle to regard everything in existence as the legitimate fruit of Evolution.

Then, instead of deriding and condemning the Bible, the Koran, the Vedas, and all the devotees of superstition, we must look upon them as in some way the legitimate necessary products of Evolution.

They are but the stepping-stones of thought through past ages. Religions, all, are the theories of the thinkers of the times in which they originated. By these theories they explained to the satisfaction of their own minds, the phenomena observed by them, but which phenomena, for want of sufficient facts, and properly developed observing powers and investigating appliances, were wrongly interpreted.

We should not sneer at these theories, creed and Bibles, but collect them, study them, compare and classify them, just as the naturalist collects and classifies fossils in order to discover the path of Evolution through the past. These fossils are the hulls or skeletons of a once, happy, active life. The Bibles are the hulls of ancient thought. Every mind *must* drop its old hull when it becomes too narrow, and clothe itself with a better one. This is why there are so many creeds, sects and theories. It will always be thus, for always, so long as thinking beings exist, there will be different degrees of ability, knowledge, different environments, and hence, difference in thought.

We are trying to force all minds to wear the same garment, to adopt the same theory of the universe, of God, of existence. It cannot be done. Even the different advocates of that broadest of all theories, Evolution, have different interpretations of it. We are only followers of the persecuting orthodox mind when we charge the superstitionists with all the evils of those old theories. Creeds and sects are but the result of minds seeking light. A wearied brain after a long flight of theory, must have rest or become insane, to avoid which, it constructs a creed out of the best material of the theory, and gets followers, according to the age and people in which it is promulgated.

The happiest and most fortunate of all theories yet, is that of Evolution, for it is as broad and plastic as the universe itself, and allows every mind to make its own interpretation.

We Liberals are yet too narrow-minded. We form a code of rules, and want to make it our confession of faith. The old Creedalists did the same to the best of their ability. But we ought, by this time, to be able to reach the broad conclusion that creeds and sects are only gradations on the scale of rising thought. But thought stops not at any of them, only as a resting spot, and then pursues its ever onward flight.

The Creedalists and we, are *not enemies*, as we try to make ourselves believe, for we all are laboring for one grand object— the amelioration, individually and collectively, of the human race, yes, more, of all conscious life, though some has to be weeded out that other more befitting us may grow. We disagree only in the method, the theory. Then let us be friends in deed and word. I include all, honestly inclined. Let us reason together in harmony, holding to those propositions as established truth, when we—anybody—can *demonstrate* again and again with known facts, and with mutual consent, relegate all else to the field of investigation, in which we all can happily compete for the discovery of truth, seeing we are inevitably forced to this at last, whenever we make an advance.

In this spirit we call upon the Spiritualist, either modern or ancient, who is such through faith in a creed, or theory, to *demonstrate* beyond a shadow of a doubt, the propositions of his theories. The labor of demonstration falls upon the author of every proposition to first give his proofs before asking its admission as a truth. Then it becomes the duty of those who are asked to accept it, to also demonstrate their objections to receiving it, if they have any. If all agree in the conclusion, that facts brought from both positive and negative sides, all go to proving the proposition, then it necessarily stands as a truth, and can be safely used as such in helping to solve other problems. We also just as rigidly, call upon the Materialist as the Transcendentalist, to demonstrate all this propositions with undeniable fact.

What a vast amount of theorizing we all do to make up for our lack of facts. On every subject, in every direction, the facts are infinite, presenting grand fields for investigation, in which there is a heaven of pure delight and oceans of progress, yet we stand idle at the street corners of time, wrangling with each other, using the same empty words and sophistries—sounding brass and tinkling cymbals—which ever have made such a din and babble throughout the world. The hull of disputation and suspicious insinuation is the last that the mind sheds before it puts on the spotless robe of *friendly investigation* and appears as a true philosopher.

Here and there we discover a Newton, a Franklin, a Kepler, a Darwin, a Humboldt, quietly working away his life, searching every nook and corner with his keen eyes, microscopes, telescopes, spectroscopes, thermometers, electrometers, reagents and every other conceivable device to unlock the hidden vaults of fact, and roll forth the illimitable wealth of great truths, thus blessing their race for ages to come, while the wrangles, like stickers, live and die paupers on the corners of a universe of infinite wealth.

By facts alone, the world advances, and reaches broader, more friendly conclusions. Then let us all do more careful investigation after, and recording of pure facts. Though we, ourselves, may never live to build them into a beautiful structure of truth, yet others may. Without the volumes of Brahe's facts, which he was unable to use himself, Kepler could never formulated the laws of planetary motions. A grand truth often lies dormant for want of a single fact, which alone can complete the chain by which it is suspended.

The investigator has a right to demand any conditions he sees the case requires, to get at facts, the "Spirits" and "mediums" to the contrary, notwithstanding. Whenever a theorizer tells you that you must not investigate, only according to *his own conditions*, it is sufficient warning to regard such a one as a mere trickster, or a dupe of tricksters, fearful lest his tricks may be discovered, or the "Spirits" offended, and his occupation—as juggler, prophet, medium, priest, or shallow quack scientist—be gone. The true investigator pursues fact, as a bloodhound pursues his victim, till he seizes it, holds it fast, and shows it to all the world, without a fear of contradiction, save by the quacks. He soon learns to distinguish the quack from a brother investigator, by the ear-marks, and passes him by, knowing it to be folly to spend time upon him in argument, for disputation is his sole stock in trade, and its chief delight, whether he proves a point or not.

The true searcher meets all other searchers as brothers, no matter how widely they may differ in their theories, knowing well there is no conflict in truth itself.

Let every lover of truth set to work at once on some line of investigation useful at once to himself and others, and his report of facts will be far more eagerly sought by true thinkers than all the jargon of theories and disputations he can ever invent.

But words are cheap, intricate syllogisms, make a dazzling show of literary attainments. The logical juggler secures the applause of the rabble. Brilliancy is mistaken for solidity, and a great reputation among the ignorant is secured, and this gives the demagogue a fat living.

The true philosopher is no partisan. He is content to live quietly, but industriously seeks useful facts. He builds for others to enjoy. The consciousness that he is increasing the sum of material prosperity of his race, whether he received praise or not, satisfies his humble ambition. He, like Paine, may die with the curse of priests upon him, and the eyes of an ignorant world jeering at him. It makes no difference to him. He has loved nature, he is her child, he falls contentedly to sleep in her bosom. He knows that the dark cloud of ignorant eyes that glared upon him will clear away and the sun of truth above them, on which he has ever had his eye, will enlighten them or their progeny after awhile. The quacks may make their leagues to frustrate the truth, but he knows that when it is once discovered, it shines on forever. The quacks and leagues perish, but the true philosopher lives through all ages in his discoveries. He co-operates with the truly good everywhere, to better the condition of life, but joins no leagues for party aggrandizement. The false juggler (an honest juggler gives good amusement), the quack, the striker, the demagogue, the pool-makers, the corner-manipulators, are his, and the races true enemy. Education enables us to discover these. Hence, the true philanthropist is a broad, liberal educator in genuine fact and truth. "Humanity is my church; to good my religion."

T. V. MUNSON

A HIGHER PHILOSOPHY NECESSARY.

NO. II

From *The Independent Pulpit*, August 1886

Written for The Independent Pulpit

In my first article on this subject, I merely desired to show that in matters of moral philosophy, the whole world is striving for the betterment of the race, and hence should be friendly in all honest attempts to better our philosophy. I also attempted to show that if the claims for inspiration and revelation through specially chosen "vessels of God" failed to satisfy the investigation of reason and the conclusions of sound logic, and that if we accept the theory of Evolution as the best yet proposed to explain the variations, revelations and developments in nature, we must necessarily admit that all religions, whether superstitions or not, are also natural products, though in principle they be false. Hence, if natural, we have become sectarian and dogmatic, whenever we condemn as wicked those who *honestly* practice and advocate such religions.

No Evolutionist can consistently condemn the intent, as wicked or evil in another, for any honest advocacy or practice, no matter what it is. Hence the Evolutionist, as such, antagonizes no individual action in his philosophy. As an individual, he may resist aggression against his person, and this he does instinctively as the "first law of nature." He does, however, antagonize in teaching, though as a friend, if his opponent is honest, every principle of which is not supported by incontestable evidence. By this I mean that the teacher should speak for all, while the individual acts for self. The teacher then, should lose his individuality—his own theories—in pure fact. According to this, we should give every teaching heed, accordingly as we find the teacher is cognizant of the facts in the case. That he clearly and impartially proves every proposition which he lays down as an additional premise from which to reason. To do this we must be well versed in facts ourselves, even better than the teacher, if possible, so that we may judge whether he is promulgating true or false propositions. Then why have teachers at all, (you may ask), if we must be even wiser than they to guard against accepting erroneous doctrines? I reply, to guard our children from receiving and practicing evil principles till habits are formed which they may reject with pain and unhappiness in after life when their reason matures. Each individual will finally entertain his own particular views in the end, if he reasons at all.

Now, if you have caught my idea, it is this: The mind or brain, in childhood, is mostly receptive. It does not stop to prove whether you have told it the truth or not, but simply accepts your statements as so much true mind-food. Accordingly as such statements are true or false, not in intention on the part of the teacher, but in reality, so will the future use of those acceptances by the pupil lead him to beneficent or injurious practices to himself and his fellow beings.;

Then what a momentous question to the parents becomes the matter of a teacher for their children.

I then come to the general conclusion that we need the most complete scholars, especially in practical matters, for our small children. Teachers who have a talent for illustrating in a correct, systematic and natural order, and the ability to combine known facts into legitimate, logical propositions. Teachers who avoid theorizing but encourage it in their pupils, only to prune off their excrescences in every product of reason. It is the pupil who should do the theorizing before the teacher, that he may justly criticise it; not the teacher who should be continually promulgating theoretical dogmas he cannot himself prove. So the public lecturer should appear before the audience as on trial to prove whether he is fit for a teacher or not. This is the natural tendency. Follow it. It will lead us on rapidly toward self-government, the most complete and nearest perfect of all rulings, when the masses are truly enlightened, or the most anarchical and destructive when ignorance prevails. A good test of the advancement of any community or people is seen in the relative support and attentions bestowed upon the ranting demagogue and the unassuming, modest, yet thoroughly demonstrative and profound lecturer.

A people may correctly or incorrectly claim great enlightenment just in proportion as it denominates simple, demonstrable, accepted facts, or faith, dogma, creed, prophecy, divine revelation and crude theory, as knowledge.

The world at large judges the knowledge as true or false, according to the results of its practice. Nature also points out by "the survival of the fittest," those who have practiced most properly those principles known to be based upon substantial fact. We see poverty, crime and misery come chiefly through the attempt to practice indemonstrable dogma. We see, too, the successful mechanic, farmer, merchant, physician rise, surely, steadily, above the dogmatists around him—like a giant oak among a forest of weeds and scrubby bushes—simply by implicit obedience to the dictates of clear-cut facts. Of course the purslane and rag-weeds which at first would rush over everything else with their dogmatic assumption of more space than rightly belongs to them, fret, growl and threaten the monopolizing oak, only to wither and die unnoticed beneath the shades of the monarch. They should either have been given by nature and education the facts, impulses and aspirations of the oak with ifs firmness, endurance and persistence, that they might grow up together as brother oaks, or else, the wisdom which begets contentment in filling the humbler and only sphere their natures could occupy.

Having now indicated rather ramblingly the outlines of a natural philosophy, I shall in my next, take up in more detail, "The Development of Moral Character."

I most respectfully invite friendly criticism, not matter from what school of philosophy, of my treatment of this subject—a subject which has ever been the most difficult, and paramount to all others in the human mind.

In the search for truth all mankind should be friendly. We grant that all who disagree with us are honest until proven otherwise. Do the same with us, and *demonstrate* to be such, what you may take in us to be *error*, and you shall have our most grateful thanks, and be made happy in seeing us abandon the error when clearly shown.

T. V. MUNSON.

Denison, Texas.

A HIGHER PHILOSOPHY DEMANDED.

NO. III

From *The Independent Pulpit*, September 1886

Written for The Independent Pulpit

Say some persons of faith and fear: "Why, if I believed as you do, I would turn to stealing, robbing, killing and all manner of crime, for I should have no fears of future punishment." What a dreadful compliment to one's one inherent tastes; upon the impulses implanted by his father and mother through all his tender years and even in his very blood-corpuscles! Acknowledges himself a base thief and murderer at heart, a sneaking coward only restrained by the flames of hell, he sees in the distance of superstitious faith! In this he gives vent to the still smoldering instinct implanted in his nature in the long past ages of barbarous and brutish life, when his progenitors prowled naked and fierce in the jungles of the Tertian ago, when death and rapine lurked on every hand in the fangs of the serpent, hyæna, and cannibal, painted red in the blood of the timid vegetarian. Resistance or flight alone could save, except, perchance, by fainting with a wish, a prayer for escape, the danger accidentally pass, thus evolving faith and worship.

But upon second thought, and observing the pure and beneficent lives of such mean as Goethe, Humboldt, Lyell, Draper, Volney, Renan, Hume, Buckle, Huxley, Darwin, Haeckel, Spencer, Tyndal, Liebig, Franklin, Paine, Washington, Jefferson, Lincoln, Downing, and thousands more in every noble pursuit of life, their better sense—the product of the reasoning experiences of later ages—dictate to them that when they by choice lay off their old hulls of faith, that they will succeed far getter and be immensely more happy in the p4ractice of the purest and most friendly morality, which makes them regard all men as brothers, and hence he desires all to have like aspirations with himself, so that the universal co-operation can the more thoroughly discover and open to all the laws of nature which lead to greater human happiness. He now does not say that the great Infidels named above are in hell. But if they are, and he is perfectly sure of it, he wants to go there too, for such associates will make the most perfect imaginable heaven. This merely as a prelude to the graver discussion of

THE LAW OF NECESSITY IN MORAL DEVELOPMENT.

Admit change in form and position, be it ever so small at a time, and infinite time to work in, with successive changes every moment in everything, as we certainly see, and infinite variation in kind and extent necessarily follows. As each change is made known to us through phenomena, or resultant effects upon us produced by the changes, we include moral attributes as natural phenomena attending the correlative actions of reasoning, pain and pleasure-feeling beings, and hence can just as consistently apply the development theory to moral character, as to the physical beings possessing it.

All changes necessarily take certain directions according to the materials and forces engaged in the change. Not even a creative act, if possible, from an outside, separate force from matter, can change the natural direction and form of existing things, even in the smallest part, without breaking the equilibrium of all nature, and thus producing universal chaos, for when the equilibrium is broken at one point, adjoining parts would have to be re-adjust the disturbance and consequently leave their present office unfilled, a vacuum absolutely, or else have it taken by adjoining atoms. Thus on, from atom to atom, would this creative shock run until the entire universe were re-adjusted, practically recreated or destroyed. As a new part could not occupy space already filled, to add a new creation anywhere would equivalent to swelling the whole. To blot out absolutely one part would shrink the whole. Hence to admit creation or destruction, absolutely, is to either swell or shrink infinity—a logical absurdity. The universe must then in time and place, eternally remain constant in its occupying capacity. But its parts, to the best of our knowledge, are all moving, changing and interchanging, adding to and taking from another equivalent, yet in absolute essence, extent, and existence the same—eternal, infinite.

To illustrate the law of necessity, take a rigid cylinder of any dimension, and it can only be passed into a rigid circle having the same diameter, lengthwise of the axis of the cylinder. To occupy the most of a given space with honey or other liquid in separate cells, the cells *must* be hexagonal. The bee starts with an irregular circle-like cell, and as she approaches the limits of extent, each cell takes on the hexagonal form.

If a mass of comprehensible spheres of uniform size and compressibility be pressed solidly together till no space remain in the mass unoccupied by the volume of the spheres, it will be found that each sphere which lay entirely within the mass, has become a dodecahedron. So with all other forms, though we may not so readily comprehend their environments, yet we can see each visible circumstance has left its impress, from which we conclude, according to the strictest inductive logic, that its entire make-up, likewise depends upon natural surroundings. But the immediate surroundings are constantly varying, either slowly or rapidly, so that an individual remains in everything absolutely the same only for an infinitely short time. "Why then, have we a continuous consciousness of our past individuality?" I may be asked by the creationists. Simply because we retain former impressions of knowledge in the sensory organs, in some yet undiscovered way. But those impressions are being constantly dimmed and modified by new impressions. The continuity is rarely suddenly broken, though sometimes, as where parts of the brain have been removed, all memory or consciousness of former impressions destroyed on particular kinds of knowledge, or in the whole, and life, as it were, begun anew.

We retain our personal consciousness of the past hour, far more vividly than that of a year or more ago. In the grown up person, the first years of infancy have been obliterated past all the powers of memory to recall. When we compare our photograph of forty with ourselves in the long dress of driveling infancy, we have to stretch the imagination immensely to fancy any resemblance at all. Nothing could more interesting demonstrate evolution than a series of photographs of our great-grand parent, from infancy onward annually, and on down through every generation in direct line to ourselves, in which series we would have both individual and family, or race development clearly portrayed. Such a series would be a great treasure as a keepsake and a teacher, showing us how fashion, association, education, each in its evolving turn has left its impress, and our present self is the result of a mighty long chain of impressions.

Thus, I conclude that the law of necessity must rule. The bee *must* make hexagonal cells to do her work to best advantage, yet she does not always do so. Valleys must lay between hills. A triangle must contain the sum of two right angles. Every angle of a regular hexagon must contain sixty degrees. A circle cannot be a square at the same time. An individual must be what is environments make it.

"Then why all this argument and haranguing at the people," you ask. I reply, that too, is a regular sequence of perceptions, experience, taste, I simply cannot help it. Self-preservation and pleasure lie at the bottom. I have eyes—through what long process of development I cannot explain fully—with which I see a danger, something approaching which will cause me pain if not averted, hence, I move out of the way. I see something else passing which will help me along more easily and happily. I seize it. One of these—the greatest of all happifiers of social beings—is to make others happy. I think over what has most aided me in getting a pure happiness with the least dregs. I enthusiastically tell it to others. To *all* who hear it, it will not give happiness. But they will receive an impression from it, which, united with other materials for judgement, brings them to a slightly different conclusion than they would have reached without it. If I am a deep philosopher and recognize the working of other minds than my own, I make my proposition broad enough to reach and embrace the workings of all minds which I see produce beneficial results to the race at large, hence I seek in my philosophy to gain the esteem and friendship of all such, though in many points we differ.

But there are others whose doctrines I see lead only to utter misery and destruction, with all my associates. Then direct opposition, antagonism, repulsion, as between the wrongly mated poles of a battery, ensue. No compromise, either absolute conversion to a new state by the destruction of the former profession—a veritable slave as one who confesses faith in that which is utterly incomprehensible to him; or the destruction of the individual himself who professes, as were the heretics served in the church at one time, or else by a cold unmingling behavior towards one's enemies as though they never existed.

The philosopher, as such, does not antagonize with material force. He simply lays down the broadest laws of which his mind can comprehend, well knowing that knowledge ever increases, mind expands, and the nearer correct any philosophy is in the absolute, the longer it will stand, and the greater the number of thinking beings will be ranged under it in friendship.

Seeing that useful knowledge, the temperate use of all our faculties, the diligent employment of all our time in securing an honorable competence or recreation; the respect for the feelings of others, the observance of personal cleanliness and order, lead to health, peace, long life, and honor in the minds of others; but that filthiness, ignorance, intemperance, fraud, indolence, and disrespect to others, leads to disease, poverty, disgrace and premature death; we observe the former and increase or the latter and perish. Where a being takes the preservative course, not so much through a process of abstract reasoning as by habit or instinct, as we term it, and flourishes, or the destructive course through accident or the intervention of circumstances its instinct could not recognize, and die out, we call the process "natural selection" or "survival of the fittest.: When this is aided by a still higher mental action, abstract reasoning, so as to formulate rules of action we have the highest form of selection possible, yet none the less natural.

We need have no fears that man will recede to ignorance and barbarism, after he has once learned to see clearly in the intellectual field. A man with eyes, hardly will depart from the plain road when he has once reached it, into a thicket of brambles, in order to increase his speed, though he may have traveled through brambles the most of his life.

My next will be: "*Selfishness and the Law of Necessity Further Considered.*"

T. V. MUNSON

A HIGHER PHILOSOPHY DEMANDED.

THE DEVELOPMENT OF MORAL CHARACTER—
SELFISHNESS AND THE LAW OF NECESSITY FURTHER
CONSIDERED

NUMBER IV

From *The Independent Pulpit*, October 1886

Written for the Independent Pulpit

Pain is a guardian angel pointing the way to pleasure. Pleasure, moderately acquired, rounds out and strengthens character, but seen too often, becomes stale, and in excess, cloys and drives back to the sharpest pangs of pain. Vibrating between the two, now touching this, now that, is all of life. If the pendulum-like swing between the two is temperate, well-timed, the wear is longer and easier, and the useful work performed greater and better; but if fitful and violent, the wear and breakage is great, usefulness destroyed, and rest—death—the sooner reached. Nature seems to be ashamed of a poor, inefficient product, and soon recalls it from the field of actions through the door of involution, reconstructs it in the laboratory of development and sends it joyfully again through the gateway of evolution. Thus, on and on forever, ever renewing, ever growing old, yet in absolute existence—always the same, eternal.

Conscious individuality implies both pain and pleasure. Hence there can be no eternal heaven of ceaseless, unmixed joy, no perpetual hell with flames of wrath and smoke of pain ascending forever and ever. All must live betimes, all must die; all enjoy; all with pain familiar grow, only to live and enjoy and pain again; not as *I*, but some *other* one. Then consciousness itself moves or stands still—lives—dies—with each individual change in form.

Pain tells the individual when it is being destroyed; pleasure when it is being built up. The one begets fear of death, the other love of life, so long as the individual moves harmoniously in its sphere, or sees a prospect of doing so; so long as the individual keeps heart, feels that it can rule that circumstances of its existence, so as to receive pleasure and avoid pain, it makes every effort at self-preservation. This is the first and deepest impulse of all consciousness. But when the being reasons sufficiently to see that its circumstances inevitably lead to a perpetual, grinding torture, a long drawn death, love of life departs, and with it the fear of death, and an impulse to suicide naturally follows. But the reason alone, may be wrong or deranged, while other circumstances remain favorable to a happy life, yet the false reasoning still leads to self-destruction. So suicide may be right or wrong. However, at this point, society steps in, and says, always such deaths shocks me, does me harm, for my sake, for your family's and friends' sake, do not the deed. Let me say when the individual shall die, and enact the law for the individual, "Thou shalt not kill," "If thou dost kill another you forfeit your own life." "If you would kill yourself, I will restore you, if I can, and doctor you till your love of life returns, when you will take care of yourself even better than I, and can go free." But in all cases, when the facts are traced out, if will be found that the weakest die and the fittest live.

In society, self-preservation depends largely upon the rules of action of the community, hence wise selfishness is long-sighted; it looks to the preservation of the body politic, without which the individual would have no safeguard against the greater forces of wild beasts, disease, storms, fire, invaders, etc., save by his own puny efforts. So the individual if thoughtful, readily submits to the voice of the community in all questions where general welfare is paramount to his individual welfare, and the man *cheerfully*, if law-loving, suffers the penalty laid justly upon him; or sullenly with desperation, if he is purely, narrowly, personally selfish. But submit at lasts, he *must*, as society is greater than the individual. "The voice of the people is the voice of God." But has society no evils? Yes, many, all bound up in the word *ignorance*. How corrected? By force? by war? by strikes? by boycotts? by lock-outs? by rings? Yes, sometimes partially, but not *radically*. These only strengthen prejudice of mind, though they may destroy strength of body. It is the mind, the reason, at last that must be changed, corrected, hence the need of investigators in moral philosophy; the lecturer, the teacher, the reformer, the highest, the noblest, the most unselfish, the poorest paid but the most beneficial employment of man. In this sphere we have both the true and the false. The Sam Jones type and the Herbert Spencer. It is good to have both, that by comparison of the practice of the teachings of each we may judge which is the better for any particular community. There are some communities which only a Jones could reach, but he could land such communities or minds but a step higher. Yet a long way below where Spencer could easily reach them. The true and false is not so much in the intention of the man as in his mistakes as to the proper application of the philosophy. This brings us to the observation again that the falsity or impropriety of the old religions, the supernatural Bible theories, is in trying to hoop the mind of all time with the rigid, inelastic band of a single age. It is education in pure, simple fact, alone, which is the one universal, everlasting creed that will prepare every mind and every community to forget its own bonds or rules of best action. Hence, Jones [Samuel Porter Jones—a celebrated Methodist minister from Georgia] is a good teacher in that he imparts some useful facts, but a terrible poor one in that he utters many things not founded upon fact. Spencer [a prominent agnostic philosopher from England] and Darwin pour forth a flood of pure, beautiful facts, great truths, and withal, perhaps some errors and theories whose foundations may not have sufficient fact to make them stand as truth. The learner simply asks himself, "to which source shall I go for most facts? I care not for their theories."

In my next, "The Moral Ladder, or Ascending Scale of Selfishness, will be viewed.

T. V. MUNSON

A HIGHER PHILOSOPHY NEEDED.

THE MORAL LADDER, OR ASCENDING SCALE.

NUMBER V.

From *The Independent Pulpit*, October 1886

Written for the Independent Pulpit
What is right action?
What is wrong action?
Is there any kind of an act which is wrong or right inherently, absolutely and for all time?

There are various answers given to these questions by various schools of philosophy. Everything in morals depends upon the answer given.

The one who has faith in a creed, in a bible or koran, or book of Mormon, which he considers a divine revelation, says "right action is conformity or obedience to the revealed will of God as set forth in the commandments and teachings of the prophets, Christ, Mohammed, Joe Smith, etc., and their apostles, and wrong action is disobedience to the will of God. God being infallible, and eternal, obedience to him is always and absolutely right, disobedience always wrong. Hence lying, stealing and murder are absolutely and always wrong.

But he who advocates a natural religion, and recognizes the law of individualization, says, "right action in any conscious being is doing that in each case which the best preserves and increases the individual acting. This includes the general conclusion of mankind as to the effects of various actions, along with special actions of the particular individual under consideration. But as the conditions of mankind at large are slowly changing, and certain acts at one age, which would bring a good result, at another bring a very bad result to the actor, and his individual surrounding are much more rapidly changing. Many kinds of acts which were right once are wrong now, hence all rightness or wrongness depends upon circumstances, is relative not absolute. Yet it is just as imperative and controlling for the time being as though it were unchangeable and eternal. Hence lying, stealing and killing are right according to *circumstances* of the case. If a lie *only* could save a man, his family, friends, country, and telling the truth would lead to the destruction of all, then telling the lie would be right and the truth wrong. Under similar circumstances, for self or community preservation, when nothing else can do it, stealing and killing become right. The world recognizes and practices this law of fitness even in the highest diplomacy, in wars and conquering territory. It is the mistake as to the fitness of an act which should be sought to be avoided. It is the one who mistakes that suffers for his action.

If it were considered a virtue in any community to lie, steal, and kill, then the one who told truth would be most suspected of evil design. He certainly soon would have least property if he did not steal, and most easily or likely be killed if he did not defend himself and kill his enemies. But a community which would practice lying, theft and killing against its own members, would soon become extinct, and some other fitter beings occupy its place.

It is only as to *self-preservation*, in an individual or community, that such acts as murder, theft, etc., are absolutely destructive to that community, and in that light, absolutely wrong. But the naturalist holds that everything, both individuals and actions, are natural, absolutely the result of conditions, hence in the abstract have no moral aspect, but only when relatively viewed as to the good of one and the damage to another, that an act takes on moral character. Hence an absolute wrong in a community, has an entirely different meaning from the world absolute, in existence, or nature at large.

But we are discussing the laws of behavior or individuals and communities, and trying to discover the fittest acts for them to do in order to preserve themselves the longest, and derive the greatest amount of happiness so long as we are sure they exist as such, believing that such acts cannot adversely affect them, should they continue a conscious individuality in the future. As to the consciousness beyond death we know naught, yet we know equally as much as other living beings of whom we are cognizant, and who may believe in a future conscious individuality.

When we view moral action as related to knowledge and reason, it classifies itself into any ascending scale, corresponding exactly with the degree of knowledge, hence we hold that moral development must come through education in actual knowledge of fact.

MORAL LADDER

Certain elements in solution in crevices of the earth, under certain condition of heat and pressure, such as silica or quartz, slowly arrange their atoms, about a certain position, in the most exact and regular form, into a crystal, whose angles always measure exactly the same, when the chemical constituents are exactly the same in the same proportions, it matters not where in the earth the crystal may be formed. The inherent force of life, even of pure chemicals, seems to possess a species of intelligence which lays hold upon and moves each atom to its nearest available position in the crystal, and when the crystal is built it seems only a dead, though strangely wrought piece of matter, yet there is essentially employed in its growth a pure organizing individualizing force, as there is in the cell of the moneron, which, like the crystals, gradually individualizes from certain combinations of matters under certain degree of light and heat. But though there is self-preserving force shown, even in those unconscious individuals, yet to them there can be no right or wrong, no moral character in action, as they have no perception of failure or success, or of mistakes. The entire body of some growing crystalline forms oscillate from place to place while forming. The moneron also oscillates, but with constantly changing form or motion within itself, as though it were constantly refitting its own atoms together. As the moneron becomes a long cell, then constricts and becomes two, three or more cells, which may entirely separate, or may remain in a cluster or string, a community—each part helping to protect or nourish the others as well as to sustain itself, we see the higher or compound, *community-individual*, is but a cluster of simpler individuals. Thus on step by step, from a speck of crystal to a cell; a moneron to a cluster of cells; an Amœba. Then specialized clusters of cells upon a large cluster begin to appear. A polyp, it may be, which now to our coarse eyes, begins to show an electrical or nervous development, by which it is attracted toward certain things from which it can derive nourishment, or repelled from other things which would consume or disorganize it. It may have become a plant which will open to the light of the sun or close at the approach of cold or light of the sun or close a the approach of cold or darkness, or even to perceive the touch of an insect, as do the leaves of the Venus Flytrap and other plants, and seize the intruder between the folds of their leaves, and hold and consume. It may have become any oyster, and yet show no appreciation of light or objects of sight, of sound, or anything more than a general blunt sensation and taste, with inherent motion enough to slowly follow the dictates of these crude senses. Sociability, music and the beautiful have never been developed in it, yet they essentially exist there, and may become apparent in time. The tendency to divide and multiply has reached the stage of sexualization and pairing. The love of young—maternity—is yet unknown to it, but it is on the upward way. It has acquired a sympathetic feeling, a feeling for others' feeling. The snail with a tentacle, half eye, half finger, goes flinching, poking, blindly, yet seeing light, though its long tedious route. Thus on and on, snail-like, through the countless myriads of ages, stumbling and staggering, part failure and part success, has matter taken to itself touch, taste, love of companions, progeny, smell, hearing and sight, and without a recording part, by which past experience were more or less retained, and these compared with the conditions of the present, gave reason, and judgment how to do better next time, until at least, man, having out-run all other earthly beings in the acquirement of the recording apparatus—the brain—and the use of "recorders," he stand at the head of all nature known to him, seeing clearly that *"knowledge is the chief thing,"* and hence he cries out to his fellows, "therefore get knowledge, but with all thy getting get wisdom," or power to correctly use knowledge. Nature, in educated man, has passed from blind *"natural selection,"* to *intelligent selection*. With intelligent selection comes the idea of right and wrong. How far back among conscious beings this conception was reached no one can say, but it is very clear that many of what we term lower animals possess it in some degree. A dog, or horse, often shows clearly that he has made a mistake, and that he regrets it. Man views all nature struggling and contending for self-preservation in all its individuals, and yet the whole, as the great individuality, the I Am, God., Universe, demands the final surrendering of all minor individualities, in order to preserve itself in eternal motion, yet only to replace an old part with a new one.

For the sake of being the better able to use his knowledge for self-preservation, man classified it. He terms the desire to preserve self, *selfishness*.

Then he divided selfishness into kinds, according to the demonstration it makes, as found among thinking beings.

1. Importunity, as in the bleating lamb, the crying babe, the sick, crippled, beggar. It is too frail to labor, too devoid of cunning to steal; it is simple want without ability to alone supply. A call for help may save it. This call it can make, and of

necessity it cries. The remedy is either death or satisfaction. Sympathy, love, philanthropy try to cure it, by kindly supplying its needs; or, if beyond the point of recovery, then palliate pain as gently and speedily as possible. But strangely, mankind in most ages and communities, allow pain to be shockingly prolonged when all hopes of recovery is past. It seems there is room for improvement here. This senseless, merciless prolongation of pain seems one of the outgrowths of trying to fossilize knowledge with faith.

2. Cunning, Lying, Theft.—The fox cannot openly catch needful prey; the greedy, ignorant man cannot gain a satisfactory subsistence by honorable completion. Lacking sufficient knowledge of, and consequently care for the rights of others, yet fearing their punishment, they steal, lie, defraud, clan together, boycott, strike, "pool" and make "corners" against their abler competitors, without a just cause, to counteract which, counter strikes, boycotts and pools are made. If of a timid nature they try to receive their wants unperceived, in the dark, with noiseless step, but if bold, they knock down, even in open day, and rob. The object is the same—to secure the labor of others, without compensation. If they succeed, they inwardly justify themselves and conclude that they have done right. But mankind at large has seen it often tried, and so generally to fail of accomplishing permanent good even to those who do it, that such acts have come to be considered wrong, injurious to the social body at large, and hence condemned and punished. Mankind has tried dishonesty, filthiness, lewdness and suffered. It has tried the opposite and been benefitted. The desire to subsist upon the acquirements of others is the most universal form of selfishness, to counteract which, almost the entire civil code is used. Its prevalence is an index of the vast extent of ignorance in which the race still wanders, and of the brutal state from which it was developed. One point however is reached—it is almost universally detested. The popular sentiment is against it.

Education as to how a better competency can be honorably obtained by converting the raw materials of nature into comfortable supports with much greater case than taking away from others is its only remedy.

3. Reciprocity—*Do to others as under like circumstances you would be done by*. The results of the reformation of the second form of selfishness, brings us to the third, which shows favor, that favor may be returned. This is the basis of all true commerce, social or financial. It knows its own rights, defends, and at the same time, respects the rights of others. It sacrifices nobly in emergencies to acquire fame or wealth, or greater social environment, but never in the manner of the cat or lion does it "stoop to conquer." It is just to others because it loves justice bestowed upon itself. It is kind to others, for kindness makes its own heart glad. It is honest for it knows the blighting effect of a bad credit. It is truthful, for a habit of falsifying, it soon learns, shows even in the countenance of its own face, and plainly placards itself to discerning eyes, a "fraud." It is no tale teller for if its own mistakes were published, it too would have a bad character. It loves, for it is in ecstasies when beloved. But the object must be attractive, it therefore tries to make itself lovable. It sharply discriminates between mere lust and intelligent appreciation. Its love is guided by education and reason, so that it finds itself at the age of maturity, healthy, robust, happy and so conditioned that it can comfortably raise a family, it seeks a mate with like adaptations, and of a congenial, sacrificing position, so that the offspring may have every reasonable chance for a long happy and useful life. Otherwise it chooses a life of single blessedness, either way making as much of a heaven of earth possible, and being prepared for all the heaven the future may unfold.

But universal equality and friendship, even of the human race, is a mere fancy. Different capacities, varying degrees of knowledge and hence varying degrees of success will always exist. As compared with Vanderbilt, Gould, Rothschild, almost the entire world is a financial failure, but the whole race accompanied with Cannibals and bushmen, is a grand success, and slowly getting better. A large fund of practical knowledge, a moderate competency with cheerful contentment, but not apathy, is probably the best acquirement.

T. V. MUNSON.

ARE "LIBERALS" PROGRESSIVE?

BY T. V. MUNSON

From *The Independent Pulpit*, March 1889

Written for the Independent Pulpit

The above is a poor question to be asked of people who really ought to be the most enlightened and actively engaged in the true work of investigation and progress. It matters not to me how much a person may *write* and *talk* Liberalism, I yet must classify him as a partisan, a sectarian, if that writing and talking is devoted to proving by argument alone that "I am right," "you are wrong." That is only *wrangling*. The world has been at it so long that it has become crazed with the idea that advancement can be made by debate and war. True, these have some beneficial results, yet such as are usually not their direct object. They are blind hazards, similar to the results of a prize fight.

Men are not converted by argument; on the contrary, they are only strengthened in their prejudices. Recall the results of any debate you please.

Men are not made loyal and patriotic to the conqueror's country by being whipped. Argument always appeals to and strengthens the combative faculty. Investigation for argument's sake is always warped with prejudice and a desire to overthrow others. These impulses are antagonistic to progress. About the only progress which comes of partisan debate, is from the accidental discoveries bearing mostly upon some side issue, or unrelated matter. How much more swift, sure, comforting and harmonizing would be the results if all our great debaters would league together in the most friendly manner, to aid each other in original investigation of every department of nature, regardless of each other's personal opinion on abstruse and esoteric questions! Then, as the facts would accumulate and be demonstrated, as each discoverer claiming it would be required to do to the satisfaction of all the others, each and all would constantly be built up in progress and strength, while their opinions would be ever readjusting themselves to the facts.

Then we would have no Buddhistic dreamers, sitting in cloisters with the only eyes they have shut stubbornly against light and observation, with the attention forever concentrated upon the Perkingee-like figures, which fill the panorama of the darkened chambers of his skull like a troop of disembodied "spirits," and from whose fantastic performances he takes his text to enlighten and convert the world. Instead of becoming spiritualists, in order to investigate spiritualism, or Methodists to investigate methodism, or Christians to investigate Christianity, or Liberalists, in order to investigate Liberalism, or *debaters* in order to convince, let us simply become *observers, demonstrators*, and *recorders* of *fact*. The greater the fund of *classified facts*, the greater the wealth of the people who discover and classify them, in all that leads to true wealth of any kind. Who leads the world to-day in matters of real action, in all that lends comfort, beauty and what happiness we have? Is it he who said "mortify the flesh?" Is it he who said "take no heed for the morrow?" Who is it that removes mountains; he that, with his eyes rolled up, asks an imaginary being to undo his own eternal work, or he who discovers dynamite and invents the drill?

Was it the coward who stood terrified at the "thunderbolts of God," or he who led the electric current captive from the clouds; that gave us the telegraph, telephone and electric railway, and let the "bolt" quietly and harmlessly down the side of the house into mother earth? Is it the gowned monk, prattling to nothing before a brassy image, and great crowds of ignorant dupes, or he who plants forests, makes lakes and canals, and underdrains land that causes rain to descend where none fell before, and the desert blossom as the rose? Is it Moses of Lyell that tells us most truthfully about the structure and age of the world? Was it Paul or Spencer who has given the most complete and reliable code of social action? Was it Paine, Voltaire, Wesley, Ingersoll, Luther, Sweedenborg, Beecher and Talmage, who have added most largely to individual and social happiness; or Shakespeare, Bacon, Huxley, Humboldt, Tyndal and Franklin? Is it the government of the popes upon a superstitious foundation, or that of Jefferson and Gladstone upon statistical facts, and the principles of statecraft gleaned from the results in all ages and countries, that has made the most enlightened, wealthy, peaceful and powerful nations? Does the observance of the principles of heredity and hygiene, as practiced with domestic animals, or allowing *chance* and "love on first sight" to rule the reproduction of the race, produce the handsomest, healthiest and happiest men and women?

Apropos: DO THE INDEPENDENT PULPIT writers gain more for themselves and the race by long-winded debates, pro and con, with no systematic scheme of investigation candidly and friendly to all, on any department of ethics, than they would by intelligence, organization and division of topics for investigation in a brotherly way, for the sake of fact and progress purely, wishing to confound, convert and suppress no one—who will tersely and *courteously* add to the general fund of facts? Could not the PULPIT be turned into a *social club room*, as it were, (but I fear I am not obtruding my nose into other people's affairs), and let a number be devoted to solving, or at least examining into and discovering if possible, the very best method of decreasing intemperance?

Then give a turn at *social entertainment* of young and old, the best form of social clubs and how to organize them.

Then some phases of the question of educating the youth *how to marry* so as to produce a constantly rising race in every desirable feature. Then the esoteric field might be discussed with all facts, if any, bearing upon it brought to view, etc., etc.

Ah! but that is too stale. It is too simple to journey always in the world of *fact* and *truth*. Investigation is too hard a task when heaven can be had of the imagination for the asking. It is so easy to sit still and wrangle, and cuddle ourself with the sweet gratification that our own arguments alone are invulnerable and contain the basis of all truth. Like the Celestials, most of us prefer to wander in the realms of dreamland than beside the real brooks, and among flowers, trees, insects, birds, in company with fellow mortals. The race has scarcely yet learned that it in reality, is *in the midst* of heaven, and persists in forever looking back into the pit of hell imagined by ignorant youth. Like a kitten at nine days of age, it is just beginning to open its real eyes. All the time before, it had them scaled and was dreaming. That state served it best then. It is a blessed thing to be an optimist. The pessimist is the kitten that either got its eyes open *too* soon, or the one that *remains with them closed till after the average time*. The mission of the race is to get all to open their eyes at the *right time*, or as near that as possible, for those with eyes closed cannot see, and, hence, believe that others see and know better than they; and those *with eyes open* cannot now understand how the dreams of the others can be taken by them as delicious realities. This difference creates endless and fruitless debate as to what is true. It is better to consider the best method of getting all eyes wide open *without making them sore. Handling and endeavoring to see the real*, under *every* light, is known to succeed best. The ideal is already overdone.

 The ablest commentary I have ever seen upon the reliability of the Bible is Mr. Shaw's "The Bible Against itself." But he has greatly weakened the force of the work by giving it a prejudiced title. Had he simply labeled it "Bible Quotations," and allowed the reader to note the against part himself, the prejudice of timid investigators would have been less aroused. But it seems to me far more important for me to teach my children the useful facts in nature, than the errors of the ancients.

ARE "LIBERALS" PROGRESSIVE?

NO. 2

BY T. V. MUNSON

From *The Independent Pulpit*, April 1889

Editor's Note: The following is a reply to *Independent Pulpit* publisher J. D. Shaw's critique of the preceding essay, "Are Liberals Progressive?" (See page 336 for Shaw.)

Written for the Independent Pulpit

In penning my first article under the above heading, I had no idea of entering into debate, nor wish I to be drawn into it now.

It was written merely as a partial expression of conclusions formed in my own mind during years of observation, both as a church member and as an independent thinker. I desired in publishing it only to give to others a reason for my own opinions, not that I had the slightest wish to compel others to have similar opinions. In accordance with such opinions, it is evident a certain course of action on my part would follow, if the opinions were deep and strong, and thought of sufficient importance, on my part, to demand special action. I was quite surprised to find friend Shaw doubling on me with four columns.

All the reply I shall attempt is to more clearly make myself understood, as it is evident Mr. Shaw even, has not fully caught my exact meaning.

Keeping in view my first rule, viz: "It matters not to me how much a person may write and talk Liberalism, I yet must classify him as a partisan, a sectarian, if that writing and talking is devoted to proving, by argument alone, that 'I am right; you are wrong'." It then appears that Mr. Shaw did not understand me as to what "has razed the battlements of superstition, etc." I confess I did not, when writing that, make the statement as explicit as I should have done, never anticipating that it would be an assertion for special consideration. But now I must give a clearer notion of my idea of the force that has done the razing.

In general terms, I would say it is the force of definite knowledge acquired by the individual, to whom superstition has been destroyed in part or whole.

To make myself so clear that no one can mistake my meaning, I will illustrate: Take the prophet's command for the sun to stand still. Without a knowledge of the laws of moving bodies under the influence of gravitation, the debaters might have eternally discussed the pros and cons of the probability of such an occurrence, without ever convincing any one. All that such a debate would do would be to cause all who gave attention to it to array themselves in two opposing ranks, according to whether the pro or con theory suited their own minds most agreeably.

But had Kepler stepped before the opposing rank with blackboard, and pendulum, and other necessary apparatus, showing, by actual sight, which courses moving bodies *invariably* take with reference to each other; that when one of a system of bodies, moving together under the force of gravitation, is stopped, or taken away, that all the others once leave their old courses and make a new arrangement among themselves, and that in a planetary system the sun is already, and always at comparative rest as to the planets themselves, and that, if the earth was the center and at rest, as supposed by the ancients, that when the sun was stopping in its revolution it would at once rush to the earth, or else, if held in position, all the planets, including the earth, must rush to the sun, or else the force of gravitation, and the previous momentum of all heavenly bodies, must be suspended so long as the sun stood still, then the hearers and viewers of such *demonstration* would be compelled to ask themselves, "Which is most probable; the assertion of this cranky prophet—always without credit in his own country—and for such a trivial cause, or these actual demonstrations which we see, and can repeat at our pleasure? But if Kepler would continue with the plainest mathematical demonstrations, the simple, easily understood, at first, then go on, step by step, followed by the people, till his great astronomical laws would stand before them in "figures that can not lie," so that every man on earth could follow the demonstrations themselves, Kepler need never say a word about the prophet and the sun standing still, nor even know that the prophet ever existed; all who had heard the story of the prophet and sun, and also the demonstration of Kepler, would, of themselves, abandon the one and adopt the other. On the other hand, Kepler would do the very worst possible thing to hint (even if he knew) about the prophet, as it would spring the stubbornness of former views and theories onto the minds of his audience, and thus obscure clear candid views.

Thus I might take up the six days creation "revelation" of Genesis. Debate never made any other view. The "Testimony of the Rocks" eternally and effectually changed the views on that point, but only when the mind comes actually to study and contemplate the rocks themselves. Likewise the "flood" dwindles into a mere ripple when placed among the thousands of subsidences and elevations which the crust of the earth has undergone in past ages, and may again happen, as the present state of the moon seems to show it has suffered, and that such cataclysms [sic] grow more and more violent as the planet grows older and the crust thicker.

The history of man's creation and life upon earth, as given in Genesis, pales into the serenest field of fiction to one who finds and studies the remains of man in the crust of the earth. The theory of special creation of species with "seed in themselves after their kind" loses all its mystery and piquancy to a person like Darwin, who fearlessly searched and studied the world of organic forms. The experimenter who produces hybrids finds nature everywhere giving the lie to such a statement. Argument *abstractly* from any of these matters convinces no one. It is the actual study of the matter itself that has "razed the battlements of superstition."

Let us now see what further is not only utterly destroying superstition, but constructing the most enlightened civilization, even in the churches themselves. Commerce, the speedy and cheap travel of all people to other parts of the globe, should stand first. Next, distribution of printed matter, especially the accounts of actual events in newspapers. Philosophical and religious papers, doubtless, are doing some good, especially where those of different view are taken and read by students who are not pinned to any specific theory, but, as in the majority of cases, people take but one, if any, paper on religious matters, and *that to suit their own pet theory*, on the whole, that class is a clog to advancement. The telegraph, the teaching of the natural sciences in most schools, especially when not in connection with religious or other theories, expositions, especially international ones; the multiplicity of religious sects, and many other general movements in society, each of which appears to maintain itself as a resultant of many forces, but whose direction is designed and directed by no one in particular, all are constantly enlarging, correcting and enlightening the race.

This all springs from the fundamental individual desire to learn and better one's condition.

I fear nothing from the "organized church in every community in this country, and a salaried preacher in every church," so long as I see that every one of these churches and preachers keep pace with the world, though at the tail of the column. Compare them with the churches and preachers of some hundreds of years ago, and they stand in comparison as rank heretics.

The "captives" whom it seems time "to prepare comfortable quarters for" are such as Mr. Shaw and myself. Those who have gotten out of their old shells, and go wandering about as though friendless and lost. There are thousands who are ready to change tenements as soon as such are in sight, of a suitable nature to accommodate their new wants, but till then prefer to remain languidly in the old, rather than formulate anew for themselves. If the new quarters are so built as to better than ever suit the nature of man, and the possibilities of progress, there will be an overflowing occupation of them, but if as narrow and unproductive of real satisfaction as the old, then the new shall remain, as they ought, empty.

I find Mr. Shaw again does not fully preach the principle under which I place Ingersoll, Paine and Voltaire with Beecher, Wesley, Luther and Talmage. I was classifying *kind*, not quality nor time, hence I committed no anachronism, nor breach, in arrangement. The kind of men who have set the world ahead are they who have *discovered* new facts, and *recorded* them where the world could use them. Franklin, for instance, destroyed the "Thunderbolts of God" by capturing the electrical disturbance of the clouds, and taking it quietly down to the earth. He did not argue against the old superstitious theory, but simply found out *more* about the *real*. In every department where real advancement has come a similar investigation will be found. What new fact or investigation did Ingersoll ever discover or make to entitle him to any such claim as has Huxley, or even Shakespeare, in the enlargement of ideas of physical or mental science? I meant that as Wesley was a debater and fighter of moral opinions so is Ingersoll; and as real investigators and recorders of new phenomena and facts, that both stand in the same category. They both assume to do that reasoning for other people, which they, the people, should do themselves if they have the data, inclination and time.

I object to Mr. Shaw's assumption as unproved that "we should most likely never have had a Huxley, a Humboldt, or a Tyndal, but for the labors of Luther, Voltaire and Paine." That is the very reason I object to most argument, because it makes assumptions that it is impossible to prove. Then uses the assumptions as established premises to build other propositions upon. That no one might mistake his meaning Mr. Shaw repeats, without any "most likelys" whatever, as follows: "But for the reformation due to the heroic labors of such men as Luther, Voltaire, and Paine, each in his generation, the long and brilliant list of scientist and economists that have since done so much for this century would not have existed."

To my mind this assumption is akin to the one of the man who might, while standing on the banks of a great river, watching driftwood float by, assert to his friend: "These logs we now see going by would never have come only for those other logs we saw go by a short time ago." As though the entire stream of events depended upon a few logs or a few men.

Having said enough to make my ideas clear, I think, I will not longer consume time and space so valuable, thanking Mr. Shaw for his kind accomplishments, and the privilege to appear before his large body of greatly respected readers.

After reading my articles and Mr. Shaw's criticism of them, the readers will be found to have arranged themselves into two or more divisions as to which is nearest correct, without having learned a single new fact more than that we have written, and not fully agreed. We probably would have recruited, our strength more, and made the boys happier, had we joined them in a game of ball, or had invented a real good puzzle, especially if it had been based upon some little understood force or phenomenon.

THE FISKEAN GOD.

From *The Independent Pulpit*, August 1891.

Written for the Independent Pulpit.

There is a class of scientific persons who, though great, profound investigators of the highest authority in their special fields, are, when it comes to matters of opinion concerning the "soul of things" or the actuating energy of the universe, transcendentalists. Such men as Emerson, Joseph Leidy, Asa Gray, are found in this school. John Fiske is its ablest special exponent in such works as "Cosmic Philosophy," "The Idea of God," and "The Destiny of Man," and the Unitarian church gives formality and ceremony to suit the philosophy, and in its folds are found the majority of such scientists as I have indicated. Unquestionably it is the most enlightened church of the age.* But it stands on a superstitious foundation, although its advocates deny this, and endeavor to prove their God by scientific, or rational process.

It is this proof (?) or, argument to prove a *purposing God* outside and above matter that I wish to consider briefly in this paper.

The scholarly, eloquent and eminent John H. Clifford, minister of the Unitarian Society of Germantown, Philadelphia, delivered and published through the Franklin Printing Company, of Philadelphia, a sermon on "Faith and Science," in which he advocates the Fiskean God, and endeavors to show there is no conflict between science and religion, or "Faith and Science," as he puts it. Would that all ministers could and would preach such beautiful sermons, so full of "peace and good will among men. He narrows the chasm between faith and rationalism, till it would seem that a child might safely stand astraddle of the yawning gulf that has, through all ages, lain between belief and knowledge, between "heaven" on faith's side and "hell" on knowledge's side. What a grand thing it has been for "hell" that "God" planted that "tree of knowledge" on hell's side of the chasm. It is perpetually attracting the superstitionalists and transcendentalists toward it, and making them feel that the gulf is very narrow, and even quite passable to all who may reach and partake of the fruit in the full confidence that it is good and wholesome. Some thinkers, like Fiske, and Emerson and Clifford are, by nature, too timid to let go the transcendental fence altogether, and content themselves with reaching into the branches of the tree that hang over on their side. When we behold the long string of "tenderfoots" astraddle that fence filching from hell its golden apples of knowledge, we are astonished that the fence does not crush beneath them. There sat Volney and Voltaire, Tom Paine, Bacon and Swedenborg and a great host of ancient followers, who died on the fence with heads, hands and pockets full of the forbidden fruit, while they were ridiculed and persecuted, with all manner of jibes and tortures, by the truly obedient, faithful and ignorant legions of every color and sect that stood aghast, back and apart from them, on their side of the fence, building fagots for them, so that if hell did not burn them the fagots would. Do I not paint the picture correctly?

Ah! what strange thing is that taking place at great intervals and distances along the line of that gulf! It is Ecclesiastes and Socrates, and Hume and Buckle and Darwin, and Spencer, and Tyndall and Huxley, and Ingersoll, utterly reckless of the fence and gulf it bordered, running at full speed from the starving land of faith, and without one fear of the mob or the bottomless pit, at one fell sweep, leaping the fence and chasm and alighting fair and square in "hell" under the broad and generous shade of the forbidden tree. With what astonishment, joy and peace they view the landscape o'er! The awful terrors of faith and hell are left eternally behind. What the faithful had thought hell, was the mist of fear that rose perpetually about the borders of faithland, and distorted and obscured all the beautiful fruits of this infinite land of freedom, where all the lovely trees of the knowledge of good and evil, grow perpetually. But one regret comes to their brave and sympathetic hearts, and that is, that Fiske and Emerson and Leidy and Clifford do not jump off that fence onto the side where the beautiful trees grow and give them company in enjoying the only true and living heaven, so long labeled hell, and let the precious fragrance of the flowers, and the ruddy glow of the fruit of the tree of knowledge shine further into that misty, foggy land of faith, and bring forward all brave, worthy persons there, to push down the old rotten fence everywhere, and bridge the gulf of fear completely, and extend the lawns and orchards of (hell) heaven throughout all regions where human beings tread. But a big ray of hope fills their hearts. The fence is getting so loaded with Unitarians, and they have lost so much faith that they can begin to see the ground of truth under the trees, and they pull so hard upon the branches that the fence must go down sooner or later; then will the lawn and orchard and fragrant groves extend to the utmost limits of human progress.

Now let us see if we cannot draw some of the rusty nails out of that dilapidated fence of faith, and thus hasten its fall and the extension of the only real heaven.

We find that fence has been made of material boards, but composed in an unnatural, or heterogeneous combination. The main board of physics commonly called "Natural Philosophy," is spiked on that fence with a rotten nail. Upon this nail have all the transcendental schools hung their Gods.

The more mystical the philosophies of these schools, the more material were their gods. Note the gods of the Egyptians, the Ephesians, the Hindoos, the Chinese and others. On the contrary, as material knowledge increases, the more mystical becomes the idea of God, till we come to the Fiskean idea, where it reaches the vanishing point, and one step more lands us squarely face to face with actual existence, and "personal omnipresent energy" is clearly ruled out of the field of knowledge. *The essence of superstition consists in personifying abstract energy.*

The Rev. Clifford exhibits a generous spirit, and comes near getting out of the meshes of superstition. But the fruit of the tree of knowledge that he gathered, seems to be not quite mellow yet, and fears yet the colic, should he take it entirely devoid of faith in the ghost he still hangs by its side.

That last, low, weakest entrenchment of all superstition, thrown up by John Fiske, namely: "Omnipresent Energy," "Anthropomorphic, quasi-personal God," catches him.

How hard it is to relinquish the ghosts altogether! When reason has discarded completely all the true Gods—personal ghosts that sit or fly somewhere in the universe and that run the inert machine matter, according to the imagination of transcendentalists, it yet fears to claim its victory, and surrenders in the last step, when that step would have set it forever free, with no glimmering ghost to mock it with the epithet "Infidel!" "Atheist!" "without God and without hope!" The childish fear of being called an Atheist, has caused many a noble reason to topple, fall and surrender its achievements at last to the monster superstition.

Those with the God-idea, finding no tangible ghost in the universe, clap their personification onto "Omnipresent Energy," and deify it with purpose, and imagine that this purpose gives a dramatic tendency" to the infinite universe, and declare with John Fiske, that "This is none other than the living God." (See The Idea of God, preface, pages ix., x., xi., xii., by John Fiske.)

Now we are better ready to examine, and try to draw that rotten spike, driven into the rail of physics on the fence of faith by transcendentalists.

Scientists of this school start in their works on physics with an impossible major premise, or proposition, and though in one aspect it appears plausible, yet it is untrue. If accepted, it requires a purposing energy—God—outside of and beyond matter.

The proposition I refer to is this: "A mass of matter, if at rest and uninfluenced by any outward force, will forever remain at rest, and if propelled in any direction at any given velocity, and uninfluenced by any other than the propelling force, will forever move in the given direction with the given initial velocity, and the motion will forever be in a straight line."

Now, that seems very plausible. It is easy to progress from that proposition to the conclusion of an "Omnipresent Energy."

As matter is assumed to be absolutely inert, and yet is clearly in every part, everywhere in motion, it necessarily follows that there must be an "Omnipresent Energy" to produce the motion. As there is harmony, or correlation of the parts, it is argued that the energy has purpose, or intelligence, This assumed abstract, purposing, "Omnipresent Energy," is Fiske's and Emerson's, and Savage's, and Leidy's, and Clifford's God; a God built upon impossibility; upon a mere assumption of weak, finite man as we shall presently see, to sustain a venerated, ancient belief, around which all faiths have grown and still cling.

Let us examine this major premise of faith calmly and unprejudicially for a moment.

It assumes a mass of matter *alone* in an empty infinity of space, which, to start with, is supposing an impossibility. Then it assumes that if it moves at all, an outside energy must strike it, coming from non-matter, or nonentity, yet possessing energy, thus ignoring all our knowledge of chemical, electrical, stellar and mechanical action and reaction. We know that the oxygen and other elements rush to each other by inherent dislikes. So we see the magnetic needle swings to or away from diverging parts of a steel bar possessing a similar inherent energy, even when thick plate-glass intervenes, albeit when abstractly viewed, as purposeless as mind can imagine, yet essentially with purpose to serve the *needs* and constitution of the *magnets*, nothing more.

Thus we trace purpose and energy in all its varieties to individual masses of matter, not to the infinite.

But to return to the assumption of inertia in matter. The assumption fails to follow the supposed *energy*, and devotes all its attention to the mass of matter, not questioning the correctness of the assumed action of the energy on matter. In the same work on physics is another law laid down and this time a correct law. It is stated thus: "Action and reaction are always equal and in opposite directions.

Applying this law in the major premise, and we have a remarkable result. As, in limitless space no fulcrum of resistance can be conceived outside the assumed mass of matter to be moved, it is impossible for any energy, however great, to exert a propelling force, hence the major assumption is impossible and false. But suppose we admit that the energy so as to cause the mass of matter to move. By reaction the matter moves off in the direction of impulsion. Here, with an equal energy of reaction, or else it not move. But we have the assumed imponderable energy acting without producing resistance in the opposite direction, or only in a single direction, which proves the major premise false by *reductio ad absurdum*. But if we give the assumed energy ponderability—make a substantial God, as did the ancients, then by the law of reaction when energy acts against the mass of matter, and the mass moves in one direction, the energy must move with the same momentum in the opposite direction, and hence could never come together gain. Applying this to the infinite universe of matter, the infinite energy that set it in motion must have receded from it an infinite distance, and hence the material universe remains without the infinite energy, without God. But this would require the existence of two infinities, at an infinite distance from each other, another absurdity, as the material universe is assumed to occupy infinite space itself.

Thus we are thrown back at every attempt to get outside of matter with energy of any kind, and are forced to the conclusion that all energy is embodied in matter. But when we try to find out the ultimate essence of matter, it becomes the great mystery, and all we do know, are impressions. The impressions come from masses of matter, and are received upon masses of matter. These masses of matter, in our most ultimate analysis, give no other intimation, than that they are only combinations of energy, whose ultimate state is incomprehensible except as matter as we know it. At this point we are truly Unitarians. That is, all our knowledge of matter and energy affirms that matter and energy are one and the same, only differently considered.

Then the far more easy and rational way is to accept the whole of *existence* just as we find it. We at once escape all the ghosts and Gods, and get right at the "soul of things" by getting the things themselves. The ancient philosopher, who defined it as: "I Am That, I Am," the eternal existence (not "ever present energy," nor "ever present matter"), had about the correct idea. "Ever present energy" is only half the real. It takes, combined with it, the idea of "ever present matter," to complete the conception so that it fully fits existence.

With this conception, how grand becomes our thoughts and lives. We look upon the face of the existence. Its countenance is charmingly lovely, or hideously awful, just as our vision is adjusted with health, and peace, and sympathy, or deranged by disease, and conflict and hatred. It is we, ourselves, who hold the thaumatrope, through which we enjoy or despise the existence.

The face of the existence is nebulæ, and sun and comets, and planets, and moons and meteorites; its delineations are oceans, and continents, mountains and lakes and rivers and clouds; its fibrous structure is chemical elements. Its energy is in itself in every part, to take care of that part, and to link it to all other parts in its combinations, where the matter and energy, or energetic matter unites into new and wonderful modes of action.

To endow it with other energy that is inherent in it, would be to destroy it. This, the destruction of matter, all experience contradicts. Nothing can be absolutely destroyed in essence, and the reverse is likewise true, nothing can be absolutely created *de novo*, but changed is in and through and over all the parts, though the whole remains eternally the same.

The cravings of the sensorium of man are to fill up the space in his consciousness for the impressions of fact and resultant truth. Failing to secure fact man satisfies the craving with fancy and theory, and when he comes to consider the infinite, he constructs himself gods. This leads us to compare Fiske's "Anthropomorphic, quasi-personal omnipresent energy with a subjective purpose," with the more orthodox "all-wise, omnipresent, omniscient, infinitely lovable, and loving, fearful and jealous, incomprehensible God, without body and with parts"—a mere myth of the idle brain, a scarecrow.

Without such fancies, humanity can and does in some individuals, still exist, and behold and admire and study the tangible existence, nature, the universe in its wonderful relationships of parts in their inherent energy, and be none the less humane, loving and happy.

It takes human intelligence a long, hard struggle to free itself from the superstitious traditions of its infancy, and realize that it is in the very presence of the Great I Am, and a very part of it.

To realize that the I Am sees in part with my eyes, with your eyes, and looks from eye to eye of himself, and that we feel the thrill that he feels, and think the thoughts that he thinks, and experience his love, is a grand, a noble, an elevating conception. What other, than the positive philosophy reaches such exalted thought? To love a woman or man, or animal or plant, is to love *God*, which only another name for the object of nature collectively considered.

The resultant energy of all the individual and atomic energies within the earth, show forth in gravitation, which links it and all there is in it to all other stellar bodies. Thus our every feeling, thought and act go into the universal resultant of gravitation, and according to the nebular hypothesis, by convergence, collision, reaction, or repulsion, divergence or radiation, the greater masses divide again in due time, proportional to their mass, and return again and again to new and marvelous individualizations.

This view may be stigmatized as Atheism, or Pantheism, but that matters not, the existence recks not. After all, here we all land at last.

It were better for the ministers to preach teach existence and human relations therewith, rather than incomprehensible assumption and transcendentalism. But if any one has a god, why, let him enjoy it to the best of his ability; but liberality would suggest to him that what is meat and bread to him in philosophy, is poison and death to his neighbor, if forced upon that neighbor as a matter of confession, to avoid criticism and persecution. None are liberal or charitable who do not stand upon this great foundation stone of opinion and investigation.

WHY THEOPHILUS BECAME AN INFIDEL

From *The New Revelation*, 1906 [Revised 1910]

INTRODUCTION.

As it is frequently stated in church pulpits, that persons who do not believe and confess the tenets of Christianity and join the church, take the position of unbelievers in order to give rein to their evil natures and to shirk moral responsibility; and because I have been so misrepresented by some, and for the sake of truth and progress, I deem it proper for me, at this time, to refute once for all such unkind and, unjust and untrue charges as to myself. As to whether I have shirked any just responsibility falling upon me as a citizen or member of human society, my very active life and its results are the only answer I have to offer.

Raised by Christian parents, I joined the Christian (or Disciples) church, at the age of seventeen, and faithfully did my duties as a member, earnestly praying daily, teaching in Sunday School, exhorting in prayer-meetings, and living a Christian life to the best of my understanding, and of course condemning unbelievers, and other Christian sects than my own, as all good orthodox Christians have generally done. This I continued to do for the most of ten years of my most vigorous young manhood.

During the last four years of this church life I was studying a course in the sciences in a Christian university, and on Sundays studiously listened to sermons by the ablest ministers in that church. I was ever honestly seeking truth. I had but one light to guide me to its recognition, and that was the senses and reasoning faculties of which I found myself possessed.

My joint studies of theology and science found numerous statements and dogmas of the Scriptures to be in direct contradiction of demonstrated facts and truths of science. But all my early life, education, associations and prejudices were with my faith, and to disavow my religion meant almost universal ostracism and loss of honorable and lucrative position. I still hoped to discover satisfactory reconciliation of my faith with my knowledge. I diligently and prayerfully reviewed the Bible and its history and the sciences. This completely wrecked my faith, and in justice to my brethren and myself, I withdrew from the church, at the age of nearly twenty-eight years, determined to stand by demonstrated truth, which I was sure could lead only to a better life and a satisfied conscience.

It is now—at the writing of this, while in vigorous health in my sixty-third year and in my calmest mood, alone in my study, facing resignedly whatever judgment the future holds for me—thirty-five years since I lost faith in priestly dogma and gave myself wholly to the control of fact and truth, as seen and understood by my untrammeled, unprejudiced reason, trained in the strictest school of logic and correct scientific investigation; for only truth can stand, while faith is variable and ever changing, and must die, wherever in conflict with truth. Truth cannot be opposite-sided.

To answer more fully why I have not throughout my entire life continued to confess and profess Christian doctrine I present the following reasons, and in doing so, it is with most kindly and respectful feelings towards all persons, but I shall be plain and candid so that I may not be-misunderstood. I contend not against honest, well-meaning people, but against the dishonest and error.

THE REASONS WHY.

(1). On the whole, in consequence of reaching years of mature manhood, after joining the church, and especially for having acquired more knowledge both of the Scriptures, their origin and history,—and of the truths of science, and thereby the capability to more correctly investigate and reason; also because I loved truth, and to get it—threw myself unreservedly and candidly upon my only means of securing it—unprejudiced, fact-enlightened reason.

(2). Because I learned. that Christianity is founded on a pure myth,—the creation and fall of Adam and Eve, and on the totally untenable claim that Jesus of Nazareth was the begotten Son of God, (i.e. of himself), in the character of the Holy Ghost, whatever that might be, and yet was the son of a carpenter, and had two distinct lines of male descent,(one of forty-one members, the other of fifty-six, see Matt, i, 1-16, Luke iii, 23-24, from Abraham to Jesus; yet Matt. in i, 17, gives forty-two generations) by a Jewish woman—one of the fallen descendants of Adam. This requires some amplification.

(a). Comparative anatomy, embryology, anthropology, archeology, and geology, prove most certainly to those acquainted with their facts and truths, that mankind originated from more primitive animal forms by gradual change through influences of changed conditions, and hence was not created all at once, full grown and perfect; direct from the earth, as stated in Genesis, but has continually advanced from a low quadruped animal, covered with hair, bearing a tail and living wild as a climbing animal in tropical forests and hence never had a moral "fall" but has been in the rising scale all along for hundreds of thousands of years, into a tailless, naked, self-clothed, upright, talking, thinking, more or less civilized being, and this augurs for man a paradisial future in his earthly home. See Darwin's "Origin of Species," and "Descent of Man," Hæckel's "History of Creation and Origin of Man," Huxley's "Man's Place in Nature," Lyell's "Geology," Owen's "Comparative Anatomy," Carpenter's "Comparative Physiology," and many other similar and later works, supported by a vast number of facts.

(b). Because, by the law of consistency, if man was created immediately of full stature and perfection by a perfect creator, he would have possessed a perfect moral character and hence could not have committed an immoral act, and consequently could not have a "fall" into total depravity, perpetually transmissible to all his descendants, thus violating the theory of free moral agency, otherwise taught in Genesis to Adam's act in eating the apple. It is totally illogical to hold that God,—an infinitely perfect being,—can transmit to his works any but perfect character, and yet, according to the story of Adam, he, after illogically becoming evil, must then transmit only evil. The Bible theory that Satan (the devil), was created by God as one of his highest archangels, and that he became totally evil, is a most absurd, inconsistency, and this is one reason for rejecting the Scriptures as a revelation of an all wise perfect being. If Adam, a perfect son of God direct from his hands, and Satan, his highest archangel, could become totally depraved, by what logic can a son of God and woman—Adam's lost daughter—be unable to sin, as Jesus is represented in the New Testament?

(c). Yet, it admitting, for the moment, for the purpose of better examination by rules of logic and justice, that man was created perfect; placed in a paradise, ignorant of what constituted good and evil, and without knowing the meaning of death, for up to that time no death had occurred, no meaning of morality or immorality, for they had not yet eaten of the fruit that alone could give it, as the story goes; that a tree filled with beautiful delicious fruit was growing in the midst of the paradise, the eating of which would confer on man the precious, useful knowledge of good and evil, and also a tree, whose fruit would confer on the eater of it eternal life, and that the wisest other creature ever created by God—Satan—whose nature was to lead men to do wrong (though perfectly illogical for a perfect creator to produce), was likewise admitted to the paradise, and who truthfully told the man's sweetheart that the fruit was good to eat, that the eating of it would bring to the eater a most desirable knowledge, and that death would not follow on the day of eating it; that Eve, Adam's sweetheart, did eat the fruit, found it very pleasant and did not die, nor experience any bad effects and hastened to tell Adam, her lover, of her discovery, and urged him to eat of it; that he did eat and did not die that day nor for nearly a thousand years afterward, as the story relates, but at once knew good from evil, and he and Eve began at once to cover their nakedness (but another Scripture states that God clothed them with skins of wild beasts), and to practice other moral acts; that God had not previously told them that he would curse them by making life hard for them and all their progeny; that then, God became very angry and jealous, and counseled with other gods,—presumably Christ the Son of God, and the Holy Ghost, as these three, according to this religion, always existed together, even "before the world was"—saying "Behold, the man has become as one of us to know good and evil; and now, lest he put forth his hand and take hold of the tree of life and eat and live forever; therefore the Lord God sent him forth from the Garden of Eden." That was, to revenge himself on his own helpless creature, and satisfy his jealousy and in addition He pronounced a terrible curse upon man, woman and Satan. Yet after about four thousand years, having in the meantime still further cursed man by drowning with a flood, he repented, and has been ever since trying to coax man to eat of that tree of life" and live forever, and has utterly failed as to the greater part of man, admitting that becoming a Christian secures such life. How much wiser and better and kinder and really beneficent, it would have been to let man in the first place eat of the tree of life, and all mankind stay eternally in paradise, where he was first placed! I have been true to the Scriptures, in presenting this garden scene, as every reader of the Bible knows.

In all honesty, who of the four persons of the story should be most reprehensible according to our-best rules of ethics today? Certainly, God, first, for he, in the story, told Adam a falsehood about dying, became jealous, angry, and cursed his own creatures for doing what their natures prompted them to do. Their natures came from God, if he created them; Satan next, although he told the truth about dying, yet he inveigled Adam and Eve into eating the fruit; Eve next, for she inveigled Adam, and Adam least, for he, rather than lose his sweetheart, chose death, that he might be with her, yet God went free and Adam and Eve were most cursed. Is this God the loving "Father" of Christianity? So the New Testament teaches. I say no, a thousand times No!! And all true history and science and plain common sense say no! No! NO!!! but deceit and ancient priestcraft *is* its father,

When the real truth of the matter was by careful study and honest search for truth revealed to me, my whole being revolted against the savagery of ancient heathenish idolatry, parading itself as the Bride of the Son of God. I was mortified and ashamed of myself for having been a duped idolater for ten of the best years of my life.

Thus, the whole foundation of Christianity I discovered in awful agony to be devoid of reason and justice and hence the entire superstructure of belief must be rejected. To me, it is blaspheming reason and justice, and mercy to advocate Christianity, as established by an infinite, all wise and perfectly good being.

But, I do not berate and abuse honest believers in it, for I too was once such a believer, and then felt it my duty to advocate it, yet I now know, that then I was too ignorant and zealous to be able to apprehend the truth regarding it. Now, that I have learned a little, it seems my duty to assist others in learning, else I should not have made this address.

(d.) If Christ is a true representative of Adam, a true second Adam, then he too, is a myth, or a deceiver, but admitting for a moment that Adam was a genuine character, and Christ also genuine, and a representative of Adam, then Christ is a creature and not the Creator as represented in St. John i: 1-10.

(e). If Adam, the perfect Son of God, direct, without any parent but God, as Genesis represents, could and did commit sin, and that too when he yet knew not right from wrong, as he had not yet eaten of the fruit giving the knowledge of good and evil, by what manner of logic was Jesus unable to sin, as the Scriptures hold, although he was the Son of Mary, a descendent of Adam, hence under the curse. If he was unable to disobey God, then he had no free will, yet free will is a cardinal doctrine of the Bible.

(f.). But to assist me and other persons to believe the above propositions, the Scriptures relate many things as having been done by Jesus, called miracles, and Jesus is represented as claiming that he was what the Hebrew Scriptures are said to proclaim him to be, and that man might believe in him. See St. John xiv:10-11, Matt. xi:2-5, 20-23. As miracles are defined as the arresting of the natural course of events, as the stopping of the sun in its course, the making of wine out of water only, etc., to believe that any person can do such things, is to contradict all our knowledge of causation, and to deny the existence of natural causes and effects, and hence we reject Jesus, the pretended miracle worker, as a fraud, or else a person of unsound mind, or that the Scriptures are untrue.

It is claimed in these gospels that the casting of devils out of the insane cured them; that is, to say, devils go into people and cause insanity. Medical science has shown that insanity is caused by lesions of brain matter, by disease, or accident, or poisons in the blood, or heredity, and that where the poison and disease can be removed without leaving the brain disrupted or disorganized, the insanity may be cured. In the miracle in which it is said that Jesus cured Peter's mother-in-law of fever by casting a devil out of her, is to hold that devils cause fever by getting into persons; but medical science has well shown that fever is caused by vast numbers of microscopic plants or animals getting into the blood and tissues, and that by eliminating them before the organization of the patient is moribund, recovery follows: On another occasion Jesus is said to have cured a boy of fits—epilepsy—by casting a devil out of him. But, like insanity and other diseases, fits have physiological, and other causes, and the existence of devils is not proven, and the devil theory belongs with that of witchcraft, and is abandoned by all intelligent people. These unreasonable features run through the whole category of Jesus' reputed miracles. Hence, this miracle testimony, instead of proving Christ to be the Son of God, proves most certainly that he was a fraud, or fanatic, or else the statements about his performing miracles are pure fabrications injected into the Scriptures by unknown persons. The history of the origin and construction of the gospels prove the latter to have been the case, and to have occurred at least seventy or eighty years after the time of Jesus. See Gibbon's, Renan's, Davidson's, Waite's and other history of the Christian religion.

But why is the believing of these senseless religious propositions so much insisted on by priests and preachers? It commits the professor of a faith to the support of that faith! To confess a faith before men commits one to the doctrine and its support,—*a constant contributor to the priesthood that runs it.* Hence the denunciation, ostracism, threats of condemnation and everlasting awful punishment by the priestly bogies—Gods and devils. This is the kernel of the whole matter. This gives the only good reason for that unreasonable, unjust, cruel Scripture. "He that believe and confesses me before men shall be saved, but he that believeth not shall be condemned," etc.

To frighten a person into confessing a proposition that his best judgment rejects, is to make a hypocrite of him, and start a life of deception, a good basis on which criminality loves to build.

If the doing of miracles proves the doer to be the Son of God, the Peter and Saul, and Simon Magus, and Apollonius and hundreds of priests in various religions throughout the world, were likewise Sons of God, for just as trustworthy history states that they worked miracles.

(g). If the Scriptural statements about Jesus are true then his character was decidedly one-sided and imperfect and his disposition and teachings by precept and example were often wrong, or else our best standards in ethics are wrong, and his teachings, if generally put in practice, would wreck society and soon depopulate the world. Take for example Matt. x:34-35,36, "Think not, that I come to send peace on earth: I came not to send peace, but a sword; for I am come to set a man at varience [sic] against his father, and the daughter against her mother, and the daughter-in-law against the mother-in-law, and a man's foes shall be they of his own household." Could anything be more fiendish than that? How it gives the lie to the song of the heavenly host mentioned in Luke ii:14, saying over Jesus, when an infant in the manager, "Glory to God in the highest, and on earth peace, good will toward men."

Jesus was a celibate and seemingly totally devoid of filial affection, in the manner he is reported to have treated his parents, especially his mother.

He is represented as morbidly ambitious for glory, as his reported prayer, just before his crucifixion, John xvii:1, 5, 10, 24, shows: "Father, the hour has come: glorify thy Son, that thy Son may also glorify thee. And now, O Father, glorify thou me with thine own self, with the glory I had with thee before the world was. And all mine are thine and thine are mine; and I am glorified in them."

"Father, I will that they also, whom thou hast given me, be with me where I am , that they may behold my glory, which thou hast given me; for thou lovest me before the foundation of the world."

Just think of an infinite God being thus vainglorious, begging himself to glorify himself. How supremely ridiculous! God, about to die, to free man from a sin that in the nature of things he could not avoid doing, and praying to himself to have *some* of this sinful mankind to glorify him in heaven!

He taught his disciples to take no heed for their future, and yet when hungry and tramping about, with his followers, entered other's wheat fields and helped themselves to other's labor. Because when hungry, (he was hunting figs to appease the hunger), coming upon a barren fig tree, he cursed it with death.

His berating, epithetizing [sic] and cursing people for not believing him to be the Christ, or the Son of God, is not God-like, but decidedly priestly. If he knew anything of the necessities of the human mind, that it is simply a question of evidence, as to whether the mind honestly gives assent to a proposition or not, he would instead of raving and cursing, have produced that evidence that would have certainly convinced. Without such conviction his followers are necessarily controlled by superstition or guile. Consider the following:

SOME OF THE EPITHETS AND CURSES OF JESUS

1. O ye of little faith! (addressed to his disciples, Matt. viii;26).
2. Wo unto thee Chorazin! woe unto thee Bethsaida! It shall be more tolerable for Tyre and Sidon at the day of judgment than for you. And thou Capernaum, which art exalted unto heaven shall be brought down to hell, Matt. xi:21-23.
3. O! generation of vipers! (to his audience for unbelief), Matt. xii:34 (because the people in these towns could not believe him and repent).
4. O thou of little faith (to Peter for sinking when trying to walk on water), Matt. xvi:31.
5. Ye hypocrites (to the Scribes and Pharisees), Matt. xv:7.
6. O ye hypocrites (to the Scribes and Pharisees), Matt. xvi:3.
7. O ye of little faith (to his disciples), Matt. xvi:8.
8. Get thee behind me, Satan (to Peter for advising), Matt. xvi:23.

9. O faithless and perverse generation (to his disciples for unbelief), Matt. xvii:17.
10. Ye hypocrites (to the Pharisees), Matt. xvii:18.
11. —17. Woe unto you Scribes, Pharisees, hypocrites (seven times), Matt. xxiii:13, 14, 15, 23, 25, 27, 28.
18. Woe unto you blind guides (to Scribes and Pharisees), Matt. xxiii:16.
19. Ye fools* and blind guides (to Scribes and Pharisees), Matt. xxiii:19.
20. Ye blind guides (to Scribes and Pharisees"), Matt. xxiii:24.
21. Thou blind Pharisee (to Scribes and Pharisees), Matt. xxiii:26.
22. Ye serpents, ye generation of vipers! how can ye escape the damnation of hell, Matt. xxiii:33.

*In Mat. V. 22, Jesus is reported to have said, "But I say unto you...that whosoever shall say Thou fool, shall be in danger of hell fire."

Do such invectives and hatred comport with the character of an infinite, allwise, merciful, loving father toward a few puny ignorant children, lost away in an obscure spot on the earth, a mere speck of dust, away in a corner of an infinite universe? No, no! It cannot be. An awful falsehood has been palmed off upon ignorant man by cunning priestcraft. That is the most charitable view we can take, the most in accordance with history, the most reasonable. To believe that the God of a universe would thus rave, and curse his own creatures, simply because they could not believe a man to be God, to be son of himself, son of a woman and son of the Holy Ghost, and yet have two lines of male descent all the way back to the first man, one of sixty-four generations, the other seventy-six generations, in less than 6,000 years, when God is said to have created Adam out of clay, is to be fanatical on religion, or a designing charlatan.

(3.) The Scriptures are greatly at variance with themselves as to who was the father of Jesus. Matthew i:18-20 states, that the Holy Ghost was his father; Luke iii:23, that Joseph was; St. John i:1 state, that he was God, and also that he was the only begotten Son of God, i:14-18, and the Scriptures in several places represent him as calling himself the Son of Man, and in others, the begotten Son of God, with Mary as his mother. Thus we have to believe, in order to be forgiven all our sins, and to inherit eternal life and be admitted into a paradise, in the skies somewhere, that Jesus is God, and the Son of God (that is of himself), son of a woman, Mary, a descendant of Adam under the curse, the Son of the Holy Ghost, and yet the son of Joseph, also under the curse, and yet cannot sin; did die, and yet cannot die; and that if I cannot believe all this and much more equally as ridiculous, and confess to believe it before men, I shall be condemned to punishment eternally in a lake of awful fire, whose smoke ascendeth forever and ever. Yet I may do all manner of evil, if I only confess belief in the above proposition as to Jesus, even on the scaffold or on my death-bed, and I will be admitted into the Christian heaven. Well, then, if the Scriptures are true, I am destined to dwell and suffer infinite torture forever in the Christian hell! for my reason refuses to believe it.

Many of the Scriptural statements about miracles, as well as other matters, clash with and contradict one another, as where one gospel, Matt. viii:28-34, states that Jesus cast some devils out of two insane men into a herd of swine, while other gospels, relating the same miracle, Mark v:1-16 and Luke viii:26-33, assert that he cast a legion of devils out of one man. Mark says it was done in the land of the Gadarenes, but Matthew says in the land of the Gergesenes, two separate countries.

On account of the numerous self-contradictions of the Scriptures, of which the following are examples:

GOD VISIBLE

"And Jacob called the name of the place Peniel; (which means the face of God) for I have seen God face to face, and my life is preserved." Genesis xxxii:30.

"Then went up Moses and Aaron, Nadub and Abihu, and seventy of the elders of Israel; and they saw the God of Israel: * * * And upon the nobles of the children of Israel he laid not his hand: also they saw God, and did eat and drink." Exodus xxiv: 9, 10, 11.

"He that hath seen me hath seen the Father," St. John xiv:9.

"And there arose not a prophet since in Israel like unto Moses, whom the Lord knew face to face," Deut. xxxiv:10.

"In the year that King Uzziah died I saw also the Lord sitting upon a throne, high and lifted up, and his train filled the temple. Then said I: Woe is me! for I am undone; because I am a man of unclean lips and I dwell in the midst of a people of unclean lips; for mine eyes have seen the King, the Lord of hosts," Isaiah vi:1-5.

GOD CANNOT BE SEEN

"And he said, Thou canst not see my face: for there shall no man see me, and live," Exodus xxx:20.

"No man hath seen God at any time; the only begotten Son, which is in the bosom of the Father, he has declared him," St. John i:18.

"King of Kings, and Lord of Lords, who only hath immortality, dwelling in the light which no man can approach unto; whom no man hath seen nor can see," 1 Tim. vi:15-16.

"God, who at sundry times and in diverse manners spake in time past unto the fathers by the prophets, Hath in these last days spoken unto us by his Son—by whom also he made the worlds;

Who being the brightness of his glory, and express image of his person." Heb. i:1, 2, 3.

"In the beginning was the Word, and the Word was with God, and the Word was God," St. John i:1.

Some two hundred or more self-contradictions exist in the Bible, hence it is fallible, and not the word of an infallible being.

FOR TEACHING ERROR IN PRINCIPLE

(4.) "For verily I say unto you, that whomsoever shall say unto this mountain, be thou removed and be thou cast into the sea; and shall not doubt in his heart, but shall believe that those things which he saith shall come to pass; he shall have whatsoever he saith," Mark xi:23.

"And the Lord said, If ye have faith as a grain of mustard seed, ye might say unto this sycamine tree, Be thou plucked up by the roots and be thou planted in the sea; and it should obey you," Luke xvii:6.

These promises of Jesus to answer prayer have never been fulfilled. For years I prayed daily and in the greatest of earnestness, asking only reasonable requests, yet never had the slightest intimation that my prayers were ever heard by any other than myself and other like persons. The same has been the case with all other persons I have known to pray. Even in the Galveston storm, and San Francisco earthquake, where thousands cried in utmost faith and agony, including whole assembled congregations, they went to destruction, and not a prayer was answered. A sweet little girl in Galveston, while on the housetop with her mother, with the awful waves dashing high, looked up hopefully into her mother's face and said, "Mamma, the Lord won't let us drown, will he?" The next wave, greater than any that had gone before, swept them away into an awful watery grave. This was reported by an eye-witness who escaped. "'Where then was he, who had stilled the boisterous waves of Galilee, and his promises to answer earnest prayer? Where!

The assumption that the Infinite has personality in form, speech, passion, etc., is totally incomprehensible, hence illogical and untrue.

A being with definite form, having head, eyes, ears, hair, mouth, tongue, body, hands, feet, etc., who hears, loves, sees, talks, gets angry, jealous; moves about from place to place, as Jesus and God are portrayed in the Scriptures, is not infinite but finite. Such is the Christian God. This God is neither all-powerful nor perfectly good, or else he would destroy the devil and hell if such exist, and all disease, or better, would not have created them. The fact that disease, poisons, venomous and carnivorous animals' tornadoes' earth-quakes, evil people with evil passions, etc., exist, testifies most certainty to the non-existence of a good, prayer-hearing, all-powerful creator and ruler of the universe. Hence, to worship the Christian God is idolatry.

The God who is omnipresent, all-powerful, whose body is the universe, and whose spirit is the energy that moves all bodies, is not the Christian God, but a pantheistic ideal of man, that hears no prayer, sees no acts, knows naught of good or evil. God for such a conception is a misnomer. The pantheist should not steal the name of the Christian deity, or idol, and apply it to his. It creates confusion. My reason rejects the Christian God or Gods; for there are three of them—God, Christ, and Holy Ghost, yet only one. Such is inconceivable to reason. It also rejects *all* man-invented gods as non-entities, so far as being conscious and having volition and intelligent action. All these are the creation of disordered imaginations, or else of dreams, or of cunning priests to deceive. I must, in order to be true to my most enlightened reason, my judgment, my conscience, my self-respect, my manhood, consign all these believed-in spooks to the limbo of superstition. Belief is superstition's handmaid.

The theories of time and material existence having a beginning, and of all material bodies being created by Jesus out of nothing only six thousand years ago, as taught in the Scriptures, are absolutely proven false by the facts of geology, astronomy and physics. They are also, as logical propositions, fallacious and incomprehensible. Hence, the Scriptures are erroneous, not infallible, and have fallable [sic] authorship.

It is infinitely more rational to me, to conceive the substance of the universe as eternally self-existant [sic], infinite in place and time, in division into connected parts, as it appears; infinitely capable, or energetic, to produce motion among its parts, and to form and reform its parts anew, by involving the old and evolving the new forms, the ultimate essence remaining eternally the same, full of potential energy and life; each form as it comes forth, giving out new phenomena of motion and degrees of consciousness, as our senses of special consciousness reveal to *us, the substance*, when in this special organic form, the body. Each form is a product exactly of environments, and the substance involved, and its motions are controlled by its form and the medium or media in which it moves, as a bird in air flies, a fish in water swims, an animal with legs and feet on land, walks or runs and loves, and thinks and talks with his whole being, but some of his parts in each case, much more active than others, and he is conscious that his *substance* is the conscious, active, being, and not some other independent being from his substance. I know that I feel most keenly with my fingers, and think mostly with my brain, but take away the blood and other tissues than the brain and nerves and I cannot think or feel. Wherever we look in all the universe, among the stars, or worlds, or continents or oceans; among rocks or plants or animals, from the whale to the microbe; among bodies, or molecules or atoms or electrons, we discover the great universal truth or law: that *as are the mass, composition,* (organization), *forms, relationship and state of things, so are their effects upon each other*. No such law could exist if everything depends upon some willing prayer-heeding being not itself, for its existence, form and motion. Hence, no prayer-heeding, non-material being (God) exists, save only as a figment of imagination. Man universally practices the laws above stated, in all cases where he really accomplishes anything. See him at work in chemistry, in mechanics, in every department, in commerce, in education, in social and governmental matters. "The Lord" is with the side that has the most, biggest, and best operated guns, so our armies and navies practice.

The universe is known by us to exist, not in its entirety, but in fact through impression of its many parts, upon our sensorium, through motion starting outside us and coming to our consciousness. Only that which can move or vibrate the same as our own substance, can or does cause it to vibrate. Such vibrations we can trace only to substantial bodies either within or without us, and hence assuming that there are beings extraneous to known substance that cause all motion, is pure hypothesis, without a fact to rest upon.

By learning the relationship of bodies and their motions to each other, we become able to plan what we may accomplish. Such accomplishment would be impossible if there be a willful being working apart from us and unknown to us, who runs the universe unless it be admitted, we are purely automatons, and know and do nothing, even in part, by ourselves, which is absurd. If such a non-material being exists apart from the substance of which we are conscious, it gives no evidence of its existence. Thus I reach the idea, that the universe is homogenous, consistent, substantial existence moving in its own parts by mutual co-operation among the parts in harmony with the universal method or necessity of action, and re-action, known in physics as the law of compensation and in ethics as the rule of reciprocity. God is not an appropriate name for the totality of existence, nor for its energy.

When all mankind come to recognize and conform to the doctrine of reciprocity, and its bearings in every field of action, the destructive practice of dualistic, priestly religions and war, and purely selfish commerce, with its combines, trusts, protective tariffs, boycotts and the like, will cease and the races will co-operate by friendly discussion and rational compromise of difficulties.

All objects of form are a perpetual *becoming*, never a fixity, or remaining at standstill, as faith religion would have it, and their motions are *phenomena*, not entities, as the spiritual religions declare, and name ghosts, and the infinite, living, eternal universe, may well be named *The Infinite Phenomenifera*, or Phenomenon Maker, but not God,—an idolatrous name.

This doctrine, Monism, in practice would preserve all the general and special good compatible with reciprocity. It encourages all of love, aspiration and hope that can beneficially exist. No doctrine or practice of blind faith can deprive existence of an iota of what it is or will be, except its subject as to his freedom of thought. To realize that all those I know and I, are very parts of the real Infinite, is exceedingly happifying. I look into the very eyes of the Infinite, your eyes, and all things, and commune directly with the great "I Am," and feel its throbs vibrating through every atom of my existence and all echo back to me from a far deeper source than that of any priestly religion, and tell me that we are all one essence, and that there is no devil, nor creator of devils and hells. These are but the nightmares of our ancient ancestors. The race is beginning to dream better dreams as it learns more of the facts and truths of existence. Civilization and enlightenment come *not with believing, but with knowing*, and hence are of slow growth. As knowledge increases, faith diminishes. The love of knowledge, when once tasted is infinitely stronger than the love of faith, hence the true scientist, the real scholar, such characters as Bacon, Schiller, Gœthe, Humboldt, Franklin, Paine, Jefferson, Buffon, Mill, Darwin,

Tindal, Emerson, Büchner, Ingersoll, Hæckel, looked serenely forward to the day when man will reach his true estate and live supreme by knowledge and reason while his ancient gods and faiths will find their proper place in works of mythology. Our better civilization is even now, demanding in ocean tones, a broader religion, a religious fully approved by knowledge, science and reason, that will use all the true and good of all the old religions; reject their dross of superstition, and build a new church, a church of and for humanity, and not for the gods. The science of superstition and mythology will be the proper dedication for the gods.

The proposition to cure violations of law by having the innocent suffer for the guilty, as taught in the Christian plan of salvation, is entirely unjust and vicious, as it acts as a premium on immortality for the confession of faith and moneyed support of the church. The confession of faith and the sale of indulgences are perfectly in accord with this plan. But faith is the cornerstone of the church militant. Should we wonder at the results?

BAD RECORD IN HISTORY

(5) The record of Christianity through nineteen hundred years, shows this faith-requiring religion to have been destructive of peace, happiness and human life, beyond any other age, just in proportion as that religion held sway. To tell the truth would be counted great exaggeration. Then go and read for yourselves about the persecutions, crucifixions, tearing to pieces by ferocious beasts of men, women and children, burning at the stake of early Christianity. It became a passion among early Christians to become martyrs, so that they defied the laws and aggravated the rulers to put them to death, and in turn put to death in many cases those who would not accept and confess their conflicting doctrines. Read of the Crusades that caused the death, so it is admitted, of some twenty millions of the most vigorous people of Europe, even whole armies of women and

children at a time, frantically trying to invade Asia against another equally fanatical religion, claiming to have also the God of Israel and of Christ! Read of the Inquisition that through the most diabolical tortures and massacres, destroyed the best minds of Europe into the hundreds of thousands. Read of the Thirty Years War between Christians, all carried on by the people in the greatest good faith under the instigations of cunning priests and popes for their own aggrandizement, and the glory of God. Europe was made a veritable hell for a thousand years, by the Christian church, and all that time held science and civilization throttled, until in the Renaissance, the common sense of many people rebelled, came to America, established government for the people by the people, and taught the world that freedom and knowledge are the only road to heaven, and that the earth is the only place for the heaven of humanity. At last, the sun of science, which had begun to rise in Aristotle, emerged from the many centuries pall of popery, in Francis Bacon, and his illustrious confreres and followers of the sixteenth, seventeenth, eighteenth, and nineteenth centuries, it now promises to touch toward the zenith in the twentieth, through the efforts of the many thousands of profound poets, authors, editors, and especially the army of scientists banded together for research in the American and British and French and German and Japanese associations for the advancement of science, and the great scientific universities, agricultural colleges, industrial schools and experiment stations the world over, teaching that knowledge and labor are not curses, as the Scriptures teach, but that they are the greatest blessings enjoyed by man; and also, teaching that woman is man's mother and rather more than his equal, and not his slave, as the Scriptures teach, but an encouraging and delightful mate in every field, when equally educated and not abused.

Thus scholarly scientists are now compiling from the facts and truths of nature the great *Bible* of the *Church of Humanity*, the numerous works of science. As this Bible grows more complete, and is more generally read and practiced the better and happier will all mankind become.

With the introduction of Christianity came not progress and enlightenment and peace, but retrogression, ignorance, religious wranglings, destruction of libraries and learning, dark ages, inquisitions, religious wars, suppression of scientists and science, until religious fanaticism became so revolting that the better elements in human nature,—true to the great natural law that action and reactions are equal in opposite directions,—rebelled against it and chose to tolerate and encourage investigation and reason, when the glorious flowers of science began to bloom, to enlighten, civilize and sweeten humanity and its religions. Science has laid hold upon the ancient's ghosts, (gas and steam) and the thunderbolts of the gods, (electricity), and with them is doing the work and carrying the burdens of the world, warming and lighting our homes, and making the cities shine gloriously by night as well as by day. The sciences have made the architecture, the furnishing, the heating, the lighting, the music, and even the literature of the churches to some extent attractive, comfortable, healthful and beautiful, and we can safely predict, will in some time banish superstition from them, and then they will overflow with attendance of free, thinking men, for information as well as with women and children, for entertainment, and gossip.

This increased enlightenment has come while church membership has decreased from near 100 per cent in the fifteenth century, to about 40 per cent of population in the United States and the most advanced nations of Europe in 1912.

(6.) Because the doctrines found in the Bible, especially those in the New Testament, are mostly not original in these scriptures and the reported teachings of Jesus, but copies from older religions, largely from Buddhism, as shown by a comparison of parallel Christian and Buddhist scriptures. (See

Edmondson, "Christian and Buddhist Gospels Compared.") This scholarly and profound work proves beyond question that Christianity is largely derived from Buddhism and in reality is a western sect of that religion, adulterated with more or less of Mazdeism, Mithraism, and Egyptian, Grecian and Roman mythology.

I hope my readers will not think that I regard all religion as an unmixed evil, on the contrary, I freely confess that it is my opinion, after carefully studying the progress of man from a wild savage to civilization, that these religions came as a necessary product of an enquiring, but ignorant being,—an evolutionary product. The doctrines of the religions when first proclaimed were the theories of the "wise men" of the time, and have been modified or discarded as man gradually learned more of nature. For the time being they served the purpose of nuclei or social (church) organizations, and the rules of organization became the moral code, sometimes correct in principle, and often erroneous, and insofar as they were erroneous their practice led to bad results, and so were modified or annulled. In the process of time the "wise men" became venerated, then idolized, then deified, and the theories we set up by priests, as revelations of the gods, and were proclaimed and established as dogmas, that must be believed (accepted without question) in or to belong to the cult, and were enforced by threats of terrible punishment by the gods, and paradisial rewards after death.

So far was effecting the organization and cooperation of society, and a brotherly feeling they were good. But the dogmatizing, and tyrannizing priestcraft was evil, and a vast clog to progress. It is this part of religion that I eschew. All of its real good I approve. Progress and universal brotherhood is what man most needs, not sectarianism, hatred and strife, which are the children of dogmas.

I have named only six chief reasons for changing my religious opinions, and they are abundantly sufficient, although there are many more equally weighty. (See "The Christ" and "The Bible" by J. E. Remsburg.)

"Read the Scriptures, for in them ye think ye have eternal life," and if you are really and candidly seeking knowledge, you will find that I have told you the truth.

DUALISM AND MONISM: OR RELIGION AND SCIENCE IN A NUTSHELL

From *The New Revelation*, 1906 [Revised 1910]

All philosophies of being, or existence of fundamental unity or substance, can be arranged in two classes, each belonging entirely to one class or the other, or in part to both, namely; *Dualistic* and *Monistic*.

DUALISTIC PHILOSOPHY.—PHILOSOPHY OF CONFLICT
This is based upon the assumption that all existence consists of two fundamental substances, Matter and Spirit, that spirit occupies all space, that matter occupies, when existing, at least some space and is created by spirit out of nothing, by fiat, and can by spiritual fiat, be reduced to nothing, as taught in Christian Scriptures. That all energy belongs to spirit, and that matter is of itself totally dead and inert, and is merely a transitional habiliment of spirit. Some dualists, however, believe that matter and spirit are eternally co-existent, as taught in Unitarianism and Pantheism.

These propositions are indemonstrable by reason, but must be accepted by assent of faith, which rests on the infallibility of an established priesthood of men, claiming to be inspired by spirits to reveal them.

There are numerous sects, or schools, or churches of dualists.

Generally dualists hold that spirits are of two classes, the creator class, gods, and the created class, angels, devils, or demons, and spirits of men and souls of men and animals. That all spirits are immortal, although the created class had a beginning. That souls are mortal as well as material bodies. Some gods such as the Christians, are believed by their worshipers, to be self-existent, alive, i.e., conscious, infinite in knowledge, in power, in place and time, yet have ears, eyes, head, hair, hands, feet, etc., get angry, jealous, etc. Some gods are believed to be a single unit, such as Zeus of the Greeks, Brahm [sic] of the Hindoos, Yahveh of the Hebrews, Osiris, of the Egyptians, while others, such as the Christians, are believed to be triune, the Father, the Son and Holy Ghost. The created spirits may be infinite in duration, after creation but are finite in all other respects. All the spirits are believed to be capable of entering into material bodies, and of laying aside such bodies; that the spiritual substance can entirely separate from and be independent and heterogeneous to matter. The believers in this totally deed, inert matter are the true *materialists*. Monists do not believe in such matter.

The tenets of Dualism are unproved and unprovable assumptions, as its thousands of warring sects clearly prove. Its preaching in its varieties has given rise to Theism, Deism, Pantheism, Polytheism, Monotheism, and all manner of Spiritualism. Organization upon and practice of its dogmas constitute religion, in its multitudinous sects, all of which rest upon the primary assumption or concept that light, electricity, heat, life, memory, thought, consciousness are real entities, imponderable, spiritual substances, and that all bodies that occupy space, have weight, can be perceived by the bodily senses, and composed of an entirely different genus of substance are dead, inert matter, hence the latter must have been created by the former,—spirit,—and may again be reduced to nothing, but the advocates of Dualism, seem not to perceive the logical inconsistency of an eternally live thing producing a finite, dead thing. Morality in Dualism, i.e., in faith—religions, chiefly consists in accepting and publicly confessing to believe its doctrines to be true, without doubt or question; and that disbelieving them is one of the greatest sins that can be committed. Fear of divine punishment and desire to secure eternal life, wealth and glory in a scripture-promised spiritual world after death are its prime motives to obedience to its code of morals, hence, it tends to make slavish ceremonial devotees of its followers.

*MONISTIC PHILOSOPHY.—PHILOSOPHY OF PEACE AND PROGRESS.

*Read this carefully, studiously, and you will get an idea of the philosophy now entertained by the majority of the great thinkers of the world.

This is based upon the testimony of the senses and logical reasoning therefrom; and the recorded clearly demonstrated facts and truths in every department of nature comprehensible to man, harmoniously classified, constitute its code, known as *Science*; not to be accepted by blind belief and confession, but to be known, or capable of knowing and demonstrating, over and over at any time for verification. This doctrine in practice has been able to demonstrate only one genus of fundamental existence, namely, that which of itself moves, within itself, or among its parts. This prime entity, or substance, is not the dead, inert matter of dualistic religions, not yet the warring spirits of religion, nor yet the combined, dead mater and live spirit of Pantheism, whose body is nature and whose spirit is God, but one consistent, homogeneous entity or existence, that occupies all known space, and eternally moves, hence has eternal energy, or capability to move. To assume that spirit occupies all space, and that matter also occupies some or all space, is contradictory to the recognized law of physics, known as impenetrability of matter, or else spirit occupies no space, which is a definition of nothing.

That motion, radiating from any body varies in intensity inversely as the square of the distance from the center of gravity of that body, proves the energy to reside in the body. The energy also varies exactly as the mass of the body varies, and this in connection with the previous law variability of energy announces most certainly that the energy resides within the body and not outside it, and is its essential property and motion its phenomenon by which we recognize its existence and nature. All motion and formation are necessary results from the nature of substance.

All our knowledge is conveyed to us through motion producing sensation, and the interpretation of this motion by our reason—brain, gives us the conception that everything occupying space is *energizing being*. This energizing being give us no further knowledge of its character than that it moves and feels. The motion may be of a general kind, common to all being, such as gravitative, electric, light, heat, cohesive, chemical, etc., or it may be of special kid, as organic life-motion, or consciousness, in its variety of touch, taste, smell, hearing, sight, etc., and of resultants from these, thought, dreaming, etc. But we know this consciousness to vary from the acute awareness of the most sensitive human being through all gradations of animals, down to mollusks, amoebas, an still less in the so-called sensitive plants, on down through tendrils and sunflowers, tropeolums and twisting vines; on down to the crystaloids,—half cell, half crystal,—thence to regular crystals, until finally in dust and solids and liquids and gasses, composed of the same chemical elements as the higher organisms, we find still the rudimentary consciousness of chemical affinity, through its action—chemical motion; yet on down till at last the consciousness of gravitation causes the worlds to dance about one another. Although the affinities change in degree of consciousness and the motions of the bodies,—the space-occupying beings,—change in length or amplitude; not the slightest indication is perceptible anywhere that a different extraneous kind of being or force exists. In fact, such cannot exist, without producing universal chaos, for then the known laws of science could not hold good a moment; hence there is no creator (God) of nature, there being no necessity for such; but to one not seeing that nature is all-sufficient within itself, it is necessary for him to invent a creator to satisfy his want of facts.

This motion-producing entity or being cannot be conceived of as an individual. That would be a paradox,—an infinite finite thing. In its entirety it is incomprehensible, i.e., infinite. We can rationally predicate of it, that it is self-existent, infite [sic] in place, in time, in division into connected parts,—we being some of the parts,—infinite in form of parts and motion of parts, the parts perpetually changing by involving the older and evolving the new, by mutual co-operation, while the substance, with all its capabilities eternally continues indestructible. Each individual part can be conceived only as a *part* of something greater.

The method or law of compensation,—of action and reaction equally in opposite directions, among the parts,—ever prevails. This law in social affairs is known as the law of reciprocity,—the golden rule. When worked out in its various ramifications in social and civil affairs of mankind, and classified logically, constitutes the science of ethics or morals and political economy.

Natural law is simply the method or course of procedure, while religious law is an arbitrary dogma, often in conflict with natural law. It then has evil results.

This scientific Monism has but one faith, that is the faith or conviction that this infinite being—nature—is uniform in all its parts in conforming to the great law of action and reaction in all its varieties and ramifications of form and motion. As is the environment so is the form and as is the form and make-up of a part so are its motions and consciousness, and that like or similar conditions produce like or similar results.

Perception and reason find no room possible for the so-called supernatural, or spiritual, any more than it finds totally dead, inert matter, hence these can be no other than idle theories of ignorant persons, and the believers in dead, inert substances are the true *materialists*.

Religious faith in the supernatural, neither makes nor annuls a fact or truth, except the fact of believing. It does, however, blind its subjects to the unprejudiced search for and acceptance of truth, when adverse to the tenets believed, and hence stands in the way of progress and ameliorations, as the history of religions prove. Hence, in so far religious faith is not a virtue but an evil, and hence the religion that requires it, and a public confession of it, is, in that matter, not good but evil, and hence punishment for not having religious faith is tyrannical and should be stopped. Hence hell doctrines are heathenish.

The true scientist is always ready for the acceptance of any new fact or truth discovered and proven and hence is progressive.

If it is a fact in nature that any individual form can exist eternally in a conscious state, and be aware of such state as a perpetual ego, or self, our knowledge knows nothing of it, and no faith in such a theory can make or annul the facts in the matter, hence worry about a future state is only the property of unthinking, faith-frightened persons, and produces unhappiness, and often causes persons, through fear to remain ignorant, and miserable, where they should be informed, wise and happy.

Faith glories in its invented spooks, yet it is frightened to death (in reason) by them.

Reason grows fat and happy on fact and truth, and hence has no ghosts to fear.

James Dickson Shaw

"The very first work possible in a reformation is to convince the intelligent that the old system is faulty, that it lacks the warranty of reason, is out of harmony with the truth, and obstructive of human progress."

JAMES DICKSON SHAW was born on December 27, 1841 in Walker County, Texas. During the Civil War, he served as a Second Lieutenant in the 10th Texas Infantry, C.S.A. After the war, he was an active member of the Pat Cleburne Camp, U.C.V.

In 1870, Shaw became an ordained Methodist minister. In 1878, he moved to Waco, where he served as pastor of the Fifth Street Methodist Church until 1882, when, after preaching a sermon that stressed good works over faith, Shaw was called before a church examining committee in Cleburne. After he admitted his unorthodox opinions, the committee stripped him of his credentials.

Later that same year, Shaw founded the Religious and Benevolent Association and in 1883, he began publishing a monthly newspaper titled *The Independent Pulp,* the masthead of which stated that its purpose was "to serve as a forum for the most liberal and independent thinkers on the moral, social, and intellectual questions of the day."

In 1890 Shaw organized the first meeting of the short-lived Texas Liberal Association in Waco, where he was elected president. He later served as secretary. The group disbanded following the 1894 convention in Temple.

During his heyday, Shaw was a sought-after public speaker who frequently traveled around the state to address his fellow freethinkers. In Waco, he served for a time on the city council. Following the death of *Iconoclast* publisher W. C. Brann in a gunfight with an offended Baptist, Shaw wrote a biography of his old friend.

In 1881, Shaw's first wife, Lucy, died, leaving him with six children to raise alone. In 1884, he married Rachella Dodson McCoy, who died in Waco in 1902.

In 1900 Shaw suspended publication of *The Independent Pulpit*, replacing it in 1901 with *The Searchlight*, which he edited until 1910, when he moved to Glendale, California, where two of his daughters and a grandchild looked after him in his old age. He died in California on December 3, 1926. He was buried at Waco's Oakwood Cemetery.

Even Shaw's theological opponents respected him. One Baptist minister, J. B. Cranfill, wrote that "while his arguments were clearcut and emphatic, he never at any time ceased to exemplify the high qualities of good breeding and gentlemaness."[2]

---

[2] *Dallas Morning News*, January 6, 1929.

THE BIBLE AGAINST ITSELF.

From *The Independent Pulpit*, January 1889

Christians affirm that the Bible is a divine revelation of truth unmixed with error; that all its utterances are harmonious and consistent, one with another; that it is without falsehood or equivocation, and that it is absolutely without contradiction.

In denial of this, Liberals affirm that it is a work of human origin, and while it contains some truth, it also contains some error; that its utterances are inharmonious and inconsistent in many respects; that it is equivocal in many of its doctrines, false in many of its statements, and absolutely contradictory.

In proof of this, the following passages are quoted as indisputable evidence, and, as they are all carefully noted as to chapters and verse, we invite the reader to examine them with the bible in hand, so that each one may be studied in its proper place, and considered in connection with other passages about it.

As a guarantee that we do not seek to misrepresent the Bible, we will most readily accord a reasonable amount of space in the INDEPENDENT PULPIT for such explanation of them, or any portion of them, as our Christian friends may deem satisfactory to them, so that all possible errors of understanding on our part may be exposed, and also that these, at present, very apparent discrepancies may be cleared up:

I.

GOD DIVIDED LIGHT FROM DARKNESS THE FIRST DAY.

And God divided the light from the darkness. And God called the light day, and the darkness he called night. And the evening and the morning were the first day.—Gen. 1:4-5.

GOD DIVIDED LIGHT FROM DARKNESS THE FOURTH DAY.

And God said, let there be light in the firmament of the heaven to divide the day from the night; * * * And God set them in the firmament of the heaven to give light upon the earth * * * and to divide the light from the darkness * * * and the evening and the morning were the fourth day.—Gen. 1:14-19.

II

GOD WAS PLEASED WITH HIS WORK.

And God saw everything that he had made, and, behold, it was very good.—Gen. 1:31.

GOD WAS DISPLEASED WITH HIS WORK.

It repented the Lord that he had made man on the earth, and it grieved him at his heart. —Gen. 6:6.

III

GOD DOES NOT REPENT

God is not a man, that he should lie; neither the son of man, that he should repent.—Num. 23:19.

GOD DOES REPENT.

And God saw their works, that they turned from their evil way; and God repented of the evil that he had said that he would do unto them; and he did it not. —Jonah 3:10.

IV.

GOD IS UNCHANGEABLE

For I am the Lord; I change not. —Mal. 3:6.

GOD IS CHANGEABLE.

Wherefore the Lord God of Israel saith, I said indeed that they house and the house of thy father, should walk before me forever; but now the Lord sayeth be it far from me. * * * Behold, the days come that I will cut off thine arm, and the arm of thy father's house.—I. Sam. 2:30-31.

V.

GOD CANNOT LIE

It was impossible for God to lie. —Hebr. 6:18.

GOD SENDS LYING SPIRITS TO DECEIVE.

Now therefore, behold, the Lord hath put a lying spirit in the mouth of all these thy prophets, and the Lord hath spoken evil concerning thee.—I. Kings 22:23.

VI.

GOD IS PEACEFUL.

God is not the author of confusion, but of peace.—I. Cor. 14:33.

GOD IS WARLIKE

The Lord is a man of war.—Exod. 15:3.

VII.

GOD IS MERCIFUL

The Lord is very pitiful, and of tender mercy.—James 5:11

GOD IS UNMERCIFUL.

I will not pity, nor spare, nor have mercy, but destroy them.—Jere. 13:14.

VIII.

GOD IS VISIBLE.
For I have seen God face to face, and my life is preserved.—Gen. 32:30.

GOD IS INVISIBLE.
No man hath seen God at any time.—Jon. 1:18.

IX.

GOD RESTS AND IS REFRESHED.
For in six days the Lord made heaven and earth, and on the seventh day he rested, and was refreshed.—Exod. 31:17.

GOD IS NEVER TIRED.
Hast thou not heard, that the everlasting God, the Lord, the creator of the ends of the earth, fainteth not, neither is weary!—Is. 40:28.

X.

GOD IS OMNIPRESENT.
Whither shall I flee from thy presence? If I ascend up into heaven, thou art there: if I make my bed in hell, behold, thou are there. If I take the wings of the morning, and dwell in the uttermost parts of the sea; even there shall thy hand lead me, and thy right hand shall hold me.—Ps. 139:7-10.

GOD IS NOT OMNIPRESENT.
And the Lord said, because the cry of Sodom and Gomorrah is great, and because their sin is very grevious [sic]; I will go down now, and see whither they have done altogether according to the cry of it, which is come unto me; and if not, I will know.—Gen. 18:20-21.

XI.

GOD IS OMNISCENT.

For his eyes are upon the ways of man, and he seeth all his goings, there is no darkness nor shadow of death, where the workers of iniquity may hide themselves.—Job. 34:21-22.

GOD IS NOT OMNISCENT.

And Adam and his wife hid themselves from the presence of the Lord God, amongst the trees of the garden.—Gen. 3:8.

XII.

GOD IS ALL POWERFUL.

With God all things are possible.—Mat. 19:26.

GOD IS NOT ALL-POWERFUL.

And the Lord was with Judah, and he drave out the inhabitants of the mountain; but could not drive out the inhabitants of the valley, because they had chariots of iron.—Judes. 1:19.

XIII.

GOD IS IMPARTIAL.

There is no respect of persons with God.—Rom. 2:11

GOD IS PARTIAL.

For the children being not yet born, neither having done any good or evil, that the purpose of God, according to election, might stand, * * * it was said unto her, the elder shall serve the younger. As it is written, Jacob have I loved, but Esau have I hated.—Rom. 9:11-13.

XIV.

GOD IS JUST.
A God of truth, and without iniquity, just and right is he.—Deut. 32:4.

GOD IS UNJUST.
For I, the Lord thy God am a jealous God, visiting the iniquity of the Fathers upon the children unto the third and fourth generation of them that hate me.—Exod. 20:5.

XV.

GOD DOES RIGHT.
Shall not the judge of all the earth do right?.—Gen. 18:35.

GOD DOES WRONG.
I make peace and create evil; I, the Lord do all these things.—Is. 45:7.

XVI.

GOD IS LOVE.
And we have known and believed the love that God hath to us. God is love; and he that dwelleth in love dwelleth in God, and God is him.—I. John 4:16.

GOD IS NOT LOVE.
The Lord thy God is a consuming fire.—Deut. 4:24.

XVII.

GOD'S ANGER ENDURETH BUT FOR A MOMENT.
His anger endureth but for a moment.—Ps. 30:5.

GOD'S ANGER LASTED FORTY YEARS.

And the Lord's anger was kindled against Israel, and he made them wander in the wilderness forty years, until all generations that had done evil in the sight of the Lord was consumed.—Num. 32:13.

XVIII.

GOD REQUIRED BURNT OFFERINGS.

And the priest shall burn all on the altar to be a burnt sacrifice, an offering made by fire, of a sweet savor unto the Lord.—Lev. 1:9.

GOD DID NOT REQUIRE BURNT OFFERINGS.

For I spake not unto your fathers, nor commanded them in the day that I brought them out of the land of Egypt, concerning burnt offerings or sacrifices.—Jer. 7:22.

XIX.

GOD FORBIDS HUMAN SACRIFICE.

Take heed to thyself that thou be not snared by following them * * * for even their sons and their daughters have they burnt in the fire to their gods.—Deut. 12:30-31.

GOD COMMANDS HUMAN SACRIFICE.

No devoted thing that a man shall devote unto the Lord of all that he hath, both of man and of beast, and of the field of his possession, shall be sold or redeemed; every devoted thing is most holy unto the Lord. None devoted which shall be devoted of men shall be redeemed but shall surely be put to death.—Lev. 27:28-29.

XX.

GOD TEMPTS NO MAN.

Let no man say when he is tempted, I am tempted of God; for God can not be tempted with evil, neither tempteth he any man.—James 1:13.

GOD DOES TEMPT MAN.

And it came to pass after these things that God did tempt Abraham.—Gen. 22:1.

XXI.

THERE IS BUT ONE GOD.

There is none other God but one.—I. Cor. 8:4.

THERE IS ANOTHER GOD.

And the Lord God said, behold the man is become as one of us.—Gen. 3:22.

XXII.

GOD IS COMPASSIONATE.

The Lord is gracious and full of compassion, slow to anger, and of great mercy.—Ps. 145:8.

GOD IS REVENGEFUL.

God is jealous, and the Lord revengeth; and is furious; the Lord will take vengeance on his adversaries.—Nahum. 1:2.

XXIII.

GOD'S STATUTES ARE RIGHT.

The statutes of the Lord are right.—Ps. 19:8.

GOD'S STATUTES ARE NOT ALL RIGHT.
Therefore I gave them also statutes that were not good, and judgements whereby they should not live.—Ezek. 20-25.

XXIV.

GOD WILLS TO SAVE ALL MEN.
Who will have all men to be saved, and to come unto the knowledge of the truth.—I. Tim. 2:4.

GOD DOES NOT WILL TO SAVE ALL.
God shall send them strong delusions, that they should believe a lie; that they all might be damned who believe not the truth.—II. Thes. 2:11-12.

XXV.

GOD IS GOOD.
Good and upright is the Lord.—Ps. 25:8.

GOD IS NOT GOOD.
Shall there be evil in a city, and the Lord hath not done it?—Amos. 3:6.

XXVI.

FRAUD AND ROBBERY ARE FORBIDDEN.
Thou shalt not defraud they neighbor, neither rob him.—Lev. 19:13.

FRAUD AND ROBBERY COMMANDED.
When ye go ye shall not go empty; but every woman shall borrow of her neighbor, and her that sojourneth in her house, jewels of silver and jewels of gold, and raiment; and ye shall put them upon your sons, and upon your daughters, and ye shall

spoil the Egyptians.—Exod. 3:21-22.

XXVII.

LYING IS FORBIDDEN.
Thou shalt not bear false witness.—Exod. 20:16.

LYING IS SANCTIONED.
And there came forth a spirit, and stood before the Lord, and said I will persuade him. And the Lord said unto him, wherewith? And he said, I will go forth and will be a lying spirit in the mouth of all his prophets. And he said thou shalt persuade him and prevail also; go forth and do so.—I. Kings 22:21-22.

XXVIII.

KILLING IS FORBIDDEN.
Thou shalt not kill.—Exod. 20:13.

KILLING IS COMMANDED.
Thus saith the Lord God of Israel, put every man his sword by his side, and go in and out from gate to gate throughout the cam, and slay every man his brother, and every man his companion, and every man his neighbor.—Exod. 32:27.

XXIX.

MAKING IMAGES FORBIDDEN.
Thou shalt not make unto thee any graven image, or any likeness of anything that is in heaven above, or that is in the earth beneath.—Exod. 20:4.

MAKING IMAGES COMMANDED.
Thou shalt make two cherubims of gold * * * and the cherubims shall stretch forth their wings on high, covering the

mercy seat with their wings, and their faces shall look one to another.—Exod. 25:18-20.

XXX.

GOOD WORKS TO BE SEEN OF MEN.
Let your light so shine before men that they may see your good works.—Job. 34:21-22.

GOOD WORKS NOT TO BE SEEN OF MEN.
Take heed that ye do not your alms before men, to be seen of them.—Matt. 6:1.

XXXI.

THE SWORD DISCOURAGED.
All they that take the sword shall perish with the sword.—Matt. 26:52.

THE SWORD ENCOURAGED.
He that hath no sword, let him sell his garment and buy one.—Luke 22:36.

XXXII.

NON-RESISTANCE IS TAUGHT.
Resist not evil, but whosoever shall smite thee on thy right cheek, turn to him the other also.—Matt. 5:39.

THE CONTRARY PRACTICED.
And when he had made a scourge of small cords, he drove them all out of the temple.—John 2:15.

XXXIII.

DEATH IS NOT TO BE FEARED.
Be not afraid of them that kill the body.—Luke 12:4.

DEATH IS FEARED.
After these things, Jesus walked in Galilee; for he would not walk in Jewry, because the Jews sought to kill him.—John 7:1.

XXXIV.

CIRCUMCISION COMMANDED.
For his eyes are upon the ways of man, and he seeth all his goings, there is no darkness nor shadow of death, where the workers of iniquity may hide themselves.—Job. 34:21-22.

CIRCUMCISION CONDEMNED.
Behold, I, Paul, say unto you, that if ye be circumcised, Christ shall profit you nothing.—Gal. 5:2.

XXXV.

KEEPING THE SABBATH ENJOINED.
Remember the Sabbath day to keep it holy.—Exod. 20:8.

KEEPING THE SABBATH IGNORED.
Let no man therefore judge you in meat, or in drink, or in respect of a holy day, or of the new moon; or of the Sabbath days.—Col. 2:16.

XXXVI.

WHY THE SABBATH WAS INSTITUTED.
For in six days the Lord made heaven and earth, the sea, and all that in them is, and rested the seventh day; wherefore the

Lord blessed the Sabbath day and hallowed it.—Exod. 20:11.

QUITE A DIFFERENT REASON.

And remember that thou wast a servant in the land of Egypt, and that the Lord thy God brought thee out whence through a mighty hand and by a stretched out arm; therefore the Lord thy God commanded thee to keep the Sabbath day.—Deut. 5:15.

XXXVII.

NO WORK TO BE DONE ON THE SABBATH.

Whosoever doeth any work on the Sabbath day, he shall surely be put to death.—Exod. 31:15.

JESUS IGNORED THIS LAW.

Therefore did the Jews persecute Jesus, and sought to slay him, because he had done these things on the Sabbath day.—John 5:16.

XXXVIII.

BAPTISM COMMANDED.

Go ye therefore, and teach all nations, baptizing them in the name of the Father, and of the Son, and of the Holy Ghost.—Matt. 28:19.

BAPTISM REPUDIATED.

I thank God that I baptized none of you but Crispus and Gatus * * * For Christ sent me not to baptize, but to preach the gospel.—I. Cor. 14:17.

XXXIX.

THE TAKING OF OATHS SANCTIONED.

He that sweareth in the earth, shall swear by the God of

truth.—Is. 65:16.

THE TAKING OF OATHS FORBIDDEN.
But I say unto you, swear not at all.—Matt. 5:34.

XL.

ADULTERY FORBIDDEN.
Thou shalt not commit adultery.—Exod. 20:14.

ADULTERY SANCTIONED.
But all the women children, * * * keep alive for yourselves.—Num. 31:18.

XLI.

KINDRED TO BE HONORED.
Honor thy father and mother.—Eph. 6:2.

KINDRED TO BE HATED.
If any man come to me, and hate not his father, and mother, and wife, and children, and brethren, and sisters, * * * he can not be my disciple.—Luke 14:26.

XLII.

DRINK DISCOURAGED.
Look not upon the wine when it is red, when it giveth his color in the cup, when it moveth itself aright. At the last it biteh like a serpent, and stingeth like an adder.—Prov. 23:31-32.

DRINK ENCOURAGED.
Give strong drink unto him that is ready to perish, and wine unto those that be of heavy hearts. Let him drink, and forget his misery, and remember his poverty no more.—Prov. 31:6-7.

XLIII.

OBEDIENCE TO MASTERS ENJOINED.

Servants, be subject to your masters with all fear; not only to the good and gentle, but also to the froward.—I. Pet. 2:18.

OBEDIENCE TO MASTERS FORBIDDEN.

Be not ye the servants of men.—I. Cor. 7:23.

XLIV.

THERE IS AN UNPARDONABLE SIN.

He that shall blaspheme against the Holy Ghost hath never forgiveness.—Mark 3:29.

THERE IS NO UNPARDONABLE SIN.

And by him, all that believe are justified from all things.—Acts 13:39.

XLV.

WISDON A SOURCE OF ENJOYMENT.

Happy is the man that findeth wisdom. Her ways are ways of pleasantness, and all her paths are peace.—Prov. 3:13-17.

WISDOM A SOURCE OF GRIEF.

In much wisdom is much grief; and he that increaseth knowledge increaseth sorrow.—Eccl. 1:18.

XLVI.

WEALTH A BLESSING.

Blessed is the man that feareth the Lord. Wealth and riches shall be in his home.—Ps. 112:1-3.

WEALTH A CURSE.

It is easier for a camel to go through the eye of a needle, than for a rich man to enter into the kingdom of God.—Matt. 19:24.

XLVII.

MAN WAS CREATED AFTER THE OTHER ANIMALS.

And God made the beasts of the earth after his kind, and cattle after their kind * * * And God said, let us make man * * * So God created man in his own image.—Gen. 1:25-27.

MAN WAS CREATED BEFORE THE OTHER ANIMALS.

And the Lord God said, it is not good that man should be alone; I will make him an help-meet for him. And out of the ground the Lord God formed every beast of the field, and every fowl of the air, and brought them unto Adam to see what he would them.—Gen. 2:18-19.

XLVIII.

NOAH TOOK INTO THE ARK CLEAN BEASTS BY SEVENS.

And the Lord said unto Noah, * * * Of every clean beast thou shalt take to thee by sevens. * * * And Noah did according unto all that the Lord commanded him.—Gen. 7:1-5.

NOAH TOOK INTO THE ARK CLEAN BEASTS BY TWOS.

Of clean beasts * * * there went in two and two unto Noah into the Ark * * * As God had commanded Noah.—Gen. 7:8-9.

XLIX.

JOHN THE BAPTIST RECOGNIZED JESUS AS THE MESSIAH.

The next day John seeth Jesus coming unto him, and saith, behold the Lamb of God, which taketh away the sin of the world

* * * And I saw and bare record that this is the Son of God.—John 1: 29-34.

JOHN THE BAPTIST DID NOT RECOGNIZE JESUS AS THE MESSIAH.

Now, when John had heard in the prison of the works of Christ, he sent two of his disciples and said unto him, art thou he that should come, or do we look for another?—Matt. 11:2-3.

L.

JOHN THE BAPTIST WAS ELIAS.

This is Elias which was for to come.—Matt. 11:14.

JOHN THE BAPTIST WAS NOT ELIAS.

And they asked him, What then? Art thou Elias? And he saith, I am not.—John 1:21.

LI.

THE FATHER OF JOSEPH, MARY'S HUSBAND, WAS JACOB.

And Jacob begat Joseph, the husband of Mary, of whom was born Jesus.—Matt. 1:16.

THE FATHER OF MARY'S HUSBAND WAS HELI.

Being * * * the son of Joseph which was the son of Heli.—Luke 3:23.

LII.

THE FATHER OF SALA WAS ARPHAXAD.

And Arphaxad lived five and thirty years and beget Salah.—Gen. 11:12.

THE FATHER OF SALA WAS CAINAN.

Which was the son of Sala, which was the son of Cainan,

which was the son of Arphaxad.—Luke 3:35-36.

LIII.

THE INFANT JESUS WAS TAKEN INTO EGYPT.

He took the young child and his mother by night, and departed into Egypt, and was there until the death of Herod. * * * But when Herod was dead * * * he arose and took the young child and his mother and came * * * and dwelt in a city called Nazareth.—Matt. 2:14-23.

THE INFANT JESUS WAS NOT TAKEN INTO EGYPT.

And when the days of her purification * * * were accomplished, they brought him to Jerusalem, to present him to the Lord. * * * And when they had performed all things, according to the law of the Lord, they returned * * * to their own city, Nazareth.—Luke 2:22-39.

LIV.

JESUS WAS TEMPTED IN THE WILDERNESS.

And immediately [after his baptism] the spirit driveth him into the wilderness. And he was there in the wilderness forty days, tempted of Satan.—Mark 1:12-13.

JESUS WAS NOT TEMPTED IN THE WILDERNESS.

And the third day [after his baptism] there was a marriage in Cana of Galilee. * * * And both Jesus was called, and his disciples to the marriage.—John 2:1-2.

LV.

JESUS TEACHED HIS FIRST SERMON SITTING ON THE MOUNT.

And seeing the multitudes, he went up into a mountain, and

when he was set his disciples came unto him. And he opened his mouth and taught them, saying.—Matt. 5:1-2.

JESUS PREACHED HIS FIRST SERMON STANDING IN THE PLAIN.

And he came down with them and stood in the plain; and the company of his disciples and a great multitude of people * * * came to hear him. * * * And he lifted up his eyes on his disciples and said.—Luke 6:17-20.

LVI.

JOHN WAS IN PRISON WHEN JESUS WENT INTO GALILEE.

Now, after that John was put in prison, Jesus came into Galilee, preaching the gospel of the kingdom of God.—Mark 1:14.

JOHN WAS NOT IN PRISON WHEN JESUS WENT INTO GALILEE.

After these things came Jesus and his disciples into the land of Judea. * * * And John was also baptizing in Enon. * * * For John was not yet cast into prison.—John 3:22-24.

LVII.

THE DISCIPLES WERE COMMANDED TO TAKE A STAFF AND SANDALS.

And commanded them that they should take nothing for their journey save a staff only; no scrip, no bread, no money in their purse; but be shod with sandals.—Mark 6:8-9.

THE DISCIPLES WERE COMMANDED TO TAKE NEITHER STAVES NOR SANDALS.

Provide neither gold, nor silver, nor brass in your purses; nor scrip for your journey, neither two coats, neither shoes, nor yet staves.—Matt. 10:9-10.

LVIII.

TWO BLIND MEN BESOUGHT JESUS.

And behold, two blind men sitting by the way-side, when they heard that Jesus passed by, cried out, saying, Have mercy on us, O Lord, thou son of David.—Matt. 20:30.

ONLY ONE BLIND MAN BESOUGHT HIM.

A certain blind man sat by the way-side begging. * * * And he cried, saying, Jesus, thou son of David, have mercy on me.— Luke 18:35-38.

LIX.

TWO MEN COMING OUT OF THE TOMBS MET JESUS.

There met him two possessed with devils, coming out of the tombs.—Matt. 8:28.

ONLY ONE MAN COMING OUT OF THE TOMBS MET HIM.

There met him, out of the tombs, a man with an unclean spirit.—Mark 5:2.

LX.

A CENTURION BROUGHT JESUS TO HEAL HIS SERVANT.

There came unto him a centurion, beseeching him, and saying, Lord, my servant lieth at home sick of the palsy.—Matt. 8:28.

NOT THE CENTURION, BUT HIS MESSENGERS, BESOUGHT JESUS.

He sent unto him the elders of the Jews, beseeching him that he would come and heal his servant. And when they came to

Jesus, they besought him.—Luke 7:3-4.

LXI.

TWO MEN COMING OUT OF THE TOMBS MET JESUS.
There met him two possessed with devils, coming out of the tombs.—Matt. 8:28.

ONLY ONE MAN COMING OUT OF THE TOMBS MET HIM.
There met him, out of the tombs, a man with an unclean spirit.—Mark 5:2.

LIX.

TWO MEN COMING OUT OF THE TOMBS MET JESUS.
There met him two possessed with devils, coming out of the tombs.—Matt. 8:28.

ONLY ONE MAN COMING OUT OF THE TOMBS MET HIM.
There met him, out of the tombs, a man with an unclean spirit.—Mark 5:2.

LIX.

JESUS WAS CRUCIFIED AT THE THIRD HOUR.
And it was the third hour; and they crucified him.—Mark 15:25.

HE WAS NOT CRUCIFIED UNTIL THE SIXTH HOUR.
And it was the preparation of the passover, and about the sixth hour and he said unto the Jews, Behold your king. * * * Shall I crucify your king?—John 19:14-15.

LXII.

THE TWO THIEVES REVILED JESUS.

The thieves also which were crucified with him, cast the same in his teeth.—Matt. 27:44.

ONLY ONE OF THE THIEVES REVILED HIM.

And one of the malefactors which were hanged railed on him. * * * But the other answering, rebuked him, saying, Dost thou not fear God, seeing thou art in the same condemnation—Luke 23:39-40.

LXIII.

VINEGAR MINGLED WITH GALL WAS OFFERED TO JESUS.

They gave him vinegar to drink, mingled with gall.—Matt. 27:34.

WINE MINGLED WITH MYRRH WAS OFFERED TO HIM.

And they gave him to drink wine mingled with myrrh.—Mark 15:23.

LXIV.

SATAN ENTERED INTO JUDAS WHILE AT THE SUPPER.

And after the sop Satan entered into him.—John 13:27.

SATAN ENTERED INTO HIM BEFORE THE SUPPER.

Then entered Satan into Judas. * * * And he went his way and communed with the chief priests and captains, how he might betray him. * * * Then came the day of unleavened bread when the passover must be killed.—Luke 22:3-7.

LXV.

JUDAS RETURNED THE PIECES OF SILVER.
Then Judas * * * brought again the thirty pieces of silver to the chief priests and elders.—Matt. 27:3.

JUDAS DID NOT RETURN THE PIECES OF SILVER.
Now, this man purchased a field with the reward of iniquity.—Acts 1:!8.

LXVI.

JUDAS HANGED HIMSELF.
And he cast down the pieces of silver in the temple and departed, and went and hanged himself.—Matt. 27:5.

JUDAS DID NOT HANG HIMSELF, BUT DIED ANOTHER WAY.
And falling headlong he burst asunder in the midst, and all his bowels gushed out.—Acts 1:18.

LXVII.

THE POTTER'S FIELD WAS PURCHASED BY JUDAS.
Now, this man purchased a field with the reward of iniquity.—Acts 1:18.

THE POTTER'S FIELD WAS PURCHASED BY THE CHIEF PRIESTS.
And the chief priests took the silver pieces * * * and bought with them the potter's field—Matt. 27:-7.

LXVIII.

BUT ONE WOMAN CAME TO THE SEPULCHER.
The first day of the week cometh Mary Magdalene early,

when it was yet dark, unto the sepulcher.—John 20:1.

TWO WOMEN CAME TO THE SEPULCHER.
In the end of the Sabbath as it began to dawn toward the first day of the week, came Mary Magdalene, and the other Mary, to see the sepulcher.—Matt. 28:1.

LXIX.

THREE WOMEN CAME TO THE SEPULCHER.
And when the Sabbath was past, Mary Magdalene, and Mary the mother of James, and Salome, had brought sweet spices, that they might come and anoint him.—Mark 16:1.

MORE THAN THREE WOMEN CAME TO THE SEPULCHER.
It was Mary Magdalene, and Joanna, and Mary the mother of James, and other women that were with them—Luke 14:10.

LXX.

IT WAS SUNRISE WHEN THEY CAME TO THE SEPULCHER.
And very early in the morning, the first day of the week, they came unto the sepulcher, at the rising of the sun.—Mark 16:2.

IT WAS SOME TIME BEFORE SUNRISE WHEN THEY CAME.
The first day of the week, cometh Mary Magdalene, early, while it was yet dark, unto the sepulcher.—John 20:1.

LXXI.

TWO ANGELS WERE SEEN AT THE SEPULCHER, STANDING.
And it came to pass, as they were much perplexed thereabout, behold, two men stood by them in shining garments.—Luke: 24.4.

BUT ONE ANGEL WAS SEEN AND HE WAS SITTING.
For the angel of the Lord descended from heaven, and came and rolled back the stone from the door, and sat upon it. * * * the angel answered and said unto the women, Fear not.—Matt. 28:2-5.

LXXII.

TWO ANGELS WERE SEEN WITHIN THE SEPULCHER.
And as she wept she stooped down and looked into the sepulcher, and seeth two angels in white.—John 20:11-12.

BUT ONE ANGEL WAS SEEN WITHIN THE SEPULCHER.
And entering into the sepulcher, they saw a young man sitting on the right side, clothed in a long white garment.—Mark 16:5.

LXXIII.

THE WOMEN WENT AND TOLD THE DISCIPLES OF CHRIST'S RESURRECTION.
And they departed quickly from the sepulcher, with fear and great joy, and did run to bring his disciples word.—Matt. 28:8

THE WOMEN DID NOT GO AND TELL THE DISCIPLES.
And they went out quickly and fled from the sepulcher; for they trembled and were amazed; neither said they anything to any man.—Mark 16:8.

LXXIV.

THE ANGELS APPEARED AFTER PETER AND JOHN VISITED THE SEPULCHER.
Peter therefore went forth, and that other disciple, and came to the sepulcher, * * * and went into the sepulcher, and seeth the

linen clothes. * * * Then the disciples went away again. But Mary stood without at the sepulcher weeping, and as she wept she stooped down and looked into the sepulcher, and seeth two angels in white.—John 20:3-12.

THE ANGELS APPEARED BEFORE PETER ALONE VISITED THE SEPULCHER.

Behold, two men stood by them [the women] in shining garments. * * And they * * * returned from the sepulcher, and told all these things unto the eleven. * * * Then arose Peter, and ran unto the sepulcher, and stooping down he beheld the linen clothes laid by themselves, and departed wondering.—Luke 22:4-12.

LXXV.

JESUS APPEARED FIRST TO MARY MAGDALENE ONLY.

Now when Jesus was risen early the first day of the week, he appeared first to Mary Magdalene.—Mark 16:9.

JESUS APPEARED FIRST TO THE TWO MARYS.

And as they [Mary Magdalene and the other Mary] went to tell his disciples, behold Jesus met them, saying, All hail.—Matt. 28:9.

THOSE BIBLE CONTRADICITONS.

The array of Bible contradictions massed under the heading, "The Bible Against Itself," will serve the important purpose of putting a quietus upon the ceaseless din of preachers and Sunday school teachers that the Bible is without contradictions. Of last this cry has become so loud, and so bare-faced, that we deem it well enough that the plain truth be placed before the people.

In this array we have only given a portion of the immense number that can be produced, and for brevity's sake we have only arranged one text on a side. There is a pamphlet containing 144 propositions, and another containing 148, in both of which a number of different texts for and against each proposition are given. Our object in giving but one is to provide a cheap tract for free distribution, and at the same time furnish an increased number of propositions. In the pamphlet we are printing, and which will be ready for delivery by the time this issue of the PULPIT reaches its destiny, there are 150 propositions.

Thus we have placed it in the power of every Liberal to keep at hand a copy of this exposition to use in offsetting the impudent claim that the Bible is without contradictions. It is difficult to remember these propositions, and more difficult to quote from memory the citations given; therefore a reference to the tract itself will often save time and trouble.

If we are encouraged with a patronage that will justify the expense we will follow this with others fully as effective in refuting the assumptions and assertions that come from men who find their living by keeping the people who furnish it in ignorance of the truth. We believe in letting the Bible explain itself, and in giving all classes a chance to use their own judgement in the examination of it. We hope our well-to-do Liberals will help us to place this tract to the best possible advantage.

MR. MUNSON ON LIBERALS AND PROGRESS

From *The Independent Pulpit*, March 1889

Editor's Note: The following piece was written in response to T. V. Munson's article, "Are Liberals Progressive?" (See page 259.)

Special attention is hereby called to the opening article in this PULPIT. The question there propounded is an important one, and, although we can not concur in all that the article contains, we regard it as an able and honest effort at the most important, problem now before the Liberals of this country, namely, how to construct a system of ethics competent to take the place of religion, and so present it to that world as to attract favorable attention. This problem can not be ignored, and there are few Liberals, perhaps, who fail to recognize its importance. The final success of our cause depend upon its solution; hence we gladly welcome to our columns any and all efforts in that direction.

Mr. Munson is a very competent person to participate in such a discussion, and now that he is in the field, we hope to keep him there and keep him busy until something definite and tangible has been developed. The bent of his mind was discovered in a brief note we published in the January issue (See "Encouraging Letters," page 258), which, being considered along with his present article, gives us a pretty good idea of his views, and what we have to say here has been prompted by having considered the two in each other's light.

We commend his desire for a "constructive department" in THE PULPIT, not, however, because constructiveness has been ignored, overlooked or even neglected in its past management. From the very beginning of its career THE PULPIT has endeavored to define the rationalistic basis of ethics and construct thereupon a system of moral culture competent to utilize all the good to be found in the old systems without perpetuating the bad with which they have been burdened. Such a system can not be perfected by a single individual, nor within the space of single individual's lifetime, much less within the space of six years.

It is true that this work has not been systematically pursued, and for the very best of reasons. Our struggle for existence and establishment has been of such a character as to render system and order in the conduct of THE PULPIT impossible. It has always been thought by many very honest and sincere people that we have no right to publish such a journal, and the determined opposition of these people forced upon us a militant struggle from which we have never been freed, by either truce or treaty.

As the movements of an army are determined largely by the enemy's maneuverings, so many of our utterances have been, and are yet, determined by the utterances of our opponents. The condition of things has not been of our choosing; indeed, we are averse to it. Our disposition is to be at peace always, and with all people, and war is accepted only when the peace would involve a sacrifice of truth, honor and principle. This condition of our existence has rendered it necessary for us to divide our time between the two equally important departments of Liberal work, namely, the destructive and constructive; and if we have devoted more time for the former than to the latter it has been necessitated by the aggressiveness of the opposition, and not because we prefer that sort of work, for, in fact, we do not.

In expressing our preference for constructive work, and in deprecating the necessity for that which is destructive, we should not be understood as considering the latter less important and necessary than the former. They are of equal importance as long as the latter is necessary at all, and at present it is necessary in order that the former may be rendered practicable. Mr. Munson's idea that we "have razed the battlements of superstition till no longer remains one stone upon another" is quite complimentary from the standpoint he is now viewing it, but in fact, at least so far as having removed the spell of superstition from the minds of the people, and free them from the fear to think for themselves and express their convictions with freedom and independence, it is far from being true. It is only an illusion. With an organized church in every community in this country, and a salaried preacher in every church, whose position and emolument depend upon his orthodoxy, who will say that the "battlements of superstition have been razed?" Mr. Munson, in a moment of optimistic exultation, may cheer a fellow-soldier by such an exclamation, but Mr. Munson, in a more thoughtful mood, and viewing the almost universal sway of superstition dominating society, the press, the schools, the courts, and the very government itself, will contradict it. His suggestion that we begin to prepare "comfortable quarters for the captives" would cause a smile, if the sarcasm of the application was not so serious and disheartening. One is constrained to inquire where and who are the captives? If, in answer to this, it be said the unbelievers, we reply with the most discouraging fact that seven out of every ten of these either belong to the church or attend its ministry, read its literature and contribute to its revenue. Of the remaining three, at least two are so raw-skinned and mercenary that they will not take any part in our work, thus leaving one in ten to be depended upon as actual, out and out Liberals. This is not the sum of our difficulty either, for among the few who dare to be Liberal and defy the great majority, there is very little unity. We mention these things to show that if we move slowly there are good reasons for it, and to show, too, that much as we desire constructive work, there is yet a demand for that which is negative and destructive.

When Mr. Munson calls for special departments in THE PULPIT he shows conclusively that our struggles is little understood by him, and supposing that there are others looking at it from the same point of view, we will make a revelation that may prove interesting to more than one of our readers.

All know that we undertook this work without either experience, capital or the influence of any organized sentiment to sustain us; that from the beginning to the present we have worked in the face of an opposition that has the experience and prestige of ages, wealth by millions, and an organized sentiment extending its power over every department of human society, a sentiment adhered to with a blindness and abjectness as servile as slavery itself. Knowing this, they ought to know that our very existence today is due to a system of economy absolutely rigid, supplemented by the assistance of a few brave Liberals, some of whom can be counted as rich; therefore, every dollar we can obtain has to be used in meeting the expenses of living, in rather a poor way, and in paying for the mechanical and clerical work incident to the conduct of such a publication, thus leaving us nothing at all with which to pay for contributions to its columns. Not being able to offer pecuniary compensation of able and trained writers, we can not control the subject matter as we would like to do, and the revelation we started to make is that we have conducted the word hitherto without ever having expended one cent in payment for the matter we have published. The friends, one and all, who have thus far provided us with this matter have gone unrecompensed for their labors, save by the consciousness of having performed, in a most unselfish way, a noble service to a worthy cause, and the gratitude of those who have been profited by it.

With these facts in view, everyone must realize at once our inability to systemize the work. We can not direct and control the offerings of voluntary contributors. They write when they please, and upon subjects of their own choosing, and we, glad enough to have whatever they may offer, seldom know what we are going to receive, or who it will be from before it is needed by the printers. We have often thought of the department plan, but unless we could control the subject matter so as to have it all in hand ere a page is printed, it is impracticable. As it is, we often begin an issue not knowing what we will end with. We do not complain of those who have aided us with their pens; no, indeed, we feel profoundly grateful to them. But in self-defense we go to show how impossible it would be for us to systemize the work by means of departments. We confidently look forward to the time when we can do so, but that time is not now.

Mr. Munson objects to the argumentative character of THE PULPIT for which, if indeed this is a fault, we shall ask him to share the responsibility with the rest of us, for, in proportion to the amount he has written for us, no one has been more argumentative than he, in proof of which we need only instance the article under consideration. Argument is often weakened by acrimony and invective, as everyone knows, but to condemn it in this wholesale way, because of the occasional indiscretion of combatants, is like condemning the art of swimming because now and then some one is drowned. We are as much opposed to the abuses that occur from time to time in the discussion between opposing schools of thought as anyone can be, but argument is nevertheless necessary to all human progress. To condemn a reformer for arguing is like condemning a fish for living in the water. There never was a reform movement without argument, and it is safe to say there never will be. To expect original investigation without argument is to suppose a disposition that is not at all human. As long as men see things in a different light, and reach different and conflicting conclusions, they will argue, and we think they should.

We join Mr. Munson in condemning argument merely to perpetuate reconceived opinions, which is quite a different thing from reasoning in search of the truth; and while we admit that, now and then, THE PULPIT contributors, not excepting the editor, forget themselves and mar their arguments with too much temper, this is only an occasional exception to a general rule that has secured for it the reputation of being straightforward, fair-minded and temperate in controversy. We challenge comparison with any and all reform publications in that respect.

Mr. Munson places Luther, Voltaire, Paine and Ingersoll in company with Wesley, Sweedenborg, Beecher and Talmage, and then crowns at their expense, the heads of Shakespeare, Bacon, Huxley, Humboldt, Tyndal and Franklin. Leaving Wesley, Beecher and Talmage out of the list in which they have no rightful place, we beg to differ very widely from the opinion of our friend. But for the labors of Luther, Voltaire and Paine (Ingersoll was not born early enough to be included here), we should most likely never have had a Huxley, a Humboldt or a Tyndal, nor is it at all likely that the present generation would have known anything at all of the labors of a Shakespeare, a Bacon, or a Franklin. Mr. Munson is only following in the footsteps of the generality of men when he honors those who, after the battle for reform has been fought and won, minister to our mercenary cravings after wealth and luxury, leaving out of sight the unpaid and unappreciated warfarings of the reformer who made these latter possible. But for the reformation due to the heroic labors of such men as Luther, Voltaire and Paine, each in his generation, the long and brilliant list of scientists and economists that have since done so much for this century would not have existed. Of all the men whose labor and toil and suffering bring glory to the race, the reformer is, somehow, least appreciated while living and least remembered when dead, yet in importance he is before all others. It is his lot to cross the current of popular superstitions, and antagonize long-cherished errors and prejudices; it is his lot to destroy false and vicious doctrines; hence against him are arrayed prejudices that extend to after generations and that are often kept alive by those who enjoy the benefit of his labors.

Referring to Mr. Munson's desire that "THE PULPIT be turned into a social club-room," we will say, that is just what we have tried to make it, or to change the phraseology a little, it is a medium for the social communion of truthseekers—a journal in which all men, who have ideas affecting the moral, social, and intellectual well-being of the race, are invited to communicate them to the world just as he has done, and as we hope he will continue to do. But in a country so dominated by superstition, and so little used to the free and frank discussion of biblical and theological questions, we cannot expect smooth sailing. If we have a medium of freethought, it must be expected that there will be some conflict of opinion. Instead, there, of discouraging argument, we want more of it; not though for argument's sake, but for the sake of the truth.

As to his criticism of our title for "The Bible Against Itself," we fail to agree with him. We are plain, straightforward and candid in this work, and do not seek to mislead any one, or catch readers by guile. The object of the work is to show our Christian friends that the Bible is contradictory, and on that account, all the more likely to be of human origin. We believe this to be a legitimate work. When we find our children, and the children of our neighbors are being taught, even in our public schools, that the Bible is the infallible word of God, and that those who doubt it are unworthy citizens fit only to be numbered with criminals, then we feel it is our duty to teach them these "errors of the ancients," was well as the truths of more modern times.

The trouble with Liberals is that they lack unity of thought, aim and purpose. In the transformation from some branch of superstition, each one has developed his individuality to such an extent that any organic movement looks to him oppressive. It is but natural that this should be so, and it will require many long years of effort, crowded with failures innumerable, for us to overcome this evil. The transition from one habit of thought to another is a slow one and cannot be otherwise. We need to have patience and a mind to work with little hope of reaping the reward of our labors in person.

As we have already intimated, Liberalism is both

destructive and constructive, and in this it is not unlike other reforms. The work of destruction always precedes that of construction, and hitherto we have been passing through this period. It is necessarily one of strife, more or less, for the world does not readily and quietly give up old established systems. The very first work possible in a reformation is to convince the intelligent that the old system is faulty, that it lacks the warranty of reason, is out of harmony with the truth, and obstructive of human progress. Until this is done, construction is impossible, and this is just what we have been and are now doing. Having advanced far enough with this to convince them that the old system is unsound, they then begin to inquire what we have to give them in its stead. We have just succeeded in provoking this inquiry, and with this triumph comes the responsibility of providing a substitute for such as can not longer accept the old system, and we are glad to have the assistance and co-operation of such able men as Mr. Munson in this work. But let no one suppose that our destructive work is ended, because we may now begin to build. There is much to be done yet in breaking down the errors and prejudices of the past, but while with one hand we strike down the bad, may we not with the other gather up the good?

In conclusion, be it said that we are for destroying every vestige of superstition, bigotry and oppression, and for the establishment in its stead that which is true, beautiful and good. It is unwise to suppose that the only mission of Liberalism is that of destruction, and it is vain to suppose that a new system of ethical culture can be established while the very worst and most obstructive features of the old one are adhered to, either actively or passively, by nine-tenths of the people. If by constructive work, it is proposed that we furnish the Christians themselves a substitute for their churches, with the expectation or hope that it will be accepted, the very thought is absurd. What we want is a system of ethical culture for ourselves. We are perfectly indifferent to the cant and hypocritical cry, "What are you going to give us instead of our religion?" Our reply to such nonsense is: Nothing! We do not want your religion. If it suits you, why, keep it and enjoy it; but it does not suit us, and we are going to look out for something better; if we find it, all well and good, but if we do not we can in no way be worsted, for yours is simply worse than none at all. If the Liberals would unite in propagating a rationalistic system of morality, and while battering the ramparts of superstition with their negative artillery, they would fortify their own position with brotherly love and charity, it would not be great while until the Christians, seeing the rottenness of their own system as it is, would reconstruct it and slough off its objectionable features.

THE PULPIT is open for the use of all who will occupy it in search for the truth, no matter whether they agree with us or not. All that is necessary to insure one a hearing here is that he be intelligent, candid and courteous. It is hardly necessary that this should be said, though, except for the information of new readers, for we believe that in every issue for more than two years our opponents have had one or more representatives, and there are now on file and in prospect enough matter from that source to insure them a representation in several future issues.

AN INFIDEL'S CONFESSION OF FAITH

From *Public Opinion*, March 12, 1896

We are asked a great many questions regarding our work and experience as a liberal. Quite frequently we are asked if we are an infidel, and relying upon what seems to be a general agreement as to the meaning of the word "infidel," we have usually answered yes. But, while there is a general agreement as to the meaning of this term, there is, nevertheless, some confusion about it, not only among Christians, but among infidels as well. It has come to us from the Latin, and originally there were two words, *in* meaning "not," and *fides*, meaning "faith." These, when used together give us *infides*, "not faith." From fides thee is fidelis, which means "faithful," hence some have used it as designating the unfaithful or those lacking fidelity to principle, but in Webster's Dictionary we have, "not holding the faith," a term as there indicated applicable to "one who does not believe in the inspiration of the scriptures and the supernatural origin of the Christian religion." It is in this sense, and this alone, too, that we accept the term and feel willing to be called an infidel. The effort of bigots to make it a term of reproach is not borne out of the etymology of the word, nor has it the prestige of common usage. In Turkey a Christian is regarded as an infidel, while in Italy a Mohammedan is an infidel. A Universalist is infidel to the doctrine of future eternal punishment, a Unitarian is infidel to the doctrine of the Trinity, a Calvinist is infidel to the doctrine of free will, and an Arminian is infidel to that of election and predestination, but common usage has applied the term more especially to those who do not believe in the divine or supernatural origin of any part of the Christian system, and looking at it from this point of view, we most cheerfully and proudly accept the term, not as indicating any moral quality whatever, but as standing for an intellectual conviction, born of reason and investigation. They err who regard infidelity as a moral force. It is purely intellectual. A liberal does not rest satisfied with the fact that he is no longer a prey to religious superstition. He sympathizes with those who are and will work for their emancipation. Infidels are more numerous than liberals, but in many instances, they are without any serious moral convictions. It is a credit to anyone to be an infidel but far more creditable to be a liberal.

"How came you to be an infidel?" This is a question that we have been asked time and time yet again. Speaking for ourself we answer, by reading, studying, and preaching the Bible. If we had not been a preacher, perhaps we would have continued to be a Christian. We were taught to believe in the Bible from childhood, and, although there were many things about it that our sense of justice revolted at, we believed it to be a divine inspiration, and, therefore, in some mysterious way correct. But, in the course of time our duty to expound its mysteries to other people, and where in trying to do this, we put it to a rational test, the conviction that it was only a fallible book of human origin grew upon us until there was no honorable escape from open and avowed infidelity. ?We reach this by a long, painful struggle that ended in the sacrifice of much that we had honestly attained by our sincere devotion to the Church. Our experience and observation lead us to fear that many preachers have realized what we did as to the truth of the Bible, but they have not been willing to make known their real convictions and accept the social consequences of revolt. The Bible is its own best interpreter, and we cannot understand how any rational person can read it with careful attention and not discover its manifest fallibility. We think it likely that many have discovered this, but from mercenary motives refuse to make it known.

In our opinion, no book has made more infidels than the Bible, and our advice to any honest thinker who wishes to know the truth about this much-abused and misused book is to read and give it a chance to speak for itself. Test it by rational processes just as you do other books, and if you are thoroughly honest with it and with yourself you will become an infidel. Reverence for the Bible as a divine inspiration is generally fastened upon people, as it was upon us, in their childhood. If children are let alone until they learn to reason logically, you can never convince them that the Bible is anything more than a human production. The method of the churches is to fill the minds of children with superstitious awe of the Bible before they are old enough to read it critically, and many go through life believing it, without ever subjecting its utterances to anything like a rational test.

Another question we are often asked is, whether or not we are as happy now as when we were a Christian, To which we invariably answer, Yes; and more so, though this is not to say that we are perfectly happy. This is not a good world to be happy in. We do not understand how any good person can be happy in the perpetual presence of so much pain, anguish, and sorrow as confronts us every day of our lives. We have never seen the day, either as a Christian or an infidel, that we would not prefer an endless sleep to life eternal, if only one soul is to be eternally tormented in a Christian hell. Perfect happiness is an impossibility in this world, unless it be to heartless beings; but, with the appalling threat of eternal punishment removed, we have found life a thousand times more endurable, and we believe that, if all men were rid of religious superstition, virtue would have a better chance. With virtue there would come a disposition to be just; justice would remove much of the evil with which we are surrounded, and in a world where everyone could have a home with food, raiment, and health, perfect happiness would be possible.

"But do you not sometimes doubt the correctness of your position?" say some. Because Christians go through the world doubting at every step, they imagine that liberals must be harassed in the same way ; but our experience is that they are not. The fundamental principles of liberalism are as demonstrative as the problems of Euclid. What motive have you for doing good?" say some, To this question we always feel like asking in reply, What motive have you for eating and drinking? If one never hungered, he would often neglect to eat, Doing good satisfies nature in the well-regulated character that is as real as physical hunger or thirst, A hunting dog will pursue the game, and a moral man will do good. If well born and well taught, men love to do good, and only wish they could do more than they do. Is it possible that men do good only through the fear of hell or the hope of heaven ? Self-preservation end self-respect beget in us a love of virtue, and supply every needed motive for doing good ; and the really good man will do good regardless of future rewards and punishments.

We have rarely been asked to express our feelings toward Christian people. As a true liberal we could have no other than feelings of kindness and good will toward all men, be they Christians or pagans. They are our brethren in a world of common strife, and common hope. No good man will dislike another because he does not believe as he does. We regard Christianity as an error, and the Christian religion as a superstition, but for Christians themselves we can have no other feelings than kindness. The bigotry and intolerance we so deprecate in Christians may exist among infidels as well, and, in fact, it does. All organized bodies are liable to become intolerant, If we all had that respect for each other that we ought to have, there is much common ground on which liberals and Christians might stand and work together in the cause of humanity, and we hope for the time when partisan strife will so far die out as to permit them to do this. Christianity, with all its harm, has done some good, and is now doing good, and we know of nothing good which it has done in the past or is now doing that could not be done by Liberals if they were what they ought to be. As we view it, the battle for freedom to think and speak has been about won in this country. We think the time has come when Liberals should go to work and do something for the general improvement and uplifting of the world. The liberals of this country have perfect freedom of the press, yet they let their papers die for want of support. They have perfect freedom to speak their thought, yet in all Texas they have not a house in which to speak, and they are too impecunious to support one regular lecturer in the field, It is not so much liberty we want now as liberality, and zeal to do the work we are left perfectly free to do. The trouble with us is that we say a great deal more than we do, We stand by and dispute with Christians about their false and foolish doctrines while they go to work and do the very things we ought to be doing. If the so-called liberals of this country had the zeal and self-sacrificing spirit that the Christians have, they could, in a few years, rival the churches in all moral and humane work, while as it is, we are talking a great deal and practically doing nothing.

ALSO AVAILABLE FROM
THE FREETHOUGHT PRESS OF TEXAS

GUIDED by REASON:
The Golden Age of Freethought in Texas
By STEVEN R. BUTLER, with J. E. Remsburg, S. P. Putnam and R. G. Ingersoll

The "Golden Age of Freethought" was a period during which American atheists and agnostics who called themselves "freethinkers," "liberals," or "infidels," sought to strengthen the "wall of separation between church and state" and to reshape American society. During this era, in which a vibrant freethought press flourished and "liberal" associations could be found in towns and cities all over the country, Texans were among not only some of the most active and enthusiastic participants but also leaders in the movement. In *Guided by Reason: The Golden Age of Freethought in Texas*, historian Steven R. Butler has combined original research with first-hand nineteenth century accounts to narrate the previously untold story of a little known but noteworthy era in Texas history.

A BIBLICAL MERRY-GO-ROUND
and Other Essays by Arthur Babb
Edited and Introduced by STEVEN R. BUTLER

Arthur Babb (1865-1951) was a farmer, railroad carpenter, building contractor and self-taught bookbinder. Despite a lack of formal education, he was also a studious man, a voracious reader and a freethinker. In 1944 and 1945, when he was seventy-nine years of age, Babb wrote two long essays in which he recorded his thoughts and opinions regarding religion. These essays, together with two short pieces composed nearly twenty years earlier and another written in 1946, make up this posthumous work in which the author asks in an occasionally humorous and conversational style of writing some of thought-provoking questions that challenge the veracity of one of humankind's oldest and most sacred concepts.

www.ingramcontent.com/pod-product-compliance
Lightning Source LLC
Chambersburg PA
CBHW071259110426
42743CB00042B/1108